D. M.

Birthright

Birthright

Christian, Do You Know Who You Are?

by
David C. Needham

MULTNOMAH PRESS
PORTLAND, OREGON 97266

Cover Design and Illustration: Britt Taylor Collins

First Printing, 1979

ISBN: 0-930014-29-4
Printed in the United States of America

Library of Congress Cataloging in Publication Data

Needham, David C   1929-
   Birthright: Christian, do you know who you are?

   Includes index.
    1. Christian life—1960-   2. Identification
(Religion) I. Title.
BV4501.2.N43   248'.4   79-90682
ISBN 0-930014-29-4

To my children, Greg and Barbara,
for whom I wish
the fullest measure of their birthright.

Table of Contents

Preface

To write concerning God's truth is a dangerous, almost frightening proposition. That danger is multiplied if the ideas shared appear to be different from traditional statements of the faith.

The danger lies in two areas. First, new expressions of spiritual truth can play right into the hands of the Christian radical whose chief delight lies in upsetting orthodox ideas. Milking every opportunity to fracture harmony in the body of Christ, this misdirected zealot willingly rearranges what is being said to suit his own purposes.

But there is another, more subtle danger.

Many sincere believers have found a comfortable security in stereotyped, neatly systematized statements of theology. Over the years, these systems have grown in prominence and familiarity until they seem as inspired as the Bible itself.

To those who subscribe unquestioningly to these traditional statements, this book will automatically raise red flags. Rather than challenging them to think objectively, it will alarm them into hasty emotional reactions.

Recognizing these dangers, I write to you, the individual in that middle group of God's people. You are totally committed to the authority of Scripture. You are also committed to remaining open to the truth. You are a biblicist. If indeed the Holy Spirit is pleased with the following study, then you too will happily respond and praise God for His truth—biblical truth.

Concerning the Notes

Many of us are accustomed to ignoring the notes at the end of the chapter. We assume that they are given to provide necessary documentations of material. In this book, for the most part, *that is not so*. I consider much of the note material to be of equal significance with the main body of the book. The only reason for placing it at the end of each chapter is to protect the crucial flow of thought. The same should be said of the appendices which follow the final chapter.

By the inclusion of statements by other writers, it should not be assumed that there necessarily exists a mutual agreement in the broader contexts of what we are saying. Nevertheless, it is my desire that I have been faithful to the writer's intent within the immediate context from which any quotation is taken.

David Needham

Introduction

*O*ne of the greatest hazards Christians face when they attempt to communicate the truth of the Bible is to assume that people (including themselves) know the meaning of the popular religious terms they employ. This difficulty can be readily seen in most popular discussions concerning the "spiritual life."

Perhaps we all think we know what a speaker means when he says, "You must deal with *self*; it must be put to death! *Self* must not remain on the throne of your life!" Yet without blinking an eye we nod our assent when the same speaker, a little bit later, goes on to assert that "most Christians suffer from a very poor self image!"

Wait a minute. If we really stopped and tried to correlate these statements, we would be forced to conclude that a victorious Christian is one who has a good image of his own non-self!

Even though we find this sort of reasoning difficult to grasp, we listen politely, sing all three stanzas of the hymn, and go on our way. To question the speaker would seem...unspiritual. So we stow the information in a vast, untidy file in the back room of our minds. It's just more talk on

11

the spiritual life. And since it's easy to forget what we don't understand, the whole thing doesn't bother us too much. But other things do. Unspoken inner things. Restless feelings of guilt. Pervasive frustration with the overall quality of our lives. Sometimes even frightening moments when a thought flashes like the glint of a faraway object in the sun...a stab of longing...a pleading inner whisper that seems both distant and near at the same moment....

Perhaps—just perhaps—might there be a deeper level of life in Christ that God had in mind for me all along? Could there be a fullness, a warmth, a joy that belongs to me and yet—somehow—I'm missing it?

If we are missing it, this is no small thing. Out of all the eternal ages of our existence as God's children, these tiny years here on earth have a destiny that can never be repeated. The Bible tells us that in the stench of a sick and rotting world we are perfume bottles for the fragrance of Christ (2 Corinthians 2:15). In the gathering darkness we shine as stars (Philippians 2:15). If only we could grasp the awesome implications of these few years! As if the mounting pain of guilt and failure wasn't enough we are tormented by the thought that we may just keep on "missing it."

Quite honestly, how much of our lives have been exactly that?

Oh, we know the doctrines. We memorize the steps to this or that. From time to time we may get swept along in the enthusiasm of some program or Christian venture as though we had been to a sales conference. We come away with excitement in our product, confidence in our techniques, and admiration for our organization's leadership. But the *power*—the revolutionary power of life in the Spirit—where is that? Where is the fullness of God?

Then there are the times when the question becomes far more than bothersome. It becomes nothing short of terrifying. Cold sweat runs and our mouths dry up when we are jolted by the news that the pastor just ran off with one of the most "godly" wives in the church. And who will be next?

These questions have returned to plague me—and I'm sure, many of you—year after year. The roads are well-worn with our hopeful footsteps. We've tried the seven-step plan to full assurance, the five steps to total maturity. We've enlisted in the latest workshops, subscribed to that aggressive organization, tuned in that dynamic speaker. We've memorized the pious technique of "accepting it by faith even though it doesn't make any sense." And we're getting tired. Tired enough and radical enough to question it all. We ask, *Is that what the Bible really says?*

Deep in our beings, many of us believe that there are some concepts clearly taught in Scripture that are so revolutionary, so startling, that if we really took them as they are, it would upset many of the applecarts of conservative evangelicalism. Assuming the power of the Holy Spirit is equal to the concepts, the implications seem staggering.

And yet, we find ourselves walled in somehow.

We find certain biblical words, phrases, and descriptions attached with super glue to almost sacred definitions...and carefully worded limitations. Terms such as "old man," "new man," "holiness," and "sin" evoke automatic, memorized explanations . Phrases such as "crucified with Christ" or "risen with Christ" elicit the same sort of sacrosanct definition.

We so readily say, "Oh, that's *positional truth,*" whenever literalism might press us to acknowledge that the power of the Holy Spirit is so little known in our experience. With fatherly rebuke, we admonish those who admittedly have a joy in Christ that we envy. "Oh," we pronounce with a knowing smile, "that is not for the church today!" From time to time, as the situation demands, we coin new terms like "Spirit control"[1] or "sin nature"[2] and invest them with sacred status.

Out of this heap of dogmatisms, our remarkably inventive and certainly sincere Christian spokesmen continue to pour out an endless supply of newly systematized notebooks for every circumstance. Up-to-date Christians display a multi-colored array of these neatly printed binders and cassette packages on their bookshelves. Crowded calendars reflect multiplying seminar circuits—each one a must for serious believers.

Shouldn't we begin to wonder how the early church ever made it? How could they have possibly turned the world upside down without cassette albums and three-ring binders?

It is my earnest conviction that we have dreadfully complicated what Christianity is all about. I'm not saying these supplemental materials are without value. God has indeed used them in wonderful ways in many lives. But I do wonder what complex, interlocking, systematic theologies were bouncing around in Peter's mind on the Day of Pentecost and in those fresh, exciting years that followed. Were the epistles only meaningful after the theologians had opportunity to tear them apart and glue them back together?

Due to differences in time, culture and language, we have both needed and greatly profited from the dedicated men who have labored in the task of translating (in the broadest sense) the Scriptures for us. But we have amassed such a vast library of "how to do it" books that their sheer quantity and complexity have placed them beyond the reach of the spiritually sensitive person. Perhaps this explains the fresh interest among Christians in seminars dealing with new techniques in speed reading!

Witness the recent production of best-sellers on everything from the juicy details of the Great Tribulation (to be sucked up by Christians who suppose they won't be on earth when it happens anyway) to equally juicy details of how to put sparkle into your sex life.

And what is the result?

We have today the most sexually-educated, prophecy-oriented generation of Christians in the history of the world. Certainly the Bible does speak to these issues, but is this really the ultimate of what God intends for us? Is this the essence? When we stand before Christ's judgment throne will even one—just one—of His questions relate to my speculations on the number 666 or the scope of my sexual experiences?

For all their lack of slick materials and theological vocabulary, the early Christians above all else knew something of the majesty of a miracle-working God. They also knew that because of a miracle they were alive from the dead, no longer "in the flesh," but rather aliens in this world. Ambassadors from another home. And this was enough! Obviously there was much, much more to know that would embellish these basics, but the essence—the all-important essence—was already there.

Because of the new covenant these men and women were alive as no humans had ever been alive before! They were a new species; they were not of this world. And they knew it. With spiritual gifts never assumed to be temporary, the early church found itself with Spirit-taught men of wisdom and compassion who both understood the Scriptures and heard the voice of God. With their own personal identity and life-course locked in, they saw a world that needed desperately to see Jesus in the flesh—their flesh. And they went out to live.

But that was a long time ago.

For too many years I refused to listen to the wistful, disturbing questions of my own soul. Then, my very patient, loving Lord broke through my deepening disillusionment. Through His gracious Holy Spirit, doors of discovery opened and I began discovering *life*. Life that was out there all the time.

This book is about those doors.

(NOTE: You may wish to turn first to Appendix A for a list of what I consider are the practical values of the emphasis of this book.)

Introduction, Notes

1. The biblical phrases are "led by the Spirit," "walk by the Spirit," and "filled by the Spirit." None of these imply what "Spirit control" would appear to suggest. I can only assume that the reason some have chosen this new terminology is because their concept of the work of the Holy Spirit is that He desires to restrain, to hold back, to work against the tendencies that a child of God normally would have. Hence He must "control" rather than "lead" or "strengthen" or "fill." This I believe fails to correspond to the emphasis of new covenant personhood.

2. The term "sin nature" finds its nearest expression in the New Testament in the statement describing unbelievers *"and were by nature objects of wrath"* (Ephesians 2:3). Though the Scriptures underline the fact that believers possess the capacity to sin—indeed there is *"a law in my members"* which if not redirected by another law will produce sin (Romans 7:23; 8:2)—it would seem to go against the emphasis of resurrection life to say that "the nature" of one who is born of God is to sin (cf. 1 John 3:7-9). Since the term "sin nature" would not have been awkward for Paul to use in view of Ephesians 2:3 it would appear that there was divine wisdom in the selection of the word "flesh" in such passages as Romans 8:3-12 and Galatians 5:16-24 rather than "sin nature." Though the general quality of the NIV translation of the Bible is very commendable, I believe the decision in this regard has not aided in the understanding of God's truth. See Appendix B for some additional thoughts concerning this terminology.

Part 1

Meaning and Identity:
Who Are You,
Christian?

Through the following five chapters we may expect to move from the dismal shadows of the absolute emptiness of most of the world's humanity to the glorious vantage point of the inexpressible fullness that God intends for all believers whom He calls "children of light." We will begin by discovering that sin is much more ruthless then simply doing the wrong thing, "missing the mark." It is the absolute madness of attempting to make some sense out of an existence in which there can be no lasting significance—no meaning. The *"empty way of life...futility of their thinking...they walked after emptiness and became empty"* (1 Peter 1:18; Ephesians 4:17; Jeremiah 2:5).

Next, I will invite you on a somewhat personal pilgrimage. The path leads out of my own frustrations as a Christian who saw himself fundamentally as a forgiven sinner into the freedom of realizing my own birthright. In this pilgrimage I soon discovered two things. (These will occupy our third and fourth chapters.) The first thing was quite uncomfortable to accept. I was out of step with much that was being taught. The second discovery seemed so difficult to grasp. I was seeing myself increasingly as a spiritual being more than a flesh-oriented mortal being. Was this biblical? Would I find God's balanced evaluation?

God's answer was Jesus, the perfect man (Of course He was God, too.). What was His evaluation of personhood? What was there about His life that gave it such significance? We all know what it was about His death, but what about His life? He talked about total dependence upon His Father. He talked about the new covenant and the Holy Spirit. And He said *"As the Father has sent me, I am sending you"* (John 20:21). And on that focus Part I will conclude.

Chapter 1

A Cry for Meaning

*T*he next few pages might not make easy sailing. We'll need to tack back and forth between our preconceived notions and our commitment to get at the essence of biblical truth.

Let's begin by asking some questions. And let's not be satisfied until the answers we find make solid sense. Since Christians rightly say that the root of all of our problems is sin, let's start there.

Just what is sin, anyway? Everyone should have some nice, neat definition filed away somewhere.

"Sin is a lack of conformity to the moral law of God, either in act, disposition, or state."

Thank you, Mr. Theologian. I guess I knew it was something like that. But now I realize that what I really want to ask isn't *What?*, but *Why?* Why do I think and act the way I do?

"Every man sins because he has a sin nature—Christian and non-Christian alike."

I see. And what is a sin nature?

"A sin nature is a governing power or principle within. It is that which excites sin from within."

19

It follows then, if my theologian friend is correct, that every human has within him some sort of sinister spiritual force or diabolic mental tumor that influences his behavior. It must be more than a capacity for sin because sin is much more pervading in human beings than the word "capacity" would imply. The Bible makes it clear that such a term would fall short, especially in describing the non-Christian.

Perhaps the clearest passage describing this nature is Ephesians 2:3. Paul tells us *"we were by nature children of wrath."* This nature, Paul says, was our very life. *"We too all formerly lived in the lusts of our flesh, indulging the desires of the flesh and of the mind"* (NASB).

What we have is a paradox. This life, he says, was really non-life. A walking death. *"You were dead in your trespasses and sins."*

You can't moderate it. So total is this state of being that God says elsewhere,

"There is no one righteous, not even one;
There is no one who understands,
no one who seeks God.
All have turned away,
They have together become worthless;
there is no one who does good.
not even one."   (Romans 3:10-12)

Back to the Roots

But why? Why does man find himself in such a state? ("Why" is the most important word.) Since we are searching for the root of the problem, we must go all the way back to the Garden of Eden. Somehow, under the tree of the knowledge of good and evil, our first parents acquired this deathly nature. Actually, to be more accurate, the Bible focuses in on what they *lost* rather than on what they acquired.

God was extremely pointed in telling them...and us. What would happen if they disobeyed their Creator?

"You will surely die."   (Genesis 2:17)

Of course He meant physical death, as so vividly demonstrated in the following chapters of Genesis. But did God mean something more than physical death? I am sure that He did. Ephesians 2:1 should settle the question for anyone. *"You were dead in your trespasses and sins."*

What then really happened to those two tragic people? Though still "living," they had lost *life*. Eventually, they would lose physical life. But right at that moment of disobedience they lost *true life*.

"You Haven't Lived Unless... "

But couldn't Adam and Eve still walk and talk and eat and love and laugh and weep and dream?

Perhaps the best way to appreciate what they lost is to think for a moment of some very common expressions we hear and see every day through the advertising media.

"You haven't really lived," we're told, "until you've tried _____, seen _____, heard _____, felt _____, tasted _____."

By the definition of some, many aren't really alive at all. You see, each of us determines the degree to which we or anyone else is alive by what we consider to be true fulfillment in life. If we or they have "that," we or they are truly living! If we or they do not have "that," then forget it. Life has not been discovered at all.

One Who "Had It"

The contradictory voices sing across the airwaves, shout from seductive billboards, passionately plead from the covers of a thousand paperbacks.

Who is right?
Is anybody right?

We will never know for sure what it is to really live unless we hear from the only One who could truly know. And that

One, of course, is the One who made us. He is the One who told Adam and Eve that they had lost it! If only we could hear from our Creator an extended description of someone who "had it," then we would know.

And has He done that? Most perfectly! There was only One—just One—who "had it" from His birth all the way through life. *That One, of course, is Jesus.* He certainly was the most alive human who ever walked this earth. (Of course He was and still is God, but that's not the point right now.) He indeed was a man, a perfect man.

And what was the essence of His life? Was it simply that He did everything right? He did; yet it was something deeper than that. The essence of His life was that all that he did—His words, His works, His entire life—came from His Father. His was a totally dependent life.[1] For a human to be truly alive—by our Creator's definition—is to live as an extension of God's own life.

Listen to what Jesus said:

"The words that I say to you are not just my own. Rather, it is the Father, living in me, who is doing his work."

"I live because of the Father."

"I have brought you glory on earth by completing the work you gave me to do....Now they know that everything you have given me comes from you."

"Anyone who has seen me has seen the Father."
        (John 14:10; 6:57a; 17:4, 7; 14:9b)

In every respect He was the perfect man. In fact, the Holy Spirit through Paul in Ephesians 4:13 tells us that the perfect man would attain to *"the whole measure of the fullness of Christ."* (See also 1 John 2:6; and 1 Corinthians 11:1.)

A Fully Operational Human

Keeping in mind that the ultimate purpose of God in all things is to display His own glory (Ephesians 1:12), let's see if we can put together in one sentence what God has in mind for a fully operational human being. How does this sound? *God's purpose in creating us is so that we, through a dependent relationship with our God, could receive and display the very life of God—the glory of God.*

Through His unique creation of man, all that God wished to show of Himself—His perfections, His purity, His love—could be seen and most fully appreciated. For a person to fulfill this function is life. And anything less than this *is less than life.*

Something Gained. . . Something Lost

What then happened in the Garden of Eden? *Adam and Eve lost life.*

At least part of what Satan told them would happen, happened. They became independent creatures, cut off from the life of God. Cut off from His mind, His perfections, His purity. Life for them (if indeed it was life) had to be found *within* themselves. It was in that tragic sense that they became "like God."

God's life flows from no higher source than Himself; He draws on no moral law outside of Himself. So now Adam and Eve were severed from any higher, outside source, any moral law to sustain them. They were on their own.

Yes, they had acquired something. They were by nature children of wrath. But far more foundationally, they lost something. They lost dependent life from God. They were now "dead in trespasses and sins." If they were to find meaning in their existence, if they were to make any sense out of the few years allotted to them before their bodies withered and died, they had to do it on their own.[2]

"Flesh,"[3] that is, everything mortal about them, became very important. Of course it was important—*it was all they had.* Brains, emotions, senses, creativity, imagination, bodies. Life was here, in the flesh. It was nowhere else. My, what a potential for those first humans! Man was like God. He was his own "strong one" (for that is the meaning of "elohim," god). The "grand adventure" had begun!

Think about human life for a moment—at its best and at its worst. Try picturing a tiny baby in her mother's arms. So soft, so loveable. Look again a couple of years later with the sun in her hair. Chubby little hands, sparkling eyes, tiny nose, delicate smile, spontaneous laugh, running across the lawn and calling out, "Daddy's home." Or look at any little boy, four years old, hanging upside down from his swing, wondering why the world looks so strange. Freckles, holes in his jeans, baseball cards—so fully alive! Fifteen years later—so beautiful, so handsome, so expectant. And then...long years, stress, illness, ulcers, wrinkles, pain, sorrow, stooping, decay, dim eyes, the wheelchair, white sheets, jumbled words, a final gasp, death, a box...a grave—that final offense against "the grand adventure."

And if that were not enough, all through those years there is the ugly side—the evil essence that haunts man's highest moments—the destructive pride, cruelty, envy, deceit. *But why?* Jesus said, "you in Me, and I in you." Man was never made for life "in the flesh."

The Two-Fold Tragedy of Eden

If only we could grasp the absolute, unutterable horror of that tragic day in Eden. It was a two-fold tragedy, both God's and man's.

Imagine for a moment that you are a judge who is also a master woodcraftsman. With supreme care you carve a gavel, uniquely shaped to be held in your hand as an extension and expression of yourself. Imagine further that somehow that choice gavel is removed from your hand, the one for whom it was made. Imagine it being picked up and used for hammering nails or pounding in bean poles or scraping the mouldy insides of garbage cans. No matter how productive that gavel might be, or no matter how destructive (if used as a club), every use, every act would be a most ugly offense to you, the gavel-maker.

So also must the human race have become an offense to God. The very creatures who were to express God's glory—His will, His purity, His love—were aborting and perverting that display. To put it mildly, God was grieved.

But the tragedy was not God's alone.
The tragedy was also man's.

Every man, unless he is able to practice some form of total deception, is aware of a strange abiding emptiness. Even in his most productive moments—his greatest hours—he senses a shallowness, a vague loneliness, a foreboding doubt that perhaps what he had assumed to be life was not really life at all.

A Fresh Definition of Sin

This, then, is the essence of sin. It is more than some carefully worded, theological definition. That locked-in statement quoted earlier simply will not do. *Sin is* more pointedly *the expression of man's struggle with the meaning of his existence while missing life from God. It is all the varieties of ways man deals with and expresses his alienation from his Creator as he encounters the inescapable issue of meaning.*[4]

Adam and Eve voluntarily placed themselves in this position of independence from God for the determination of significance in life. They would decide what was to be good and what was to be bad; where values were to be found; where life was to be found. Thus *"sin entered the world through one man, and death through sin"* (Romans 5:12).

Sin *is* a transgression of the law of God. And to reject life, to determine a will different from the will of God (which is the law of God) is the most heinous crime a person can commit. *The essence of sin, then, cannot be separated from the issue of meaning.*

Perhaps someone is voicing an inner objection at this point.

"I think you are playing lightly with the horrible nature of sin. How can you describe it so casually as a struggle with 'meaning'? Doesn't the Bible say 'The heart is deceitful above all things and desperately wicked'? You are not doing justice to that forceful biblical description."

Just the opposite is true! Isaiah 53:5 most literally says, *"He was pierced for our **rebellion**; He was crushed for our **perversions.**"*[5] In rebelling against God's perfect intention and perverting the qualities of humanness toward non-God oriented ends, man has committed the ultimate offense. For the wrath of God to be aroused—for the lake of fire to be man's ultimate end—is justice in view of the terrible crime committed.

Because of that crime a curse settled over the whole earth. It settled most pointedly upon man, who was now mortal. It settled on all creation so that it too was *"subjected to frustration* (aimlessness)" (Romans 8:20). It was heard in the form of a shout from the crowds as they erected the tower of Babel. *"Let us make a name for ourselves"* (Genesis 11:4). It was repeatedly echoed in the words, *"everyone did as he saw fit"* (Judges 17:6, 21:25). Perhaps Solomon gave it its most eloquent expression when he cried:

> *"'Meaningless! Meaningless!'*
>   *says the Teacher.*
> *'Utterly meaningless*
>   *Everything is meaningless.'"*

(Ecclesiastes 1:2)[6]

The Master of My Fate; the Captain of My Soul

And so it has remained. Through all the centuries. As a representative child of Adam I have rejected all of God's efforts to communicate with me. I stoned His prophets. I mocked His Scriptures. And then—2,000 years ago—I killed His Son. The One who came to bring me the only hope, His very life. Since that day, my journey through the darkness has only accelerated. I have become adept at inventing counterfeit lights — bright-colored, flashing lights. Pseudo rainbows; artificial sunsets; celluloid stars.

More recently I discovered that God is dead, anyway. I am a product of organic evolution. A cosmic accident. A unique moment in a mysterious 30-billion year process. It is an adventure filled with suspense — *and* cruelty *and* meaninglessness. And though I do not know what is ahead, never fear, I am on my way!

"I do not care what Gods there be;
I am the master of my fate,
the captain of my soul."
(Lord Alfred Tennyson)

Even today, after reading the morning news and the latest issue of *TIME* magazine, and even though I acknowledge countless gallons of human tears, the endless cycle of agonizing tragedy, I, along with the world's majority, maintain that Adam made *the right decision.* Even as I swallow my tranquilizers, rush to my psychiatrist, take that extra drink, endure my third divorce, and watch my children reject all the ideals I have tried to pass on — I still say there is hope!

"You were wearied by all your ways,
    but you would not say, 'It is hopeless.'
You found renewal of your strength,
    and so you did not faint."
(Isaiah 57:10)

Portrait of a Gallery
I wonder if you could imagine for a moment the entire human race as though it were an art gallery full of picture frames. Long, long halls. Billions of picture frames — *without any pictures!* Empty. Can you visualize it?

Some of the frames are very carefully carved. Some with delicate gold leaf. Some rather gaudily painted. Others dirty, chipped. But every frame wrapped around — *nothing* — emptiness.

It is possible that the human race is seen in such a way by God. An art gallery with no paintings.

Each human being was intended to frame an inimitable, individual masterpiece of God's own reflected glory. But where God should be, there is only emptiness — a bare patch of wall. Since the frames are conscious, however, the fact of emptiness is simply too devastating — too self-destructive — to acknowledge. And so humankind becomes obsessed with the only thing left to it — its own flesh. The frame. "Life," if it is to be found at all, must be found in one's own frame and the frames around him.

So, ingeniously and carefully, man lights his gallery, carpets and air-conditions the halls, creates all sorts of special displays, and leads community crusades to clean up the dirty and broken frames. In solemn conferences he formulates long-range plans to deal with the rapidly increasing quantity of frames brought about by mass production and new preservation techniques. The antique section of the gallery presents a special challenge. Detente must be made between frames demanding individualistic displays and frames committed to a group identity. Calm must be restored to those remoter wings of the gallery which have been so neglected and now demand equality with the more privileged galleries.

But since one must naturally protect the welfare of one's own frame, and since growth now appears beyond control, it seems that the gallery rules must be changed. Forget that dark hall, those jumbled halls. Dismantle those old frames. Abort the delivery of new frames...no...wait...it wasn't supposed to work out this way...we thought all our new inventions and progress would solve the difficulties and...if only we had more time...but the air's getting foul...lights are beginning to flicker...sounds of confusion are coming from every corner.

And—anyway—**There Are No Pictures.**
We all know that.
Emptiness.
Everywhere emptiness.
What difference does it all make anyway?

Where Then, Is Life?

In the Bible, the concept of sin is inseparable from the issue of meaning. Certainly this is the thrust of the book of Ecclesiastes. In chapter two of that book, Solomon carefully listed for us the variety of ways he attempted to find meaning in life.

> *"I thought in my heart, 'Come now, I will test you with pleasure to find out what is good.' But that also proved to be meaningless. 'Laughter,' I said, 'is foolish. And what does pleasure accomplish?' I tried cheering myself with wine, and embracing folly—my mind was still guiding me with wisdom. I wanted to see what was worthwhile for men to do under heaven during the few days of their lives. I undertook great projects: I built houses for myself and planted vineyards.... I denied myself nothing my eyes desired; I refused my heart no pleasure. My heart took delight in all my work, and this was the reward for all my labor. Yet when I surveyed all that my hands had done and what I had toiled to achieve, everything was meaningless, a chasing after the wind; nothing was gained under the sun.... So I hated life, because the work that is done under the sun was grievous to me. All of it is meaningless, a chasing after the wind."*
>
> (Ecclesiastes 2:1-4, 10-11, 17)

Two things made Solomon quite different from most people. Because of these two things, his book becomes especially helpful to us. First, he had the position and the finances to try all of the options that he imagined might give some sense of meaning to life. Second, David's son had the brains to see through to the emptiness of everything he tried. I'm no Solomon. Neither are you. But the core issue is still just the same for every man, every woman: *Where do I find life?*

Although we do not possess Solomon's gold, we have our own ambitions and fragile fantasies. For these we struggle and sacrifice, envy and steal (quite subtly of course). Unfortunately, we do not possess Solomon's wisdom either. Thinking we've "made it," we cling tenaciously to our idols and respectable pride, unwilling to admit to ourselves or anyone else "Is not this thing in my right hand a lie?" (Isaiah 44:20).

By nature (because of Adam) man is committed to this sometimes colorful, ofttimes suspenseful, but always "dead end street" existence. *Sin, then, is not simply some capacity or sinister inner force. It is rather the fundamental necessity for every person who does not possess life from God.* He has no alternative but to struggle with the "futility" of his mind (Ephesians 4:17-18), forced by birth to live in a world environment subjected to futility (Romans 8:20).

We humans have no choice but to deal with the issue of meaning—

> to search for it,
> fight for it,
> envy it in others,
> react against those who might take it from us,
> grieve because it has been lost,
> or perhaps (most deceptively and pitifully)
> be deluded into thinking we have found it.

To give up is suicide. But to continue existing in meaninglessness—is that so much better?

This *is* sin. It is not merely something a non-Christian "has," it is his most basic nature.

It would appear that through much of history it was the rare person who ever stopped and asked why. Probably for most, the job of survival was so demanding there simply wasn't time to ask questions. For others, their unquestioned commitment to family or king or religious system appeared to fill the vacuum. Yet the question *Why?*, ever lurking in the shadows, has never left. The conscious or unconscious issue of meaning has driven every man who ever lived.

Some of us can appreciate the dramatic effect the last 200 years of industrial revolution have had upon man and his struggle with meaning. For multitudes, it has given them the time and means to discover entirely new counterfeit reasons for living. The multiplied billions spent each year on advertising has not been a poor investment. Spot TV commercials and lavish full-color magazine ads confidently point us to where we can find life. Whether it's a new car or a humble deodorant, the line is the same.

With more leisure time we grab at entertainment with its many faces, each one beckoning us away from our own world into someone else's world. And whether their world is a real one or simply another fantasy it doesn't make much difference—at least it isn't mine!

For some, the continuing revolution itself represents meaning in life: the dedicated executive, the political activist, the innovative public relations man, the loyal employee who attaches a father image to either his company or his union.

For others, the industrial revolution steals the only meaning left to them—survival. Cradle-to-grave security results in psychotic boredom. It is all too evident: the epidemic of drugs, growing fascination with gambling, sex perversion and exploitation, thrill killings, zealous crusades for empty causes. Then there are those far more socially acceptable symptoms which surface in an addiction to television or an insatiable appetite for more and more spectator sports. Most recently the rash of revolutions and counterrevolutions have raised the whispered why's to loud voices no thinking person can fail to hear.

"The Deeds of the Flesh"

For the non-Christian, the combined will to live and the will to discover meaning find expression in what Paul calls "the deeds of the flesh."

> *"Now the deeds of the flesh are evident, which are immorality, impurity, sensuality, idolatry, sorcery, enmities, strife, jealousy, outbursts of anger, disputes, dissensions, factions, envyings, drunkenness, carousings, and things like these..."*
>
> (Galatians 5:19-21, NASB)

The first three "deeds," *immorality, impurity,* and *sensuality,* obviously relate to man's attempts to get at meaning through his body—his glands and senses, his fantasies. *Idolatry* is very broad. An idolator is one who has made up his mind on where and how he will find life. And whatever it is, he will work feverishly to get it, guard it, sacrifice to it, and worship it. To lose it is to lose life.

Sorcery focuses on the search for meaning in the occult. *Enmities, strife, jealousy,* and *outbursts of anger* reflect the standard reactions of one who is frustrated with a given set of circumstances. Either some supposed meaning in life has been taken from him, or threatened, or kept just beyond his reach.

Disputes, dissensions, and *factions* point to conflicting ideologies as to where life really is—where values are. *Envyings* is clear enough. Someone else has "made it," and I want it.

The final two "deeds," *drunkenness* and *carousing,* evidence the fact that I have now given up.

I have no will to seek meaning anymore.
I've tried and tried to make some sense out of life.
I'm through trying.
I want out.

Please Don't Tamper with My Idol

Of the various expressions of the "deeds of the flesh," *idolatry* seems so uniquely captivating. Especially the socially acceptable types of idolatry. I grasp so tightly to my fulfillments. And from a purely human welfare point of view, it is better for others that I do. I find meaning in my work, my artistic creations. My idealistic humanism, instead of attacking others or escaping responsibility, is actually contributing to the well-being of others. But let someone threaten my idol and...watch out! You'd be surprised how quickly I can react.

Perhaps my particular idol is that of being a popular, much-admired teacher. And then some better teacher comes along. I begin to hear that students are flocking to sign up for his section to the exclusion of mine. Stand back! My protective reflexes are as quick as a laser. I say to myself, "That new teacher seems smooth enough...probably covering his own insecurity! Just give him a few weeks and the veneer will wear thin. Anyway, students are poor judges of what makes a good teacher."

Those "wholesome" idols are so terribly subtle because I can say to myself, "But isn't 'being a teacher every student would love to have' a worthy goal?" And of course the answer is "Yes!" But a goal can so easily become *the* goal and as such it becomes *the* measurement as to where life or meaning for me is to be found.It is then an idol and a very fragile idol at that. As an idol, it cannot help but cast a shadow on the priority of God—His joy, His sufficiency, His glory—and my relation to that priority. It is so difficult to separate one's *identity* from the particular *channel* through which God might desire that identity to flow.

There are so many potential idols. Maybe yours has been to be very attractive to the opposite sex. And at last your efforts appear rewarded. Someone has found you attractive. Ah! It's a great feeling! And then comes that faint coolness and reserve followed by tactful rejections and finally that blunt, cold breakup. That would be devastating enough to your idol, but then you discover that she (or he) has not only rejected you, but has found someone else. Someone wittier—more attractive than you. Shattering, absolutely shattering. Out of this terrible hurt you either slip into depression as you feel life ebbing through your fingers, or you fight to protect your idol.

"She wasn't good enough for me, anyway. Didn't appreciate my fine, inner qualities. Knew all along she couldn't be trusted. They deserve each other. She'll get burned by him for sure."

With that, your idol, your sense of meaning and fulfillment in life, is once again safe and secure.

Some idols are especially wholesome, but they are still idols.

An individual's life may be entirely submerged in his family. He has carefully constructed his priorities and his family is number one. Then one day some drunk careens across the center line and his entire family is wiped out in an instant. He's not only lost his family, he has lost life—meaning. What's left? Now unless he soon discovers some other goal, some worthy idol, he will turn to embrace any one or more of the other works of the flesh we've discussed from Galatians 5.

It is both surprising and discouraging to discover how many sins we Christians commit which are really nothing more than flesh level efforts to protect some idol.

Remember how you felt when someone said, "Say, you're putting on weight!" or "I didn't know you were losing your hair." Maybe you controlled it, but it was there nevertheless—you were angry, offended, just a little bit hateful. This was especially true if you were criticized in some area in which you had taken pride in yourself such as in speaking or sports, or in being a good cook or a loving, generous person. Inwardly at least the sparks fly and you flush with emotion. You might even tell just a little lie to keep your idol intact.

Meaning: A Burned Out Bridge

Oh the tragedy of Eden! Rejecting dependence upon the will and character of God, Adam and Eve rejected *life*! Looking for fullness they found instead a fathomless despair. Their one bridge to meaning—their fundamental reason for existing—lay in charred and hopeless ruin before them. Man's essential nature was now "in the flesh." And the Bible says that "those who are in the flesh cannot please God."

> So, by his very nature, man is a sinner.
> Cut off from his Creator.
> Cut off from any hope of meaning.
> That's what sin is all about.[7]

Summary

To appreciate the wholesomeness of authentic Christian personhood, it must first be seen over against the biblical picture of the lostness of man and the fundamental nature of sin.

In drastic contrast with God's original and ultimate intention for human beings to be receivers and displayers of His very life in a dependent love relationship, man rejected God. Since this dependent relationship as seen most perfectly in the life of Jesus would have given meaning to existence, to lose it was to lose life. Thus man forced upon himself the consequence of hopelessly struggling with the issue of meaning. This *is* sin—a tragedy for man, an offense to God.

Note: It will be important to keep in mind the focus of this chapter in terms of the relationship between sin and the problem of meaning because the rest of the book builds on this fundamental concept.

Chapter 1, Notes

1. The biblical concept of dependence is inseparable from faith. It is in this sense that the following quotation is valid. "The opposite of sin is faith and never virtue." H.A. Williams quoted in *Sources and Resources, A Newsletter for Christian Leaders*, Vol. I, No. 12, February 15, 1978.

2. See D. Martin Lloyd-Jones, *Romans, the Law and Its Functions, Exposition of Chapter 7:1-8:4* (Grand Rapids: Zondervan, 1974), p. 125, in which he emphasizes the inseparable relationship between sin and independence.

3. "The word *sarx* in Paul's epistles has various shades of meaning ranging from the strictly literal usage in such a phrase as 'flesh and bones' to the idea of carnal sin. But in the great majority of passages it stands for human nature on its material side. It includes 'all that is peculiar to human nature in its corporeal embodiment.' Elsewhere Paul has used the contrast of *hŏ ĕsō* and *hŏ ĕsō anthropos*—the inward and the outward man—and the flesh comprises everything (impulses, thoughts, desires, and the like) belonging to the latter.... It is human nature in its frailty and weakness and in need of help. It is man apart from God.... It is not in itself base; and it is well to remind ourselves that of the notion of the inherent evil of matter, which was a characteristic of Gnostic doctrine, there was not a trace in Paul. His dualism is not cosmic nor metaphysical, but practical and moral. But though not evil in itself, the flesh is that part of man's nature which gives sin its opportunity" (James S. Stewart, *A Man In Christ* [New York: Harper and Brothers, n.d.], pp. 103-104). See also *The International Standard Bible Encyclopedia*, 1949 ed., s.v. "Flesh," by H.L.E. Luering.

4. It is in this sense, I believe, that the following familiar expressions of the sinfulness of man can best be understood: *"There is no one who does good, not even one." "All our righteous deeds are like a filthy garment." "The heart is more deceitful than all else and is desperately sick." "For I know that nothing good dwells in me, that is in my flesh"* (Psalms 14:3; Isaiah 64:6; Jeremiah 17:9; Romans 7:18).

In view of the relative lack of literature from an evangelical point of view concerning the issue of meaning, it is important to show that the Bible is anything but silent. The Hebrew word *hâbal* and the Greek word *mataiŏs* both convey the idea of emptiness or futility. Notable references in the Old Testament are Jeremiah 2:5 and Psalm 39:6, plus the repeated occurrences in Ecclesiastes. In the New Testament see 1 Peter 1:8; Ephesians 4:17; Romans 1:21; 8:20.

Richard Trench describes the Greek understanding of the idea of emptiness. *"Mataiŏs,* as observed already, will express the aimlessness, the leading to no object or end, the vanity, of all which has not Him, who is the only true object and end of any intelligent creature, for its scope." (p. 181).

Trench elaborates on the background of this word form. *"Mataiŏtēs* is a word altogether strange to profane Greek; one, too, which the old heathen world, had it possessed it, could never have imparted that depth of meaning which in Scripture it has obtained. For indeed that heathen world was itself too deeply and hopelessly sunken in 'vanity' to be fully alive to the fact that it was sunken in it at all; was committed so far as to have lost all power to pronounce that judgment upon itself which this word pronounced upon it." (Richard Chenevix Trench, *Synonyms of the New Testament* [Grand Rapids: Eerdmans, 1948], p. 182). See also Vine's comparison of *kĕnŏs* with *mataiŏs.* W. E. Vine, *An Expository Dictionary of New Testament Words,* 2 vols. (Old Tappan, N.J.: Fleming H. Revell Company, 1966), 2:25. Also, Colin Brown, ed., *The New International Dictionary of New Testament Theology,* 3 vols. (Grand Rapids: Zondervan, 1975), 1:549-553.

5.   Gleason L. Archer, *In the Shadow of the Cross* (Grand
      Rapids: Zondervan, 1957), pp. 13-14.

6.   See 1 Samuel 12:20-21, *"...but serve the LORD with all
      your heart. And you must not turn aside, for then you
      would go after futile things which cannot profit or deliver,
      because they are futile."* Also 2 Kings 17:15, *"...they re-
      jected His statutes...and they followed vanity and became
      vain."* (In both passages the word "futile" or "vain" is the
      same word as in Ecclesiastes.)

7.   C.S. Lewis, *The Problem of Pain* (New York: Macmillan
      Press, 1948), pp. 70-71. "The process (of the fall of
      Adam) was not, I conceive, comparable to mere deterioration
      as it may now occur in a human individual; it was a loss of
      status as a species. What condition was transmitted by hered-
      ity to all later generations, for it was not simply what
      biologists call an acquired variation. It was the emergence of
      a new kind of man; a new species, never made by God, *had
      sinned its way into existence....* It was a radical alteration of
      his constitution."

Chapter 2

The Wonder of Who You Are

*U*p to this point we have been thinking about the human race in general and the tragedy of sin. We've looked at the negative side long enough. It's time we focused in on what it means to be a Christian.

I hope it will become obvious very soon that the answer to the problem of sin is deeply rooted in the discovery of who a Christian actually is. In this discovery the problem of meaninglessness dissolves.

Self-consciousness, God's Special Gift to Man

I doubt if you'll ever bump into a turtle or a frog who is seriously contemplating his own existence. I may be wrong, but I have difficulty picturing such a creature involved in the act of self-interrogation as it basks in the afternoon sun.

"I wonder who I really am?" Or, "I wonder just why I am at all?"

I can't see it.

But God has made man a self-conscious being. He has an ability to think in terms of his own identity. It is a mark of humanness that sets him apart from animals.

Listen to man's voice:

"When I consider your heavens,
the work of your fingers,
the moon and the stars,
which you have set in place,
what is man that you are mindful of him,
the son of man that you care for him?"

(Psalm 8:3-4)

I believe that God has given to us this unique ability of self-consciousness, of thinking in terms of who we are and why we are alive, for a very important reason. Without it, no one would ever respond to Jesus.

By the Way, Who Are You?

With many non-Christians, it was this very questioning that broke down the barriers of resistance to the conviction of the Holy Spirit. Perhaps this was the way it happened in your life. You came to the place where you began asking yourself,

"I wonder what life is all about, anyway. This squirrel cage existence really doesn't make sense at all. There has to be something else."

This same ability of self-awareness can also serve as a special means of grace to lead a believer deeper and deeper into the real meaning of his life.

We all do a fair amount of thinking about ourselves. And yet, I've been surprised to discover that many people don't like to be pressed too far in answering the question of their own identity.

"Excuse me, but, who are you? Have you thought about it?"

'Well...sure. I'm Sam Jones."

"No, I mean *who are you*? Not just your name."

"Oh...well, I live in Portland, and—"

"Excuse me. But let's try again. Who *are* you?"

"Aw, you know. I'm the guy who drives the yellow Corvette. I work at the service station on the corner. My sister married the mayor's son."

"No—you misunderstand me. I'm asking you who *you* are—way down deep inside. Who are you?"

"Come on now, this is getting stupid. I'm a member of the human race. What planet did you come from?"

No, people don't like questions like that. Even Christians become ill at ease.

"Who am I? I'm a Baptist. Sure am. No—wait—I get you now. I'm a Christian—you know."

"Tell me."

"Well, he's a person who has accepted Christ."

"But I didn't ask you what you've done. I asked you who you are."

After fumbling around a bit he might respond with, "I'm going to heaven when I die" or "I'm a person who has been forgiven of all my sins—I'm a believer." Then again, he might think he knows what you're driving at and say, "Sure, I know who I am. I'm just a plain old sinner saved by grace."

In this chapter my hope is that you will come to grips with yourself in a way you never have before. Just who are you?

Fragile Identities

Generally, when we think of our own identity, we respond in terms of some particular position we have—or hope to have. We are fathers or mothers, students or teachers, baseball players or farmers. Yet when we stop to think about such identities, we have to admit that they are all so fragile—tenuous.

"I'm a mother!" you say. And that is beautiful. Just great. As long as your children are alive. But who would you be if a tragedy takes them away from you? What is your identity then?

"I'm a businessman." That sounds solid—until the bottom drops out. You're bankrupt. Business gone. Who are you then?

"I'm a vocalist." Yes you are. Until that dreaded surgery makes a mockery of the title.

"Who are you?"

"Oh, someday I hope to be...."

"Who are you?"

"Aw, I don't have to worry about that. I'm retired!"

An Identity Pilgrimage

I wonder if you would be willing to follow me on an identity pilgrimage. It is a rather private one. My own. Parts of it are rather stupid or silly. Some of it, sad. But it all leads to the most glorious event that I have ever consciously experienced. Actually, a new beginning.

I'll have to go back to when I was a little boy, walking down an aisle at the end of a church service to let everyone know I was trusting Jesus as my Savior. From then on I knew that I was forgiven; that I would go to heaven when I died; that God heard my prayers. I was a Christian.

As time went along, I did most of the things a Christian boy was expected to do—Sunday school and church, evening youth group, rallies, summer camps. One camp was decisive. I remember saying to God (with considerable fear of the consequences), "Oh God, my life is Yours to do anything You want with it." I was fourteen. Six feet tall, gold-rimmed glasses, embarrassingly skinny. The biggest reason for my decision was that it was the lesser of two fears. Sitting next to me in his wheelchair was a boy terribly crippled by polio—my own secret fear. It wasn't as though the speaker used the crippled boy as an illustration, but he did send shivers down my spine as he spoke of the seriousness of commitment to Christ. Thus, 90 percent out of dread and maybe 10 percent out of love for God, I responded. "Lord, if I don't give my life to You now, You're going to take it one way or another! So here it is."

I was now a dedicated Christian.

A Sack of Weed Seeds

But I soon discovered that my decision seemed to create more problems than it solved. First of all, my concept of dedication kept colliding with all sorts of self-centered desires and fantasies. And second, these repeated collisions underlined more than ever before how sinful I was. What little positive self-image I had was now pretty well shattered. I knew that "in me dwelleth no good thing." I was a sinner—a dedicated Christian sinner. So much for self-image!

Soon after that a youth rally speaker shared (with considerable enthusiasm) that we were God the Father's love gift to His Son. He had us turn to the seventeenth chapter of John where repeatedly the expression occurs: *"those whom you gave me."* As I listened, I thought to myself, if someone gave me a gift like that I would call it a dirty trick! For God to give *me* to Jesus would be like giving a doctor a bottle of germs or a farmer a sack of weed seeds. Yet as I read John 17, it sounded as though Jesus actually was pleased with His gift. How could that possibly be?

Oh, to Be Somebody

So very much I wanted to really *be* somebody. Just to hit a home run at summer camp with all those girls cheering along the side. But every time at bat was the same old thing. My middle name could well have been "Clumsy." Compounding my awkwardness, I refused to wear those ugly, wire-rimmed glasses. Naturally, the balls just swished past my bat and home run glory became just one more fantasy.

In this struggle for some sense of personal worth friends are terribly important. A friend is someone who thinks you are somebody even when you don't see how you could possibly be of value to anyone. There was the one cute girl with long, blond hair who actually wanted to walk with me to the last campfire. Grasping her hand, I glanced up through those tall, dark pine trees and thought, "Say, God, maybe I'm not such a nobody after all!"

One day walking down the hall in high school, the basketball coach spotted me—now 6-feet-3-inches of bone tightly wrapped with skin. He told me I would make a fantastic basketball player. "Say, maybe he was right!"

And I really tried. Being a Christian would be so much easier if Coach's prediction proved true. But somehow my elongated appendages wouldn't cooperate with my fervent desires. I might as well have dressed the part of a clown out on the court—I had everything but the costume.

But there was one day of glory. Right in the middle of an exciting game I found myself loping down court rather than occupying my usual niche on the bench. Someone threw the ball at me. Hard. Right at my stomach. Doubling up and falling to the floor, I desperately threw the ball up and made a basket! The hometown crowd erupted! I read my name in the school paper, even the town paper. But I didn't have the courage to tell anyone I hadn't even aimed for the basket. It was sheer chance. I simply hurt too much to do anything else. But oh, *it felt so good to be somebody!*

"In Me Dwelleth No Good Thing"
The time finally came when I couldn't put it off any longer. I had to decide what I was going to do with my life. Wouldn't it be great to have such evident talent that I didn't even have to decide? An artistic flair, a mechanical knack, a beautiful voice...I had a friend in college with a voice like that. All he had to do was learn a few more things about music, get up, open his mouth, and everybody would marvel. They still do. Self-worth, identity, meaning? He had it made!

As a Christian, I often struggled to live up to an appropriate level, whatever that was. But always lurking close to the surface, a surging supply of feelings and desires served vividly to support my "biblical"[1] conclusion "that in *me* dwelleth no good thing." I was told that God would take away all my old desires. He didn't! No, I didn't drink, didn't smoke, didn't go to dances. But what I couldn't do in public, my active imagination dreamed in private. Somehow, my heart was wrong, and I knew it.

I remember the warm, summer evening when two girls from the East visited our youth group. As the group's president, I was more than willing to extend a very friendly welcome. Especially to one of them. Simply beautiful. My thoughts flickered rapidly as we smiled through small talk. With the local girls, I had to maintain my "committed Christian" image. No fooling around. Word spread fast in our group. But a visitor...I drove her home. She was as delightful to sit next to as I had imagined. But to my disappointment, all she wanted to do was talk about spiritual things—all the way to the door. I didn't even get to hold her hand.

With all my burning fantasies still intact I drove back home. A long, long drive home. Piercing me deeper than any disappointment was the knowledge that my heart was "deceitful above all things and desperately wicked." How could it be that my desire to please God and all those other fleshly desires could fit into one person? What was I anyway? A spiritual failure, that was for sure.

Trying Harder

In order to assuage my constant guilt, I tried even harder to do the things I figured God wanted me to do. I took every college Bible course available. Every weekend, all the way through college, I worked in struggling rural Sunday schools. Not that I wanted to. But it seemed the way to please God. Then there were four years of seminary, four years of youth ministry, four years in the pastorate. I was committed to become someone for God—a youth leader, a pastor, a husband, a father, a teacher, a *something*.

And God was gracious. Again and again He showed me mercy and honored His Word—He loved me. I knew "the answers" and I taught them well, with all the sincere emotional energy I could muster. Yet I remember one night driving home after speaking on the subject of spiritual victory. "David," I said to myself, "what you told them tonight is true. At least according to the way you were taught. But David...it isn't working for you, is it? It isn't working at all."

I had reckoned myself "dead unto sin" dozens of times; often with a great surge of faith. I pled with God with all my heart for victory and joy. I confessed countless times. I memorized dozens of Bible verses. I claimed the fullness of the Holy Spirit in earnest faith. It was real faith. *And it did not work*. Then, God opened a door.

The Christ Filter

To appreciate that door, let's see if we can get a composite picture of the common, contemporary teaching on the spiritual life.[2] To do this, let's imagine God in all His absolute holiness at the very top of the picture. Then down at the bottom, let's place me, a SINNER. Because I have received Christ, God has performed a remarkable thing. Since He obviously cannot associate with sinners—light cannot fellowship with darkness—He has inserted a miraculous filter between Himself and me, the sinner. That filter is Jesus. His death, His resurrection. Therefore, as God looks down on me, He doesn't see me as I really am, but rather He sees all that is right about Jesus. Because of that wonderful filter, God's record against me is wiped out. Everything I was and am, a sinner who sins, is completely erased. And further, everything that Jesus is has been written in place of that record. I am justified. I am "positionally" righteous. I am judicially righteous. This is the way God sees me. But if for a moment—horrible thought—that filter were not there and He saw me as I really am, He would call me what I am, a SINNER.

But God has done two other things. First, He has sent the Holy Spirit, the Comforter. Someone called alongside to help me, teach me, give me power. And secondly, God has given me a new nature.[3] Therefore, though I am essentially a sinner, I do have this fresh capacity. So who am I? I am a SINNER with a new nature and the Holy Spirit.

The Tragic Flaw

Praise God there is some solid truth in this picture. It is true that all my sins, past, present, and future, have been paid for by Jesus' death. They are nowhere to be found in God's records concerning me. And, praise God, I rest in the fact that there has been no dubious "book juggling" to bring this about. As an objective fact, all of Christ's righteousness has been correctly credited to my account.

But there is one serious error—a tragic flaw. An error that pervades dozens of popular books on the Christian life. I wish I could shout these next lines around the world! A Christian is not simply a person who gets forgiveness, who gets to go to heaven, who gets the Holy Spirit, who gets a new nature. Mark this—*a Christian is a person who has become someone he was not before.* A Christian, in terms of his deepest identity, is a SAINT, a born child of God, a divine masterpiece, a child of light, a citizen of heaven. *Not only positionally* (true in the mind of God but not true in actuality here on earth), *not only judicially* (a matter of God's moral bookkeeping), but ACTUALLY.

Becoming a Christian is not just getting something, no matter how wonderful that something may be.

It is becoming someone.

Only Saints Go to Heaven

Perhaps you are saying, "I thought that's what everyone believed." Most emphatically, it is *not* what everyone believes. In the deepest sense of personhood, if you have received Jesus Christ as Lord and Savior, you are not a sinner. You are righteous. But what "you" are we talking about? Not some ethereal, "positional" you. But that most fundamental you, that "you" which most deeply and eternally gives you authentic personhood. The "you" that goes to heaven someday. Forgiven sinners can never go to heaven; they would only dirty up the place. Only saints can go to heaven and you are a SAINT. If you are really thinking with me right now, there are probably dozens of reactions and questions that have a right to be considered.

I can hear some of you say,

"Isn't it the idea that Jesus is in me? Isn't it His righteousness that makes me right with God?"

"I know how bad I am. If you knew me the way I know myself, you wouldn't doubt that for a moment."

"Yes I know the Bible teaches that my old sin nature has been crucified, but it still has to be controlled, doesn't it? Doesn't the Bible say, 'put off the old man'?"[4]

"Are you saying that a Christian doesn't sin?"

These are very important questions which we will need to consider very carefully. But first let's listen to the exceptionally strange answer Jesus gave one night to an earnest, searching Jew.

"A New Kind of Species"

Nicodemus was hungry to know the way to God. All his learning left him empty, questioning.

Jesus could have said, "Nicodemus, you must be forgiven." But He didn't.

Jesus said, *"Unless a man is born again, he cannot see the kingdom of God.... You should not be surprised at my saying, 'you must be born again'"* (John 3:3-7). Clearly Jesus did not mean "birth" as some vague, symbolic, initiatory term[5], but rather an actual, radical change in one's essential being. Notice our Lord adds, *"Flesh gives birth to flesh, but the Spirit gives birth to the spirit."* To enter the kingdom of God requires that one be of a different species!

Consider physical conception and birth. Being born isn't simply someone getting something more that one didn't have before (like getting the Holy Spirit). No! Being born is becoming *someone who was not there before.* And that is exactly the issue in spiritual new birth!

My parents gave me "flesh" birth. I became somebody. A real, fullfledged person. Similarly, by the new birth I became a brand new person, *a spiritual person.* One writer describes a Christian as "a new kind of species." He goes on to say:

These two segments of the human race are at opposite poles, they are basically in antithesis. They dwell together because they are both members of the *Family* of man. They are one *Genus*, to use the zoological term. But something has happened to cause them to separate into two *Species* within that *Genus*, and this separation is at a far deeper and more fundamental level than mere genetics. The division is the result of a spiritual transformation that really constitutes a new creation—nothing less, in fact, than rebirth. It is not a symbolic rebirth, like that achieved by ritual in some pagan religions of antiquity and even of today. It is a fundamental change in human nature, so great a change that it amounts to a genuine form of speciation....We indeed remain *in* the world, but we are no longer *of* the world.[6]

You Are not the Same

This concept of identity, so fundamental and yet so mysterious, was well known within the leadership of the early church. Their words were clear words, their analogies simple and striking. They spoke without hesitation, unencumbered by the creative complexities theologians have dreamed up over the centuries.[7]

Perhaps this "new personhood" idea seems far away from the daily reality of your life. That still doesn't change the basic fact: if you have received the Savior, you simply are *not* the same person you were before. When you were *"in the flesh"* (Romans 8:9, NASB), life and meaning for you had to be found right there—and there alone. Your brain, your emotions, your senses, your creativity, your glands, your world environments, your relationships—this was life. It could be found nowhere else.

But if you have been born again, this is not so anymore, *whether you know it or not!*

You may weigh the same,
Look the same,
Feel the same,

But you are not the same.

Jesus could look a man or woman straight in the eyes and say, "I have come that you might have life. You may think you are alive, but you aren't." What? Weren't they doing everything "live" people were doing...eating, walking, loving, dreaming, planning, working? Yes. And yet, the Bible says "in Him was life!"

Don't Water It Down

That's radical. Terribly radical. Don't water it down!

How could you water it down?

By saying: "Yes, I know I have a new nature. He has 'clothed me with righteousness!'"[8] What you *have* isn't the point. *It's who you are* that's the issue.

By saying: "Oh, I'm just a sinner saved by grace. I'm just a sinner indwelt by the Holy Spirit"—that's watering it down. That's casting an undeserved shadow on the greatest miracle God has ever performed concerning you. Don't do it.

(Even as I am writing this, anticipating this present moment right now as you are reading, I struggle with the fact that I am writing to your mind. It will handle these words and sentences in different ways depending on your I.Q. and your ability to read and to think logically. But your mind is only an access into your deepest self. And since I.Q. tests are meaningless to your truest personhood, I must consider two things. First, I must communicate in such a way that no one will conclude that the smarter one is, the greater is his capacity for true spirituality. And second, both you and I must be trusting in that most miraculous ministry of the Holy Spirit Who alone is in a position "to bear witness with our spirit." True spirituality ultimately has to do with "the eyes of your heart" and with information "which passes knowledge." How far more fundamentally is this true as we read the unique, divinely inspired Scriptures! Praise God! "The anointing which you have received from Him abides in you, and you have no need for anyone to teach you; but as His anointing teaches you about all things,

*and is true and is not a lie, and just as it has taught you,
you abide in Him" [1 John 2:27].)*

Listen to John's voice for a moment... *"How great is the
love which the Father has lavished on us, that we should be
called children of God! And that is what we are!... Dear
friends, now we are children of God"* (1 John 3:1-2). It is
almost as though the apostle was writing along and as he
came to the words "children of God" he paused in
amazement.

Could this really be?

Did the love of God go that far?

That we should be called *the children of God*?

It's really true.

John was deeply moved—stirred to his innermost being—"And that is what we are!"⁹

Please don't take the edge off John's excitement. God
says *"We are God's workmanship, created in Christ Jesus"*
(Ephesians 2:10). Does God create something dirty? Is God's
workmanship—His masterpiece—simply adding a little
spiritual lump onto sinful clay? Let's let Paul answer that
question:

> *"Therefore, if anyone is in Christ Jesus he is a new
> creation; the old has gone, the new has come!"*
> (2 Corinthians 5:17)

Right now, as you are reading, I wish I knew what was
going through your mind. Perhaps some of you are saying,
"Sure. I know all of that. I thought he was going to say
something really new."

Maybe it's new; maybe it's not. That isn't the point right
now. I simply know that in my own life, I have read Bible
verses like 2 Corinthians 5:17, Ephesians 2:10, and Romans
8:16-17 hundreds of times over dozens of years. Yet now I
feel as though I'd never read them at all. And if right now you
are still saying that a Christian is one who must say "No" to

himself in order to say "Yes" to God, I think you are not reading those verses either.

I Am No Longer the One Doing It . . . "

Let's take a closer look at this by taking Romans 7 as our focal point. In this chapter Paul is describing the struggle of a person with sin from an old covenant legalism perspective.[10] The sense of the spiritual was so fundamental to the apostle Paul that he states twice (and infers several more times) that when sin occurs, *"it is no longer I myself who do it, but it is sin living in me"* (Romans 7:17-20). Though he acknowledges personal responsibility, *he denies that sinning is part of his essential, deepest nature.* This is extremely important for us to see.[11]

John goes so far as to say, *"Dear children, do not let anyone lead you astray. He who does what is right is righteous, just as He is righteous. . . . No one who is born of God will continue to sin, because God's seed remains in him; he cannot go on sinning because he has been born of God"* (1 John 3:7-9). Do we really have any right to tamper with these words? Can I really conclude that God isn't speaking about me, but rather some new nature which I possess?

I Am Now Someone Else

Many contemporary sayings and illustrations roll in like a fog to obscure our true identity. You've heard a few.

Like the bumper sticker: "Christians aren't perfect, they're just forgiven."

Like the pious little saying: "A Christian is just one beggar telling another beggar where to find bread."

Really? Peter says we are a royal priesthood!

Perhaps you've encountered this illustration used to explain Paul's statement that our "citizenship is in heaven":

> I was a native of a very wicked country. Satan's country. I stood for everything my country stood for. And then came the day I received Christ. Jesus

took over that part of Satan's territory where I lived. The boundary lines were changed. Then Jesus came to me and said, "By the way, you're in my territory now. So you'd better start changing the way you act to conform to your new citizenship."

Maybe the little story has a point, but it misses the biggest point. Being born again involves a radical change of being. It is not simply a change in citizenship papers; it is a change in me! I *was* "by nature a child of wrath." No more. *By nature* I am now someone else: a child of God.

Here's another touching illustration:

I've been a wicked boy. Recently I was caught in the act of one of my many thieveries, and was brought before the judge. Looking down on me, he pronounced a huge fine which I could never pay. But then the judge paused, stepped down, and stood beside me. "I will pay your debt," he said. "In fact, I will take you into my own family to live in my home and eat at my table. You will be trained by a private tutor." So the judge took me home. The tutor has taught me how to wash my hands and hold a fork and how to be polite and clean up my language. . . .

But I'm still me! You see, the illustration simply doesn't go far enough.

Filling in the Gaps

We humans try so hard to adjust truth to be more understandable, more systematic, more related to life as we see it. Yet so often we accomplish precisely the opposite. We press it all out of shape.

Consider the truth of Romans 6:6. We read there that "our old self was crucified." That's clear enough. But as I look at that concept and look at my own behavior, I find that the two simply do not agree. So I go to work with my imagination to fill in the gaps. I conclude that since crucifixion is a very slow death, I can explain my behavior by saying it isn't quite dead yet. But then the passage goes on to say I've "been buried." Buried alive? Again I go to work with my mental gymnastics and come up with yet another conclusion. Paul must have meant that my "old self" was crucified from God's perspective—but down here on earth it's different.

Ah, that's it! This then allows me to say "the old man has died," and then turn around a few sentences later and say "the old man is very much alive but—of course—his power has been broken." Whatever that means. It's so easy to push and poke and embellish a truth until we end up with something that doesn't even resemble the original.

Is Discipline the Key?

Apparently when writers make the statement "sin's power has been broken," they are really saying this: Romans 6 teaches us that we don't *have* to give in to those sinful desires because the power is gone. Before we were saved we couldn't say "No!" But now we can. From this some Christians falsely assume that some particular sin is conquered because they have found the strength not to do it. But is this unique to Christians? Of course not. All around us we see examples of non-Christians who have broken the power of swearing, stealing, or being immoral. It is quite obvious by the fact that they no longer engage in these things. They are either very disciplined people or they have become involved in other activities (perhaps quite wholesome) which have sublimated those previous ones.

How easy it is to forget that sin is not simply what we do or don't do; sin relates to our independence from or dependence upon life from God! As Jesus said, *"Without Me, you can do nothing."*

Personhood Precedes Power

We've all met Christians (we've met ourselves!) who have had to admit that the power of sin in their lives seemed to be more intense *after* they received Christ. In many cases, they are really saying: "It isn't just the 'doing' of sinful things which bothers me, it's the 'wishing'."

It was hardly by chance that Paul selected the sin of coveting in Romans 7:8. It's the most secret of all sins. It can exist when by all measurements I am enjoying "the broken power" of my "old sin nature." For you see, true victory over sin is only a reality when not only am I not doing the sin but (1) I honestly *do not desire* what my flesh finds tantalizing, and (2) in place of that desire there is also *positive life* flowing from God, manifested in holy living. This is why spiritual power is so crucial (Ephesians 3:14-16).

But power must be linked to an awareness of person-hood.

The Door and the Doormen

A few pages back I spoke of a wonderful door. A door God opened that changed my entire perspective. Well, God had a doorman. His name is John Murray, who wrote a classic commentary on the book of Romans.

I will never forget the day I read a portion of Murray's commentary. I was so excited I literally sat on the edge of my chair. This is what I read:

> It is a mistake to think of the believer as both an old man and a new man or as having in him both the old man and the new man, the latter in view of regeneration and the former because of remaining corruption. That this is not Paul's concept is made apparent here by the fact that the "old man" is represented as having been crucified with Christ and the tense indicates a once-for-all definitive act after the pattern of Christ's crucifixion. The "old man" can no more be regarded as in the process of being crucified than Christ in his sphere could thus be regarded.[12]

I just about shivered with amazement. After hundreds of hours of reading and listening to what I thought my teachers said, at last I was listening to a man who let the Bible speak! And Murray was a godly, respected scholar. Listen to another of Murray's statements:

> Paul announces the definitive cleavage with the world of sin, which union with Christ insures. The old man is the unregenerate man; the new man is the regenerate man created in Christ Jesus unto good works. It is no more feasible to call a believer a new man and an old man, than it is to call him a regenerate man and an unregenerate. And neither is it warranted to speak of the believer as having in him the old man and the new man. This kind of terminology is without warrant and is but another method of doing prejudice to the doctrine which Paul was so jealous to establish when he siad, *"our old man has been crucified."*[13]

Was this man Murray an isolated renegade? With great relief I discovered that the much beloved W. H. Griffith Thomas said the same things. Where had I been all these years, assuming that I was still in some way the "old self" that I was before I was saved? Listen to Thomas:

> The old man *ceased to exist* (italics mine) at our regeneration, when it was "put off." We are never exhorted to "put off" the "old man." An exhortation to "put off the old man" would be tantamount to an exhortation to become regenerate.[14]

God had another doorman, D. Martyn Lloyd-Jones, to whom I will be forever indebted. By producing an entire book on just the sixth chapter of Romans, he forced me to slow down enough to discover the amazing implications of Murray's brief statements. His book, *Romans, The New Man,*

Exposition of Chapter 6, (published by Zondervan) should be a "must read" book for every Christian!

The door was now wide open. I embraced the new understanding with a joy that seemed too good to be true. According to God I was a new person—no matter what my experience shouted out. I actually—right down here where I live—was God's born one.

His actual child.

His masterpiece.

In the deepest sense of being, I was a saint. I was somebody![15]

The Twin Bins

I really believe that the major reason this revolutionary truth never hit home with me was due to the fact that many Bible teachers automatically assume that all biblical truth falls into either of two big bins.

They call the first bin *positional truth*. That's like our filter illustration. God sees something as true because He sees it through the filter of the death and resurrection of Jesus. As I stated before, there is a proper place for this idea.[16] But if one is not careful to spot its limits he will find himself parroting the standard double talk that a person must see himself as "positionally" dead when in fact his old self is very much alive.

The other bin, *experiential truth*, is simply anything that is truth that I am consciously aware of in the process of living. Therefore as I read my Bible it is my task to decide whether the truth I am reading about is to be understood as being either "positional" or "experiential."

A Third Category

But I am convinced there is a third classification which deserves the title *actual truth*. It involves facts which certainly are not positional and they may or may not be experiential.

Maybe an illustration would help. Let's suppose a young girl possesses a very beautiful singing voice. Because her parents are fearful she will become proud, they keep telling her that she has a terrible voice—nobody would want to listen to it. Assuming that her parents must be correct, she carefully avoids singing where anyone might possibly hear her. Years go by. Silent years. Then one Sunday in a worship service she becomes so caught up in a melody that she forgets herself. With an overflowing heart she sings out—strong and clear—in full voice. Immediately the people around her cease their singing in order to hear this lovely, haunting voice.

"My!" they exclaim after the song. "You have a wonderful voice!"

"Oh no," she stammers, embarrassed. "I—I know I have a terrible voice. Please forgive me. I'm sorry I bothered you with it. I'll try to be more quiet."

"No! Really your voice is beautiful—exquisite. Please sing more!"

This is what I mean by "actual truth." All through those songless years this girl actually had a beautiful voice—that was the real truth. But it wasn't experiential. And it certainly wasn't positional (that is, a recording of someone else's voice but with her name put on the label).

Many Christians assume that unless something is being experienced, it must be "positional" truth rather than actual truth. If I don't *feel* a given truth from Scripture, I throw it into the positional bin. The Bible says I am a new creation (2 Corinthians 5:17). But I don't feel like a new creation; it must be positional.

From the Burrow to the Sky

This crucial third classification, *actual truth,* is so very important to appreciate, maybe a more extended illustration will help to underline it. This one will require that you stretch your imagination with me a long way. . . . Ready?

Let's imagine that you are a bird who, by some strange series of events, was hatched into a family of rabbits. Your entire world was a rabbit's world. You learned to eat rabbit's food, you shared the warmth and security of a rabbit's burrow, you played rabbit's games. You considered yourself a rabbit. What reason was there for you to assume anything else? The rabbits gave you full acceptance as one of their own. Somehow your difference in appearance didn't bother them. So why should it bother you? It was as though they really didn't see any difference. This was home; this was life. Yes, there were those times, like when the dog chased you, that for an instant—just an instant—you flapped those strange appendages on your sides and almost thought you could fly. But then you caught yourself. That was stupid; rabbits don't fly. Sure, you hopped a bit differently than the others—but you got around as well as any of them. No, there was really no question at all as to your identity; you were a rabbit indeed!

And then one day someone came by and said to you, "By the way, did you know that you are a bird? A real bird? A bird who was built to fly?"

"What? A bird! Ridiculous. I know who I am—I'm a rabbit!"

But this someone was very persistent. You couldn't hop away from him. Day after day he was there to remind you, to taunt you with a new identity. Not that the idea lacked fascination. But it was so...so cross-grain to everything you'd been taught. And you'd been comfortable being a rabbit.

Persistence finally won, however, and this someone began to teach you to exercise those strange flappers (wings, he called them). He spun all sorts of stories, tantalizing stories, about birds. Birds in flight...soaring high above trees...with the dogs below.

Gradually you found yourself wondering, Could it really be? Perhaps a rabbit could be carried aloft by a bird—a big bird or—or perhaps one could hop so high and so far that it would almost *seem* like flying. But to really BE a bird...?

Then at last that momentous day arrived and that someone led you high up to a bluff overlooking the rabbit world far below. This was the moment. You hopped right to the edge. With a most contagious shout your companion cried, "Now! You ARE A BIRD! Jump! Fly!"

And you jumped. Flapped. You fell for a moment that seemed forever. And then...you flew! You soared. Higher and higher. With the sound of wind swishing through your feathers you cried, "I am a bird, I am a bird! I can fly!"

A silly story? Of course it is. But please—don't miss the point. How many sincere Christians have willingly accepted and adjusted to a fake personal identity during their life as believers? Their concept of themselves was that really they were just like anyone else in the world. Just human. And fundamentally sinful. Therefore, to be a dedicated Christian was to somehow say "No" to one's essential nature in order to say "Yes" to a God who was contrary to that nature. To say "No" to what one really wanted in order to say "Yes" to what God wanted.

"Fly? Oh no. I can't fly. It's not my nature to fly. But I willingly submit to be carried on the wings of the Holy Spirit."

With massive relief it was so good to know that when God looked their way they were always hidden behind Jesus (remember the filter?) They were saved from that unspeakable embarrassment of being identified as rabbits and not birds after all. It was the Holy Spirit that was the "bird," not themselves. But if that were so, how would they ever go to heaven? Well, somehow (though you won't find it in the Bible) at that moment of death God would change their nature from sinner to saint—from rabbit to bird. Or maybe, if that's not the way God does it, He would simply and eternally remove at last all individual "selves" and heaven would just be Jesus! Of course, if that were true, then they would be "non-selves"—non-persons. But who wants to think that far anyway? Somehow it would all work out.

Christian, are you listening, thinking? What does the Bible say? Who do you think you are? Is the Spirit right now bearing witness with your spirit that you are a born one of God? Do you hear His convincing voice?

Summary

Contrary to much popular teaching, regeneration (being born again) is more than having something taken away (sins forgiven) or having something added to you (a new nature with the assistance of the Holy Spirit[17]); it is becoming someone you had never been before. This new identity is not on the flesh level, but the spirit level—one's deepest self. This miracle is more than a "judicial" act of God. It is an act so REAL that it is right to say that a Christian's essential nature is righteous rather than sinful. All other lesser identities each of us have can only be understood and appreciated by our acceptance and response to this fact.

But awareness of identity only brings us to the threshold. Through the door now opened in front of us, the ultimate issue becomes not identity, but meaning or purpose in life based upon this awareness of biblical self-identity. This discovery of meaning alone is the adequate foundation upon which one can confront sin and build a life of holiness. With this in mind our next step will be to consider the relationship between identity and meaning.

Chapter 2, Notes

1. "Biblical" is put in quotes because I follow this with a misquotation of Romans 7:18 in which the important phrase, *"that is, in my flesh,"* is omitted.

2. It is common, in fact automatic with most of us, that as we read something we either say "I agree" or "I disagree" as though our mind were already made up and that our purpose in reading was mainly to confirm our convictions and increase our capacity to oppose everything that is not in agreement with our convictions. This especially is a hazard for anyone who is looked to as an authority even in a minimal sense. My earnest prayer as I am anticipating this moment when you are reading these pages is that you will find grace to be open to *the possibility* of the fresh teaching by the Holy Spirit either in addition to or in place of convictions you may have.

3. Two of the more commonly used terms in Christian literature are *sin nature* (or old nature) and *new nature*. *Sin nature* is commonly defined as that capacity within me which causes me to sin and to serve self. The *new nature* is described as that capacity within me which desires to do the will of God and which is related to the presence in the believer of eternal life. Cf. Charles C. Ryrie, *Balancing the Christian Life* (Chicago: Moody Press, 1969), pp. 34-35.

4. See footnote 14, this chapter.

5. It was common for a Gentile who chose to enter into the Jewish faith, that is, to become a proselyte, to be described as a "child new born."

6.   Arthur C. Custance, "Man in Adam and in Christ", in
      Doorway Papers, 3 vols. (Grand Rapids: Zondervan,
      1975), 3:343-344.

7.   Our theological systems were originally built, I would
      imagine, as a sort of scaffolding around the truth of
God. Not to support it, and certainly not to build it, but
rather in order to get up close to it and observe its marvelous
structure. Too easily, the scaffolding has replaced the
building as the point of focus.

8.   A casual reading of Isaiah 61:10 *"He has clothed me with
      garments of salvation, and arrayed me in a robe of right-
eousness"* could lead one to conclude that the "new nature"
was like a robe God gives me to cover over the "old man", the
sinful person, that I really am underneath. One could then
add the "putting on" passages in Colossians 3 to go along
with the idea that the positive qualities a Christian is "to
wear" are a covering to hide the scars and blemishes of the
"real me." Praise God this idea finds no support in the Scripture! First of all, in Isaiah's overall description of the prospects of the age of the new covenant (on the far side of Isaiah
53), his focus is on a change in essential personhood. In
Isaiah 60:12 God's people in that day will be called both
"righteous" and "the work of My hands" (see Ephesians
2:10). They will also be described as "oaks of righteousness"
and "the holy people" (61:3 and 62:12). Precisely the same
analogy is used of God himself in 59:17 where God is seen as
putting on "righteousness as a breastplate, and a helmet of
salvation upon His head" (cf. Ephesians 6:11-17). Certainly
what God "puts on" is harmonious with the Person
underneath. Note that Isaiah depicts this against the black
contrast of Isaiah 64:6, *"all our righteous acts are like filthy
rags,"* as he views himself and his people under the old covenant. Colossians 3:12 follows with another positive parallel
by referring to new covenant saints as *"God's chosen people,
holy and dearly loved."* Finally this "clothing" analogy is used

in Revelation 19:8 in expressing the clothing of the saints as *"fine linen, bright and clean"* certainly not as something to cover the sinner but as descriptive of "the righteous acts *of the saints*" (italics mine). Hallelujah! The Christian life is no costume party, no disguise (see 1 Peter 2:9).

Indeed it is possible for saints to lose perspective concerning both themselves and the issue of meaning and therefore attempt to dress themselves with counterfeit clothes to match their false concept of life. This is exactly what the Christians in Laodicea were doing. And like the child in the children's story, "The Emperor's New Clothes," God found it necessary to bring them back to reality and describe them as they were, "naked" (Revelation 3:17-18).

9. It is quite popular these days to use the statement "God loves me and accepts me as I am." I would imagine this means different things to different people. To some it's simply another way of expressing the thought of the invitation hymn, "Just As I am." As such, it communicates the truth that an unsaved person has nothing to offer God toward his own salvation. He comes to God as the sinner that he is, casting himself upon God's grace. To someone else this expression may point to the fact that since we as Christians are waiting for *"the redemption of our body"* (Romans 8:23), God does indeed accept our mortality as it presently is, including all its weaknesses (Romans 8:26). Even more than "acceptance" is the tremendous encouragement that Jesus *fully understands* because He once shared in our weaknesses even to the degree of *"being tempted in all things as we are"* (Hebrews 4:15). More than "understands," He "empathizes!"

But beyond these ideas this statement may lead one to several erroneous impressions:

a. If God "accepts me as I am" then there is no need for regeneration. But a holy God can accept me into His holy family *only* because He has made a radical change *in me,* *"as God's chosen people, **holy** and dearly loved"* (Colossians 3:12, italics mine). Salva-

tion means that I will never be again what I was
before. By contrast, to use this statement with the
idea that the "I am" is the sinner that I am, is to
reduce salvation to the idea that God accepts me
because He has forgiven me. *His own pure character
demands more than that* (1 John 1:3-6; Ephesians
5:8).

b. Most people, I would imagine, assume that to say
"God loves me" means that He finds me (and
everybody else) "loveable." By all means He loves
them with *agape* love which involves an act of the will
on the part of the one who chooses to give himself to
another for their welfare *totally apart from* their being loveable. *Phileo* love, which is "Love as a natural
response to a delightful object," is never used of God's
love for people except toward His responsive
followers. (The one apparent exception is Revelation
3:19, *"as many as I love phileo, I reprove and
discipline."* The context justifies the conclusion that
these Christians were not so much rebellious as they
were ignorant and deceived. They thought all was
well.) Cf. John 16:27 *(phileo)* and Mark 10:21
(agapao).

10. I believe that it is completely illogical to hold that
Romans 7:14-25 is describing the typical experience of a
believer who is looking at life through the truth of Romans 6
and 8. "The Apostle in this section is not primarily concerned
to 'give his experience'; he has not set out to tell us something
about himself. He is telling us and setting out before us his
view of the Law—the nature of the Law, what it was meant to
do, and what it was not meant to do, or the limits of the Law"
(D. Martyn Lloyd-Jones, *Romans, The Law: Its Functions
and Limits, Exposition of Chapters 7:1-8:4* [Grand Rapids:
Zondervan, 1974], p. 182.) To assume that Paul is using a
"dramatic present" tense seems much more reasonable than
to force upon this passage the numerous outright contradic-

tions with the practical holiness emphases of both Romans 6 and 8. In view of this fact, the exclamation which closes this section, "Thanks be to God through Jesus Christ our Lord!" (verse 25) is to be understood as "a parenthetical expression." "As St. Paul momentarily contemplates His own position in Christ, he gives vent to his feelings in the parenthetical ejaculation of thanksgiving, that through the mercy of God the experience just described was no longer his" (W. H. Griffith Thomas, *St. Paul's Epistle to the Romans* [Grand Rapids: 1946], p. 196). See also an extended defense of this interpretation in Lloyd-Jones, ibid. pp. 225-237.

Verse 25 then concludes with a general summary of verses 14-24.

11. "In the struggle between God's will, expressed in the law, and sin, the self stands on God's side. And yet the Christian cannot declare himself free from participation in sin, for it does not come to him simply as an external force; rather must he confess that sin dwells in him, present in his carnal nature." Anders Nygren, *Commentary on Romans* (Philadelphia: Muhlenberg Press, 1949), p. 300.

Referring to Romans 7:17-18, Bruce Narramore states, "Paul is saying that it is not his 'I' (ego—his total self) doing the evil, but sin that dwells in him. If we stopped reading after the first part of verse 18, we would have the impression that there is nothing worthwhile in Paul. But the last part of verse 18 makes it clear that he is referring specifically to his sinful tendency and not to his total person. In verses 21-23, Paul explains that his rebellious tendencies are not the same as his self. He delights in the law of God with his inner man, his deepest nature desires to do good and follow God." S. Bruce Narramore, *You're Someone Special,* (Grand Rapids: Zondervan, 1978), p. 50. Narramore appears to trace this deep level of self worth back to God's original creation of man in His image, rather than to the point of regeneration. Note his distinction between "self" and "flesh," the latter being that which awakens sinful tendencies (pages 38-39, 49).

12. John Murray, *The Epistle to the Romans* (Grand
    Rapids: Eerdmans, 1968), pp. 219-220. See extended
    quotation of Murray, Appendix C, footnote 3. Though I
    wish to underline my indebtedness to John Murray, it should
    be noted that since he did not make any connection between
    the nature of sin and the problem of meaning, there are dif-
    ferences between his understanding and mine as to the issue
    of sin in the life of a believer.

13. John Murray, *Principles of Conduct; Aspects of Biblical
    Ethics* (Grand Rapids: Eerdmans, 1957), p. 218.

14. W. H. Griffith-Thomas, *St. Paul's Epistle to the
    Romans* (Grand Rapids: Eerdmans, 1946), p. 168.
    The only passage using the terminology "old self" which
    might be seen as contradictory to this point of view is Ephe-
    sians 4:22-24, in which the "putting off" of the old self is
    commonly translated as being a command. (See NASB, NIV,
    RSV, KJV.) In contrast with the translators who give the in-
    finitives, "to put off" and "to put on," an imperatival force,
    John Murray believed that both the grammar allowed and the
    exegisis demanded that the infinitives were "infinitives of
    result." His resultant translation then was "so that ye have
    put off, according to the former manner of life, the old
    man." (See his extended argument in *Principles of Conduct*,
    pp. 214-218. See also L.S. Chafer, *Systematic Theology, 8
    vols.,* vol. 6: *Pneumatology* [Dallas: Dallas Seminary Press,
    1947-48], 6:270, and John Eadie, *A Commentary on the
    Greek Text of the Apostle Paul to the Ephesians* [London:
    William Mackenzie, 1854], p. 346. H.C.G. Moule also ex-
    presses a past tense perspective in his paraphrase, "you were
    taught in Christ with regard to the fact that your old man was
    laid aside" (*Studies in Ephesians* [Grand Rapids: Kregel
    Publications, 1977], p. 118). Martyn Lloyd-Jones, while ac-
    cepting the standard translation, believes that it in no way
    contradicts the past tense perspective of the "old self" of
    Romans 6 and Colossians 3. "What the Apostle is saying in

effect is 'Do not go on living as if you still were that old man, because that old man has died; do not go on living as if he was still there; put that off.'" (*Romans, the New Man, An Exposition of Chapter 6* [Grand Rapids: Zondervan, 1973], p. 64.) He felt Paul's terminology was comparable to someone today saying to a full grown man, "Don't be a baby because you are indeed a man." Though the Ephesians passage may be debated, there is no question as to the past tense perspective concerning the old self in Colossians 3:9. In spite of this fact the NASB has used the imperative in the heading, "Put on the New Man" at the top of the page containing this verse!

15.   Though Paul may indeed have had in mind a corporate "new man" as referring to the entire body of Christ in Romans 6, the overriding emphasis is upon the individual believer and his victory over sin. See Herman Ridderbos, *Paul, An Outline of His Theology* (Grand Rapids: Eerdmans, 1975), pp. 206-209; cf. p. 224.

16.   For examples of a correct use of the phrase "that is my position in Christ," see D. Martin Lloyd-Jones, *Romans, The New Man, Exposition of Chapter 6* (Grand Rapids: Zondervan, 1972), pp. 118, 119, 262.

17.   Lest for a moment a shadow be cast on the fundamental place of the Holy Spirit in a believer's birthright, it should be noted that an entire chapter (Chapter 9) focuses on this most wonderful Individual.

Chapter 3

Old Man, New Man...
Which Is It?

*I*n our first chapter as we considered the tragedy of sin and its relationship to the issue of meaning, I stated that "the conscious or unconscious issue of meaning has driven every man who ever lived" (p. 31). Yet always lurking behind this "drivenness" is that deeper question of identity. Whenever one's sense of purpose and one's evaluation of himself are in harmony, life has a good chance of making some sense—if only to the one doing the "living." But if the opposite is true, life becomes existence—frustrating existence. For instance, what could be more frustrating than being a Christian who thinks himself to be primarily a self-centered sinner, yet whose purpose in life is to produce God-centered holiness? For him, identity and meaning are worlds apart! Could this actually be God's intention? Thank God the answer is "No!" Let's listen to Him.

> *"But you are a chosen people, a royal priesthood, a holy nation, a people belonging to God* [that's identity] *that you may declare the praises of him who called you out of darkness into his wonderful light* [that's meaning]. *Once you were not a people, but*

now you are the people of God; once you had not
received mercy, but now you have received mercy.
Dear friends, I urge you, as aliens and strangers in
the world [that's identity], *to abstain from sinful*
desires, which war against your soul. Live such
good lives among the pagans that, though they ac-
cuse you of doing wrong they may see your good
deeds and glorify God on the day he visits us [that's
meaning]." (1 Peter 2:9-12)

By the way, did you notice in this passage that "sinful
desires" are the enemies of our immortal souls[1] (our deepest
selves)? If you can tell a man by his enemies, what does that
say about our souls? Those few words speak volumes!

Now let's listen again to what God has to say about
meaning and identity.

"Since then, you have been raised with Christ [that's
identity], *set your hearts on things above, where*
Christ is seated at the right hand of God [that's
meaning]... *Therefore as God's chosen people,*
holy and dearly loved [that's identity], *clothe*
yourselves with compassion, kindness, humility,
gentleness and patience [that's meaning]."
(Colossians 3:1, 12)

"For we are God's workmanship, created in Christ
Jesus [that's identity] *to do good works, which God*
prepared in advance for us to do [that's meaning]."
(Ephesians 2:10)

"For you were once darkness, but now you are light
in the Lord [that's identity]. *Live as children of light*
(for the fruit of light consists in all goodness,
righteousness, and truth) and find out what pleases
the Lord [that's meaning]."
(Ephesians 5:8; cf. 2 Corinthians 6:14-15)

"You've Forgotten Who You Are!"

Is there a biblical relationship between awareness of personal identity and finding meaning in life? Indeed there is!

In 1 Corinthians 6:1-7, Paul is attempting to intervene in some hot lawsuits between fellow believers. They were taking each other to court before unbelievers in order to get justice and thus protect their belongings. Paul had apostolic authority. He could have simply said, "Stop doing that." But he didn't. Instead, he encouraged the frustrated believers to focus on the problem on the basis of their true identities. "Don't you remember who you are?" Paul was saying. "Do you not know that we shall judge angels?

"You saints in Corinth, you've lost the sense of personal dignity that comes with who you are. This very fact should cause you to take a second look at the conflicts you have among yourselves. If there are not adequate wise men among you, then be willing to be cheated. Striving and fighting to get all that you 'deserve' is beneath the dignity of who you are. Real meaning in life is somewhere else!"

Now let's look over at 1 Corinthians 3. Here Paul is addressing himself to their fleshly obsession of jealously following one spiritual leader rather than another. A very loose paraphrase of Paul's response would run something like this:

"You fellows are acting like mere men. You've forgotten who you are! You are scarcely 'mere men'; you are God's temple! Meaning in life is not what man you follow. . . all things are yours and you are God's! Now come on! There's work to be done."

Paul tells these bickering believers that if a Christian thinks of himself as a "mere man," it is bound to color his concept of values.

What Jesus Told Satan

We can trace this line of reasoning back even further — into the early years of our Lord's earthly ministry. We find Him in the wilderness being tempted by Satan. "If you are the Son of God," suggested Satan, "command that these stones become bread." Remember, Jesus has gone without food for 40 days and was terribly hungry. Was this a real temptation? Of course it was! But notice His response:

"Man does not live on bread alone, but on every word that comes from the mouth of God." Or to put it another way, "Satan, if my identity was essentially flesh, 'meaning' for me this moment would certainly be bread. Fresh, buttered bread—right from the oven. Ah! But that's where you are wrong, Satan. I am, first of all, a spiritual being who lives on words from God's mouth. Did you really think I would forget my identity and attempt to satisfy some shallow meaning for a shallow identity?" (See Matthew 4:1-4.)

In Search of the Deepest Meaning

Are you ready for another illustration—a mini-melodrama? This time imagine that you are a very typical boy in high school who likes two things most of all: food and girls (in either order). If someone asked you who you were and you were quite honest you would have to express both your identity and your reason for living in those terms (with a long list of other ones, of course).

One day you're standing by your locker in the hall and the track coach spots you. He takes you by surprise when he strolls purposefully over to your locker to talk to you. (The *track* coach talking to *me*?)

"Say, I've been watching the way you walk—gotta lot of bounce to your step. Whether you know it or not, you're a sprinter. With a little training you could be setting records in the 100-yard dash. I just know it!"

"Aw c'mon, Coach. I'm no sprinter. I might win a gold medal in eating or girl-watching, but a sprinter? You've got to be kidding."

"No, I'm not kidding. And I'll prove it to you. This afternoon—at practice."

Now he's hooked you. You go to practice that afternoon...and every afternoon for weeks to follow. Your first clockings aren't that outstanding but you sense a strange exhilaration as you run that maybe—just maybe—the coach was right. In the days that follow you read biographies of great sprinters; you watch films of great races. You run and run and run. It hurts so much sometimes, yet always deeper is a growing sense of identity. You *are* a sprinter! Before long the whole shape of your life bends to this new sense of personhood. If someone walks up to you on the street and asks, "Who are you?", even before you can even give your name you spontaneously respond, "I'm a sprinter at Madison High! The big meet with Wilson High is this Saturday—you gonna be there?"

And Saturday comes. The crowd stirs as you walk across the cinders to your starting block. Suddenly the prettiest girl from Madison High walks straight up to you with a large, juicy piece of apple pie fresh from the oven and topped with a big glob of ice cream. "Hi," she coos. "I brought this for you...just for you."

Now comes the decision. You are free to do what you want. But what will you do?

It all depends on your concept of those two words: IDENTITY and MEANING.

Who are you? Are you a skin-wrapped package of taste buds, salivary glands, and sex drives? If this is your identity, there isn't much question where you will find meaning.

Or are you aware of something else? A new identity. An identity reinforced by warm, relational times with your coach, by a new focus on personhood, a new set of values. If these things are true, your response to sweet Sue will be automatic—and conclusive. On the other hand, if you have missed out on track practice, if you have allowed your mind to focus on those very tangible, "fleshly" things where you had always found life before, you will respond in one of two ways: "All right! Who cares about the race anyway; you're quite a gal, Susie." Or, if not that it will be, "Sorry Sue, I want that hunk of pie but I can't have it."

What is your response as the sprinter you now know yourself to be? With scarcely a second look at her pretty face, you turn to focus on that tape 100 yards away.

"Sorry, Sue. I'm a sprinter. I don't *want* that apple pie (not simply I can't have it). Life for me is touching that tape before anyone else. What you offer just doesn't fit in. Thanks anyway."

"Oh! You must want it...and me."

"No, Sue, you just don't realize that there's something far deeper about me than that. I'm not just a mouth connected to a stomach; I'm not just a guy who gets turned on by good-looking girls. *I'm a sprinter*, Sue. That's who I am. That's living. There's nothing like it in all the world. I'm gonna win, Susie!" BANG! Off you go...and you win.

Oh Christian, do you get the point? If you don't know most deeply who you are—if you have allowed your sense of personhood to be shaped by your own flesh, by Satan, and by the meaning-mad media that saturates the world, you are either consciously or unconsciously a most miserable, frustrated Christian. Your Bible reading, such as it is, is self-condemning. 1 John 1:9 is your life verse. God is almost your adversary. Strange that He could be both Savior and adversary. But it's true. It seems as though the things you want most in life He says you should want least...or not at all. In your view, a Christian is one who must continually say "No" to himself, "No" to his dreams, and "No" to his desires, all the while saying "Yes" to God and His demands. *Surrender*. That awful word.

To such statements Paul would shout with flaming indignation, "God forbid! What travesty! Whoever had the audacity to paint the Christian life in such a way? What a shambles of God's truth. For me *to live* is Christ!" For you see, even as Sam discovered a deeper identity, so God's intention is that every believer become literally obsessed with his own true IDENTITY — MEANING — LIFE!

God's Masterpiece

Who is a Christian? *He is God's ultimate spiritual masterpiece. God's purposed new man. Created clean as a flawless prism, progressively being facetted more fully to receive, transform, and display the otherwise invisible glories of the infinite God into limitless, visible colors—the rainbow of His own attributes—so that all creation might see GOD!*[2] This is life. The outflow of meaning. The Divine perfecting of your own truest, deepest, eternal identity.

> *"But you are a chosen race, a royal priesthood, a holy nation, a people belonging to God, that you may declare the praises of him who called you out of darkness into his wonderful light."* (1 Peter 2:9)

"You are not in the flesh but in the Spirit" (Romans 8:9, NASB). *"The Spirit gives birth to spirit"* (John 3:6). Deepest identity is spiritual, not flesh. You are distinctly alive!

Who are you, Christian? Are you fundamentally flesh? If that indeed is so, then that *is* where life will be found for you and you are not really a Christian after all. Or are you most deeply a spiritual being? If you are to be true to your *self*—your deepest, truest self—where is life for you? Where *are* your "wants"? Not your "oughts," but your "wants." When one stops to think about this it is asking quite a bit of our flesh brain to adjust to that idea that it is not the "gang boss" of our total personhood. That shallow level of mortal consciousness has to back off and admit to a deeper level of being—a spiritual level that will eternally outlive its own mortality. To really accept myself as fundamentally a spiritual being is not easy![3]

That Sounds Great, But...

Perhaps at this moment a reader is saying, "Sure, that sounds great. Too bad it doesn't work out that way. I'm jealous. I'm lustful, proud, materialistic, and a whole lot more. If I really expressed what I am both you and I would be very embarrassed, Needham. You're not only a radical, you're just plain *wrong*. Every Christian knows that real victory occurs when the Holy Spirit is allowed to control *what I am* in order that Christ can produce in me *what He is.* That, Needham, is orthodoxy!"

I hear you...I honestly hear you. I've said those very same words many, many times myself. Whether it's accepted orthodoxy, I don't know. But I do know this—it isn't biblical.

Listen to the Bible: *"For in my inner being I delight in God's law."* And preceeding that are these startling words, *"Now if I do what I do not want to do, it is no longer I who do it but it is sin living in me that does it"* (Romans 7:22, 20).[4]

John says, *"He who does what is right is righteous, just as he is righteous...No one who is born of God will continue to sin, because God's seed remains in him; and he cannot go on sinning because he has been born of God"* (1 John 3:7,9). Added to these passages are numerous positive expressions of the believer's nature. (See John 17:14-16; 1 Peter 2:9, 11; Ephesians 2:10; etc.)

Portrait Number One

I would like to try right now to paint two totally different portaits of a believer. The first portait is a common one. Familiar in many conservative, evangelical circles. It looks something like this: I am a person with two natures. One of these natures is called "the old man" (otherwise called "the natural man," "flesh," "sin nature," "old nature," "body of sin"). The other is "the new man" (otherwise called "the new nature," "spiritual nature").

Got it? One man; two natures. I, the person, am in some sense between these two capacities. I, the person, am mind, will, personality, body, and emotions. This is my personhood. What my personhood manifests in behavior depends upon which capacity is energizing me. A victorious Christian, according to this viewpoint, is the one whose new nature is so energized by God that his behavior is Christlike. (Incidentally, no matter how much emphasis this "two nature" approach might place on the "positional" death of the old nature and the living presence of the new nature, as long as Christians feel at home thinking of themselves as "forgiven sinners," it is obvious that they still understand that their "old sin nature" is really their most fundamental nature.)

Before going any further, I am convinced this first approach—this first portrait of a Christian—is inconsistent with the teaching of the New Testament, even though isolated verses could be seen in such a light.

Let's project this first perspective into a familiar life situation. Put yourself at home alone one evening, sitting in front of your TV set. Perhaps quite unexpectedly a new program begins. It takes only a moment for you to realize that this is not a show for a Christian to be watching. You are immediately aware that the program's sole purpose is to stir you to lust (whatever kind of lust you happen to be tantalized by). You know you shouldn't be watching it. But in a few moments, you're hooked. Then the thought comes flashing into your mind, "What if somebody caught me watching this? I'd better turn it off. I don't want to, but I don't dare take a chance." So reluctantly you turn the switch, taking one last, longing look. It that a spiritual victory? Hardly. But let's take it a step further.

Same program, same circumstance. You're sitting there absorbed in the program when the thought hits you, "Goodness, *God is watching me*! I sure don't want His heavy hand on me! He can be pretty tough." So once again, with equal reluctance, you turn the switch. Savoring that last delicious look. Victory? Obviously not. Let's try again.

Same thing. Same place. Watching the show, you're hit by a thought. "You know, if Jesus were here it would certainly disappoint Him to see me watching this thing. And I love Him. Anyway, I don't have to yield to this sinful temptation. By the Holy Spirit I have power to reject what I am doing. I will." Marching to the set, you grasp the switch, hesitate long enough to see just a little bit more, and flip it off. You hesitate because you've just said "No" to yourself using strength from your new nature. And it hurts to do that. Why? Because you, the person, really wanted to keep on watching. Your curious mind, your churning emotions, your glandular body. But Jesus died for you—you want to please Him. So who are you? You are a person who wants on one hand to please the Savior and on the other hand to sin. A split personality. A house divided. Is this then what Christian victory is all about?

Not according to Paul. Not according to chapter 7 of Romans. It's hard to know how Paul could have made it any clearer. He stated that when a Christian sins *"it is no longer I who do it, but it is sin living in me that does it."* And where is it dwelling in me? Paul answers, *"in my flesh"* . . . operating *"in the members of my body"* (Romans 7:18-25).[5]

Portrait Number Two

We've been looking at that first portrait of a Christian. Commonly taught, commonly believed, and commonly confusing. But look at another portrait. See if it squares with Scripture; see if it makes more sense. Ready?

I am a person who in terms of my most essential nature (deepest self, inner man, new man) is a creation of God who does not sin.[6] I am righteous—by nature delighting in the law of God. This new man is not simply a capacity; it is the real me. The person I once was (the old man) I am no more. I am not by nature a "child of wrath" anymore. I am a child of light. If I died right now, I would be fit for heaven. And heaven is not a place for people who go against their natural tendencies to do what is right. It is a place for those who *by nature* do what is right!

You know, that's an amazing thing to say, but it's true. If you have received the Savior and five seconds from now you fell over dead, you—YOU—would be at home in heaven. And according to both Peter and Paul, the only thing you would leave behind is your mortality. Peter says, *"I think it is right to refresh your memory as long as I live in the tent of this body, because I know that I will soon put it aside . . . I will make every effort to see that after my departure...."* And Paul says *"away from the body and at home with the Lord"* (2 Peter 1:13-15; 2 Corinthians 5:8). There is not a single word anywhere implying that at death the believer is finally separated from his "old man" or his "old self." Not a single word. Why? Because that happened when you were saved, not just positionally, but actually.

But even though all this is true—even though God describes us as His children (saints)—He never wants us to forget that we are for a while inseparably linked to unredeemed flesh. Our bodies are mortal. Not just the bones and muscles, glands and senses, but mind[7] and emotions as well. That vast, unbelievably intricate, electronic, chemical complex which is culturally, genetically, diabolically (at times), geographically, and pathologically-influenced mortality.

There is indeed a proper dualism in being human. Paul said, *"I see another law at work in the members of my body...within my members...this body of death...my flesh"* (Romans 7:23-25).

Remember the TV illustration? Let's look at it one final time from this *second* perspective of a Christian. There you are. The program intended to stir you to lust is doing just that. It is of the flesh—for the flesh. And your flesh—your unredeemed flesh—likes it. Wants to watch.

For a moment you find yourself saying, "I want to watch this even though I know I shouldn't." Then with a sudden jolt the gracious Holy Spirit reminds you of something so very important. "Hey, wait a minute!" you say. Who am I, anyway? Is watching this stuff truly compatible with who I really am? *I essentially am not flesh* (eyes, ears, nose, etc.). Life for me is not sleek cars, fantasy vacations, quadraphonic sound, a perfect figure, an envious reputation. Who am I? I know who I am—I am fundamentally a spiritual being created by God to display Jesus. Life—real life—is right there."

So I walk to the TV set and turn it off. No last, longing look this time. I flip it off.

Not just because I should.

Not just because I love Jesus.

But because *I want to.*

My flesh may protest.

So what? It's really pretty stupid to allow *"fleshly lusts which wage war against the soul"* (1 Peter 2:11, NASB) to continue when the war is against me, and all I have to do is turn it off.

"Oh thank you, God! Flesh, that's just your tough luck. Go ahead and cry. Go ahead and suffer. Go ahead and bombard my brain with angry signals. I have put to death the deeds of the flesh! This time you lost and I am free to live."

This, and this alone, is the victory.

You Are Not Two "You's"

Do you see it? Do you see the fundamental difference between these two portraits of a believer?

The first concept places you as a person standing between two capacities. The second equates you and your "new man." Not merely as some secondary capacity, but rather as the person you most deeply are.

You are not two "you's" (which agrees precisely with Romans 7), nor are you both "old man" and "new man."[8] In no sense is it proper to conclude that Romans 6 views "old man" and "new man" as capacities. It distinctly speaks of the old man as having been crucified and buried! Paul does not refer to the old man as an "it"; rather he says "we died," "we were buried," "we shall live."[9] The presence and potential for sin is not explained by some scripturally-contradictory continuance of "an old man whose power has been broken" capacity. Rather, sin is explained by the fact that your deepest personhood is housed in a most demanding, creative, easily-influenced mortality—flesh. This very tangible, though shallow, level of your total personhood happens to be well equipped to function in that crucial realm of meaning in life.[10] It is in this sense that the term "flesh" takes on a negative moral character.

Crucial Distinctions

Sin, remember, *is the expression of an individual's response to the issue of meaning apart from the life of God.*

Awareness of identity determines meaning in life.

Fulfillment of meaning in terms of true identity for a believer is righteousness.

The "sin nature" concept of necessity assumes that there is always somewhere inside of me something that is essentially evil. And whether or not those who hold this view actually say it, that something clings so tightly to my essential personhood that it is right to describe myself as sinful.

Indeed, it is true that there is an operating "principle" at work in every believer. That "principle"—not evil in itself—*is the incessant demand for meaning.* (This basic demand, by the way, is found in every thinking creature.) The moment that demand for meaning becomes dominant in my flesh rather than in my deepest personhood—at that moment that "principle" is producing evil within me. When flesh determines its own meaning, it always produces sin.

Yet when that determinative search for meaning flows out of the deepest self, empowered and directed by the Holy Spirit, there is at that point *nothing inside of me* that is essentially evil. My flesh at that moment is a slave to righteousness. My members are yielded to God and the result is purity—holiness in both the inward and outward man.[11]

But since we are still waiting for the redemption of our bodies, the flesh-slave idea must always be reckoned with. Left to itself, the "will to meaning" (the "principle") will always produce sin. As Jesus said, *"apart from me you can do nothing."*

One must be very careful to guard these distinctions. Otherwise, he may fall into the trap of viewing flesh as essentially sinful, or he may move to the other extreme and conclude that through some special work of God a person arrives at a state of absolute perfection. Both are tragic distortions.

The Real Conflict

The "principle" of independent discovery of meaning in life is always ready to surge into the vacuum whenever true meaning is not coming through loud and strong. And what is true meaning? Once again it is receiving and displaying the risen life of Christ.

All of this points toward a battle. An intense battle. At times, an overwhelming battle. Our flesh is constantly receiving independent "meaning possibilities" from its vast, computerized brain reservoir. It is also almost incessantly bombarded with counterfeit meanings from the world and the devil. So we war.

> *"For the flesh sets its desire against the Spirit* (or "spirit") *and the Spirit* (or "spirit") *against the flesh; for these are in opposition to one another so that you may not do the things that you please."*
>
> (Galatians 5:17)

This second portrait of a believer is not simply the first portrait with a new coat of paint. It is not simply a fresh slant or a new perspective. It is radically different. And I am convinced that the portrait is a true one; the only perspective that fully harmonizes with what the Bible says.

Summary

True meaning in life for a Christian is in receiving and displaying the risen life of Christ. Rather than this being contrary to one's essential nature, as is taught by some, it is in perfect harmony with the miracle of regeneration by which we became "holy...God's workmanship...children of light." To fulfill the will of God (righteousness) is to do what we most deeply desire to do even though this may be contrary to the desires of our flesh. This fundamental awareness of identity brings a believer into the wholesome, positive atmosphere in which God's intention of manifesting His holiness in the world can be fulfilled.

Chapter 3, Notes

1. See David H. Wheaton, "1 Peter," in *The New Bible Commentary, Revised,* edited by D. Guthrie and J.A. Motyer (Grand Rapids: Eerdmans, 1970), p. 1242.

2. The individualistic emphasis of this statement might be opposed in view of the corporate concept of the church as being God's "new man" (Ephesians 2:15). By all means the Bible underlines this concept as being most significant (see Chapter 10). But we dare not so focus on this that we ignore the fact that the successful functioning of a local body of believers (or the whole body of Christ) is dependent upon individual faith and individual obedience built upon individual awareness of personal salvation. When a believer someday stands before Christ's judgment seat, he stands alone.

3. Earl Jabay underlines this difficulty in perceiving oneself as a spiritual being by saying, "Man's existential identity can no more be conceptualized than the being of God. God is divine spirit, a reality which evades capture by human thoughts and ideas. Man is made in God's spiritual image and is fully nondefinable as God. Ideas about feelings of spirits can be conceptualized but not man's identity as a human spirit." (Earl Jabay, *Search for Identity* [Grand Rapids: Zondervan, 1967], p. 56.)

4. Referring to verse 22 in light of verses 17 and 20, Murray states, "In a word, he [Paul] identifies himself in his deepest and most determinate will with the law of God which is the good. What is more reasonable than to infer that he calls his determinate will to the good (with which he identifies

his self) 'inward man'? As he makes moral assessment of himself, as he analyzes himself and his conduct in the light of ethical criteria, he finds that which represents his deepest and truest self is the determinate will to the good and it is that deepest and truest self he calls "the inward man." (John Murray, *The Epistle to the Romans* [Grand Rapids: Eerdmans, 1968], p. 226; see also p. 263.) This did not mean, though, that Paul disassociated himself from personal accountability for the actions of his flesh.

5.   One must be careful to guard against going beyond what the Bible says by concluding that "I the person am not responsible for the behavior of my body." It is both required and reasonable that I as a Christian *"beat my body and make it my slave"* (1 Corinthians 9:27; see also repeated emphasis on this in Romans 6:15-19; 8:13.). It should also be noted that though Paul very closely relates the terms "flesh" and "members of my body" in Romans 7:18-25, the term "flesh" often is used in a negative, ethical sense.

6.   See Lewis Sperry Chafer, *He That Is Spiritual* (Wheaton: Van Kampen Press, 1918), p. 148, for a view in support of this statement. By contrast, see John R.W. Stott, *The Epistles of John, An Introduction and Commentary* (Grand Rapids: Eerdmans, 1964), pp. 127-136; John F. Walvoord, *The Holy Spirit* (Wheaton: Van Kampen Press, 1954), p. 213. Their point of view rests largely on the convenient though inadequate argument of the Greek tense in 1 John 3:6-9 and the writers' prior interpretation of 1 John 1:8. See Appendix B, p. 261 ff. It is somewhat difficult to pinpoint Walvoord's position as to the sinlessness of the "new nature" with reference to this passage. A reader might even interpret him as saying that the new nature can sin occasionally. Yet elsewhere he describes this nature as "divine." (p. 135)

7. I am using the term "mind" here in a purely mortal sense as originating in the brain and expressed by intelligence. I would agree with Murray that this is not the sense in which Paul uses "mind" in Romans 7:23 and 25. By contrast, Paul appears to equate it with the expression "inner man" of verse 22, meaning "that deepest, truest self" and parallel with the usage in 2 Corinthians 4:16. One's outward man, including his intelligence, can be deteriorating while at the same time his inner man is being renewed. Of course, when one's mental faculties are functioning properly, the reality of one's truest self as a "new man" will be perceived at least to some degree on an intellectual level. (See Murray, *Epistle to the Romans*, pp. 265-266.) Also I suppose it is possible that there may be some parallel between the use of the term "mind" here and the phrase "the spirit of your mind" in Ephesians 4:23.

8. Though Lloyd-Jones used the terminology "two 'me's'," to understand a true duality in a regenerate individual (see *Romans, the Law: It's Functions and Limits, Exposition of Chapters 7:1-8:4* [Grand Rapids: Zondervan, 1973], p. 227; see also pp. 204-207), I am quite confident that he would agree that the "me" which delights in the law of God is that "self" which most truly represents the regenerated person that I am. (See *Romans, the New Man, Exposition of Chapter 6* [Grand Rapids: Zondervan, 1973], p. 83, in which he states, "Is not that a marvelous thing to be able to say? I am not doing this or that, it is this sin that remains in my members that does so. Sin is no longer in me, it is in my members only. That is the most liberating thing you have ever heard. That is the Apostle's assertion.") Nevertheless to say this in no way removes from the believer the full responsibility for the actions of his members. He must make his body his slave.

9. An illustration of the confusion that can arise in a reader's mind over this distinction between "person" and "capacity" is seen by examining one author's explanation of the first view. In one place it is stated that the "old man"

refers to the total unregenerate person rather than simply a capacity. "Now, the old man refers to the old sin nature, the total personality, corrupted by the fall of Adam." See Dwight Pentecost, *Pattern For Maturity* (Chicago: Moody Press, 1966), p. 91. Then in another place it is stated that the "old man" is something "within us." Repeatedly the "sin nature" is distinguished from oneself (cf. pp. 99-102).

10.   This distinction would seem to parallel the point of view expressed in the diagrams and description by Ray Stedman in *Authentic Christianity* (Waco: Word Publishers, 1975), pp. 91-95.

11.   Issue might be taken with this statement in view of the fact that James specifically calls believers "sinners" (James 4:8, cf. v. 4). The context though looks at their specific behavior rather than their essential nature. In the same manner he calls them "double minded" (James 1:6-8). One other passage which might be used to support the "sinner" concept as the essential nature of a believer is Matthew 7:11, *"If you then, though you are evil...."* It would appear that his audience to some degree at least still faced the crossroad of the "narrow way" and the "broad way" (7:13-14). Also he may have been thinking of the natural tendency of the flesh toward independence (i.e., sin) rather than the fundamental essence of a regenerated person as described in 1 John 8:7-10. Elsewhere, the term "sinner" clearly has reference to the unbeliever. See Romans 5:8, 19; 1 Timothy 1:9; 1 Peter 4:8.

Chapter 4

The Essence of Personhood

S ince we have been using the terms "deepest self" and "shallow (or mortal, flesh) self" quite often, I think we should stop and get our bearings as to what is at the root of this idea of "self." Just what *is* included in being a person? Only when we answer this question will we be able to see the broader picture of authentic Christian personhood in terms of identity and meaning.

In approaching this issue it should be noted that some Christian writers regard any hint of dualism in the make-up of man as forbidden territory. Man must be viewed as an inseparable entity, they say. To focus on any one part—body, soul, or spirit—as having significance by itself is to nullify true personhood. [1]

But what does the New Testament tell us? I believe we will discover that there is indeed a proper biblical dualism to man.

Listen to Paul's voice:

"I know a man in Christ who fourteen years ago was caught up to the third heaven. Whether it was in the body or out of the body I do not know—God knows" (2 Corinthians 12:2-3).

Earlier in the book, the apostle had said:

"We are confident, I say, and would prefer to be away from the body and at home with the Lord" (2 Corinthians 5:8).[2]

In his later years, Paul wrote from prison:

"For to me, to live is Christ and to die is gain. If I am to go on living in the body, this will mean fruitful labor for me. Yet what shall I choose? I do not know! I am torn between the two: I desire to depart and be with Christ, which is better by far; but it is more necessary for you that I remain in the body" (Philippians 1:21-24).

Spiritual Personhood

These passages are by no means isolated from the overall New Testament descriptions of man. Their import is clear. *True personhood does not require a body.* Otherwise... poor Paul. According to the passages given above the apostle was at one time temporarily less than a person. And could it be that Paul was longing for the day when he would not qualify for personhood?

It is certainly true that God's original and ultimate intention for man is that he exist bodily. Our bodies, both our present unredeemed ones and our future glorified ones, are not to be thought of as sinful in themselves or of minimal importance.[3] But time after time God takes pains to remind us that we are most essentially spirit beings.[4]

How could He have expressed it more pointedly than through the apostle Paul in 1 Corinthians 14:14? In this passage concerning praying in tongues, Paul says, *"For if I pray in a tongue, my spirit prays, but my mind is unfruitful."*

In other words, there was actual, meaningful, productive communication with God who is Spirit. A person was in some way edified (14:4), even though he had no intellectual awareness of the specific nature of the communication (unless he also was able to interpret his prayer). His worship and thanksgiving to God were not dependent upon the workings or reservoir of information of his physical brain. It was his spirit that prayed. (Note: It should be understood that the fundamental point I am making does not focus on the tongues issue. Rather, I am focusing on the validity of communication on the level of the spirit.) This same idea would also seem to be in Romans 8:16, *"The Spirit Himself testifies with our spirit...."*

"Body-Spirit?"

Apparently this supposed danger of dualism is so repugnant to some that they actually go so far as to equate man's spiritual nature with his emotions.[5]

Listen to one such writer as he attempts to portray man as "body-spirit":

Our tempers can affect our digestion and our digestion can affect our tempers; it is the interlocking of the two which is a mystery and the point of the mystery has never been cleared up.

Another writer elaborates:

Man is a single being, a self, an I, or a you. Scientifically man's integrated nature becomes apparent in the study of emotions. The individual receives a message from a loved one or bad news, or he tells a lie. Automatically, in normal circumstances, his heart beats fast or slower, his breathing amplitude and rate change, adrenalin may be discharged into the blood stream.[6]

But you have a problem on your hands if you follow this logic. Any farmer knows that emotions such as fear or envy will directly affect a cow's milk production. Or a hen's inclination to lay eggs. Are they too, then, "spiritual beings"? Are humans to be thought of in the same terms as animals?

No, man's spiritual being lies much, much deeper than his emotions.

What Is Man?

"When I see Grampa in heaven...will he look like he did just before he died?"

"Will babies who die always be babies in heaven?"

"Am I stuck with my 70 I.Q. forever?"

What is man? Are there any answers to these questions? Yes, there are answers.

Perhaps known only to God is an understanding of the full-fledged personhood of every "new man" He has created. In some cases that "new man" is inseparably linked to a mortality that drastically limits the full expression of personhood. In all of us the process of decay modifies (sometimes radically) the persons we actually are.

Think of the multitudes of dear people who in years gone by were locked away in mad houses because they were epileptic or suffered from some endocrine or blood sugar problem. Who were they? Perhaps the cruelty of their very circumstances turned them to madness.

Many of us know someone who has suffered extreme brain damage due to some accident. We say, "He's just not the same person he used to be." No, in the flesh, he is not the same. But even if he was...are you certain the person you knew him to be was a true representation of who he really was? What circumstances, what performance demands, what internal or external pressures caused him to appear as something other than the distinctive, God-shaped spiritual being you will know him to be when you meet him in heaven? (See Appendix D.)

Hidden Identities

Imagine the thousands of truly born again people whose identities have been blurred by some fulfillment that was simply flesh. As you think of them, you find it very difficult to separate them from that particular obsession that gives them an identity. Perhaps it was some sport. Or some consuming commitment to build a business empire. There was always some "deal," some product, some activity, something around which all else seemed to revolve. Was this their true, unique identity? Of course not. Perhaps you wouldn't even have recognized them if they had discovered in an equally consuming way what their identity and thus their life really was.

Overreacting

In our largely justified reaction against the mysticism of Eastern religions, we Christians now find ourselves spooked by the idea that man is essentially a spiritual being. In our false assumption that Christians are simply forgiven sinners who have the Holy Spirit to control their badness and produce Christ's goodness, we have denied spiritual personhood. We have traded it for "in the flesh" identities which draw their meanings from the world's measurements of a man. This is no minor thing; it is unspeakable tragedy.

And yet, to suggest anything away from that particular point of view is to invite immediate attack by a host of evangelical writers. "Gnosticism!" they cry. "False mysticism!" "Perfectionism!" For many, the whole area is so emotionally charged that even discussion of the issue becomes impossible. Proof texts shoot up the mainmast like signal flags in a convoy.

To those of such a persuasion who even now would like to reverse the direction this book is moving, may I urge you to wait...and read.

Of Peanuts...

Two very different illustrations come to mind which may help to clarify what we have been considering: a peanut and a diamond. In its simplest form the first illustration is expressed in the little epitaph:

Here lies Sam Pease
Beneath the sod.
It's not really Pease;
It's just the pod.
Pease shelled out
And went to God.

But let's consider this more carefully. Let's imagine a human being, inward man and outward man, like a peanut with its shell. Normally, the shape of the shell gives us some idea of the shape of the peanut inside—big or small, fat or skinny—but not always. Sometimes, for any number of reasons, the shell may be covered with warts, bumps, or creases. And yet, when we remove the shell, we may find that the irregularities have no connection at all with the nature of the peanut inside.

You look at me, you live with me. Do you know me? I hope so. I sincerely hope the outward "flesh" man that you see bears a close resemblance to the shape of the deep person I most truly am. It would be so good if my spirit and my behavior were saying the same thing. No, I am not two people, but there are most certainly levels to my personhood. There is a deep self (inner man)[7] and my more shallow self. Shallow self is so quickly affected by circumstances. And if shallow self is not made a *"slave to righteousness"* (Romans 6:19), there's no telling what strange warts and bumps and creases you may see. My mannerisms, voice pattern, even my temperament may be circumstantial rather than reflective of my true personhood. You may observe me when I'm so busy protecting some supposed "self-image," or catching one I think I'm supposed to have, or grieving over one I think I've lost, that you won't have the faintest idea of who I really am. And neither would I. But I have a dream—

I hope it is more than a dream—

I dream that you might see when you look at me...live with me...a unique, human, personable expression of Jesus. Like no one else.

...and Prisms

Which brings me to the second illustration. First the peanut and then...the diamond. Just now I took out of my desk an object I've used so often in recent months I've acquired several holes in my pocket from carrying it around. (No, it's not a diamond.) It's a glass prism. Without light it really isn't much at all—just a hunk of glass. But with light, oh! It reflects all the colors of the rainbow.

This, to me, is the most expressive illustration of a Christian that I know. In terms of his deep, spiritual personhood, he is a uniquely designed prism. *A prism formed by the Creator to receive His very life (invisible to the world) and translate that light into the visible colors of the character of God.*

To most fully appreciate my prism, I must hold it in direct line with the sun. I must also choose a good surface to display the resulting colors of the spectrum.

This is what I most truly am—a God-created being with no capacity whatsoever within myself to produce real life. I am built rather to receive life. And as God shines into me, life is received.

> *"For God who said, 'Let light shine out of darkness,' made his light shine in our hearts to give us the light of the knowledge of the glory of God in the face of Christ. But we have this treasure in jars of clay to show that this all-surpassing power is from God and not from us."*   (2 Corinthians 4:6-7)

This life is best seen when displayed upon some surface. That surface is my flesh in all its varied relationships with others.

That is why Paul said, *"to remain in the flesh is more needful for you,"* because it was in that state he could productively manifest the Lord Jesus. *"For me to live,* [in the flesh] *is Christ"* (Philippians 1:21). It is these hands, this voice, this mind, these emotions, which are to be the display surfaces for the vivid colors of His attributes. His love, His power, His beauty, His patience. It is indeed the "fruit of the Spirit!"

There may be times, in medical isolation or solitary prison confinement, when "the light of the glory of God" is only observed by angels, principalities, powers, and God Himself. Yet even this may be far more precious in God's evaluations than we could possibly know.

There may be times when some type of illness or inherited defect or changes brought on by old age may greatly limit what anyone sees of Jesus. Is life then without meaning?

Let's consider this for a moment.

The Cutting of a Diamond

My prism has three facetted surfaces. Though the color spectrum displayed by it is perfect, the extent of that display is limited by the number of surfaces. If instead of a single prism you could imagine a flawless diamond with dozens or hundreds of facets, then you might get a better idea of God's purposes in making you His child. Life here on earth is not solely for the purpose of displaying the Savior, it is also the time during which God adds new facets to His original, flawless diamond — *you.*

God's intention for you and me is not only to manifest His glory in time, but also for eternity.

"There are also heavenly bodies and there are earthly bodies; but the splendor of the heavenly bodies is one kind, and the splendor of the earthly bodies is another. The sun has one kind of splendor, the moon another and the stars another; and star differs from star in splendor. So will it be with the resurrection of the dead. The body that is sown is perishable, it is raised imperishable; it is sown in dishonor, it is raised in glory. . . ."

"Those who are wise will shine like the brightness of the heavens, and those who lead many to righteousness, like the stars for ever and ever."
(1 Corinthians 15:40-42; Daniel 12:3)

There may be times, extended times, when God as a master diamond cutter is adding new facets to our spiritual beings which will be seen only in eternity. Oh dear Christian, perhaps right now you are being rather painfully facetted. Remember Peter says, *"These (trials) have come so that your faith—of greater worth than gold, which perishes even though refined by fire—may be proved genuine and result in praise, glory and honor when Jesus Christ is revealed"* (1 Peter 1:7).

"Endure hardship as discipline," says the book of Hebrews. *"God disciplines us for our good, that we may share in his holiness"* (Hebrews 12:7, 10, cf. 18-28). The next time you find yourself thinking, "I'm just not good for anything...I'm a burden to everyone around me," *stop it.* First of all, it is probably not true. And second, do you really doubt the wisdom and eternal purposes of God?

He has called you to eternal glory.

With such an important destiny, do you actually believe that God would mishandle so precious a treasure as you are to Him? You...and everyone else but God may be surprised beyond words some day. Surprised at the multi-facets of your eternal being as they multiply the beauty of God throughout the ramparts of heaven.

Perhaps this same illustration may help us to understand in what way a young child may appear in heaven in contrast with some old saint who has walked with God for a lifetime. Each will be distinctive persons...flawless diamonds. One however, will be mini-facetted, the other, multi-facetted. Through each one God will be perfectly glorified, but as Paul says, even as "star differs from star in splendor." [Note Appendix D for a brief consideration of "Spiritual Identity and Physical and Psychological Problems."]

Our Responsibility

All of us should wish that forever the glory of our God would be magnified and multiplied through our presence in heaven in the greatest way possible. To this end, the disciplines of the Christian life are not only for our sake and for the sake of our effectiveness as ambassadors on earth, but they are also for God's sake—both for time and eternity.

The sanctifying miracle of the new birth guarantees the quality of the diamond. But you and I have a most responsible role to play in determining the quality of facets as we willingly submit to the Master Diamond Cutter (Hebrews 12:9-15).

Radical Christianity

Spiritual personhood! Don't be spooked by it. Glory in it! Don't allow anyone or anything to so degrade your concept of personhood as to measure it with a flesh-level yardstick.

Remember, too, that a diamond isn't much of anything without the light. This takes us way back to chapter one. The great tragedy of Eden was man's choice of independence and its consequent meaninglessness. The great miracle of the new birth is in the establishment of true personhood, inseparable from dependence upon God. Full of meaning...forever.

Is this as radical as it sounds? Jesus said, *"they are not of the world any more than I am of the world."* His expectation was that your life would be as revolutionary as His was. He ate and slept, breathed and walked as anyone else, yet He could say *"anyone who has seen me has seen the Father."*

And before you file that verse away as simply one more proof of His deity, remember that He also said, *"that all of them may be one; Father, just as you are in me and I am in you. May they also be in us...I in them, and you in me. May they be brought to complete unity to let the world know that you sent me"* (John 17:21, 23; emphasis mine).

"For to me, to live is Christ."

Now, *that's* radical.

Summary

In describing the nature of man, God places a strong priority on spiritual personhood, although in doing so He allows no room for devaluing all that is mortal about man.[8] Therefore, a man is no less a person through the loss of any or all of his physical, mental, or emotional faculties even though the expression of his personhood may be severely warped or restricted. The necessary mortal frame of reference in which we all find ourselves requires that we make evaluations of ourselves and others as we perceive one another on this level. But even as we do this (aptitude tests, personality profiles, position, relationships, etc.) we must keep in mind that underneath the "appearance" is "the heart"—that truest, deepest self (2 Corinthians 5:12; *cf.* 5:16-17).

Since by the new birth a person becomes alive spiritually (he lives by the Spirit's gift of Jesus' risen life), he has a right—in fact, a duty—to evaluate himself in a most positive way. As a "prism" his worth is of the highest order—to receive the light of the glory of God and translate that invisible light into the visible attractiveness of Christ on the "screen" of his mortality. Due to the varying limitations and the certain decay of those "screens," Christians should take great pleasure in realizing that their significance will find its highest expression in eternity.

Chapter 4, Notes

1. A refreshing, balanced, biblical defense of dualism in humanness is found in Robert Gundry's book, *"Soma" in Biblical Theology with Emphasis on Pauline Anthropology* (Cambridge: Cambridge University Press, 1976). Note especially pages 146-56, 187-89, 201-03. An excellent brief analysis is found in *Systematic Theology* by L. Berkhof, (Grand Rapids: Eerdmans, 1953), pp. 192-96, in which this quotation is found:

   "Body and soul are distinct substances, which do interact, though their mode of interaction escapes human scrutiny and remains a mystery for us.... The operations of the soul are connected with the body as its instrument in the present life; but from the continued, conscious existence and activity of the soul after death it appears that it can work without the body." pp. 195-96.

   (In this context, Berkhof uses the term *soul* as synonymous with *spirit*.)

2. We must not assume that from Paul's statement here that he considered the body to be of no lasting value. On the contrary, he states earlier that *"we do not wish to be unclothed but clothed with our heavenly dwelling, so that what is mortal may be swallowed up by life"* (2 Corinthians 5:4). Indeed, we will yet possess a body that will be *"like his [Christ's] glorious body"* (Philippians 3:21). Yet what will be the nature of that future body? We do know that it will be *"a spiritual body"* (1 Corinthians 15:43). And the spiritual, rather than the purely physical, will be so dominant that Paul

could say that our present possession of the Holy Spirit (Who certainly is not body at all) is our *"deposit, guaranteeing what is to come"* (2 Corinthians 5:5). Regardless of the complexities of this mystery, the fact remains that Paul did not consider his present body or even his future body an absolute necessity in order to be a person even though the thought of being "unclothed" was not desirable.

3.   *"For we must all appear before the judgment seat of Christ, that each one may receive what is due him for the things done while in the body, whether good or bad"* (2 Corinthians 5:10).

4.   Any thought of the superiority of the spiritual over the physical in the nature of a believer is Platonism warmed over, according to Ranald Macaulay and Jerram Barrs. In *Being Human: The Nature of Spiritual Experience* (Downers Grove, Ill.: Inter-Varsity Press, 1978), they conclude that such an emphasis leads either to the acceptance of man's physical nature as being sinful or to some form of mysticism in which "self" must be rejected or at least must lose its distinctive identity by being incorporated into Christ. (See pages 38-52.) I am convinced that the New Testament does indeed give priority to the spiritual essence of man without succumbing to either of these errors. In spite of this criticism, the positive perspective of their book is to be commended.

An occasional reading of C.S. Lewis's book, *The Great Divorce* (New York: The Macmillan Company, 1946), would do us all good in allowing our minds to be stretched by the realization that the dimension of spiritual reality is certainly far more "solid" than mortal flesh existence. Is man somewhat *more than* God because God is essentially spirit?

5.   There appear to be times when the Bible does use the term "spirit" to refer to feelings or desires, though these certainly are exceptions to the normal deeper meaning. See Matthew 26:41; Acts 17:16; Genesis 26:35.

6.   Paul Meehl et. al., *What Then is Man, A Symposium of Theology, Psychology and Psychiatry* (St. Louis: Concordia Publishing House, 1971), p. 318.

7.   " 'The inward man' is the true self, which answers to the Divine pattern; which is contrasted with the 'outer man' (2 Corinthians 4:16), the material frame, through which for a time the 'self' finds expression in terms of earth." See B.F. Westcott, *St. Paul's Epistle to the Ephesians* (New York: The Macmillan Company, 1952), p. 51.

8.   By using the terminology "that which is mortal" contrasted with what is immortal about man (and, for that matter, terms such as "deepest self," "inward man," and "shallow self," which often is equivalent with the term "flesh"), I am purposely attempting to avoid the unresolved debates surrounding the terms "soul" and "spirit." Rather than take a position that man is body, soul, and spirit, or body-soul and spirit or body and soul-spirit, I am hoping that the truth God wishes us to see will be plain enough to all regardless of one's views about these terms.

Chapter 5

A Declaration of Dependence

*T*he "prism" illustration used at the end of the last chapter underlines a crucial principle that in a very real sense ties together the various lines of thought of Part I of this book. Fundamental in that illustration are not only the concepts of identity and meaning, of spiritual personhood and the proper appreciation of one's flesh, but of the absolute necessity of dependence on the flow of God's life if indeed we are to truly live at all. It is this principle of dependence that now demands the best of our thinking.

To do this, let's first take a brief look at what I think is the most remarkable unfolding of God's loving purposes for His people in all the Bible. It involves the radical change from life under the old covenant to life under the new covenant — life before Christ's resurrection and the day of Pentecost, and life after those events.

Old Covenant vs. New Covenant Righteousness

One of the most remarkable differences between the old covenant (the main perspective of the Old Testament) and the new covenant is the two very different ways that human right-eousness is handled.

101

In the old covenant, the most wicked man was the one who saw no greater purpose in life than his own pleasure. The idea of God simply got in the way. He was a hedonistic (self-seeking) humanist (one to whom human welfare is primary). If he knew of Jehovah, it only made his wickedness worse. If in his godlessness he chose to consider the welfare of his loved ones or his country he would have been considered as somewhat less wicked than his contemporaries. At least his humanism was directed toward the welfare of others. If he further attempted to keep on God's good side out of the fear of God's anger, he would have been thought of as even less wicked.

But righteous? Hardly that.

A righteous man was one who acknowledged and responded to the worthiness of God. He was a worshipper. He recognized that whatever he knew of God's law was right, and should be obeyed. He therefore set out with humility to do it.

"He has showed you, O man, what is good.
And what does the Lord require of you?
To act justly and to love mercy
and to walk humbly with your God."

(Micah 6:8)

To some degree this was actually possible.

There were righteous men under the old covenant. It wasn't impossible. Do you remember what God told the Israelites?

*"Then the Lord your God will make you most prosperous in all the work of your hands. . . if you obey the Lord your God and keep his commands and decrees that are written in this Book of the Law and turn to the Lord your God with all your heart and with all your soul. **Now what I am commanding you today is not too difficult for you or beyond your reach.**"* (Deuteronomy 30:9-11, emphasis mine)

This type of righteousness could be well illustrated even in the life of the apostle Paul before his revolutionary encounter with Jesus. He could say of his whole life *"as for legalistic righteousness, faultless."* He could also say, *"I have fulfilled my duty to God in all good conscience to this day."* Of his actions in persecuting the Christians he could say with sincerity that he acted as one "zealous for God" and that they were things he felt "he ought to do" as expressions of his zeal (Philippians 3:6; Acts 23:1; 22:2; 26:9).

There is really no question that Paul (Saul) had been a sincerely devout man though terribly misled by his own blind commitment to a prevalent Jewish concept: God never would nor could become a real man. Later, reflecting back on those pre-Jesus days, he acknowledged that he was *"once a blasphemer and a persecutor and a violent man."* But, he quickly added, *"I acted in ignorance"* (1 Timothy 1:13).[1]

Under the old covenant a "righteous" man was aware of how much he needed God's gracious help. (Paul very likely spent earnest time in the temple praying for God's blessing before he started on his way to persecute Christians in Damascus [cf. Galatians 1:14]). It was this very kind of person (though far more open than Paul) that the life of Jesus touched again and again.

When He was a baby, it was Anna and Simeon. At the start of His ministry it was Nathaniel. After His death it was Joseph of Arimathea and Cornelius. Yet it was to this kind of people, "righteous" people, that Jesus said in anticipation of the new covenant, *"You must be born again."* New covenant righteousness was a new proposition altogether.[2]

God My Helper/God My Life

At the risk of oversimplification, the differences between old covenant righteousness and new covenant righteousness could be compared to the difference between "God, be my Helper," and "God, be my life."

Look at it another way. In the Old Testament, God's people were characterized as His vineyard. God was the owner and protector of this vineyard, as well as the One who deserved the harvest (Isaiah 5:1-7). In anticipating the new covenant, however, Jesus told his disciples, *"I am the vine; you are the branches"* (John 15:1). The difference is a radical one indeed.

God's Highest Desire for Man

Quite mistakenly, we get the idea that God's highest desire for humans is that they do right things—godly things. That they express concern for others, obey the laws, reflect proper respect and appreciation for God. This is simply not so! God's purpose for humans *is that they become actual extensions of His life through a dependent relationship with Him.* This, above all else, is new covenant righteousness. Of course such a life will express itself in righteous acts, but the foundation for those acts is *dependence.* Not in the sense of God helping us, but in God living through us.

This whole point becomes very important to see when we face up to the problem of sin in our lives and our concern in pleasing the Savior. If righteousness is merely a matter of avoiding bad things and performing good things instead, then "victory" may be considerably easier than we think.

The Search for a Better Butterfly

Are you ready to use a little imagination again? Let's suppose that I am a young man who has become fascinated with...butterflies.

Before long I become a consummate expert. My collection knows few peers. Every waking moment of my life is utterly captivated by these amazing, colorful, infinitely varied creatures. Finally I arrange my adventure of a lifetime—a trip far up the steaming reaches of the Amazon in search of a rare, exotic species. With scarcely a second thought I turn my back on the world's materialism, its air-conditioned comfort, pretty girls, soft music, new car show rooms, moonlight shopping center sales, the love of money, my physical appearance, my health, and other people's opinions of me. It's easy to leave those things behind; they never really bother me much anyway.

Really? Yes, really. With full sincerity I would tell you that I have found a highly fulfilling reason to be alive. I've found meaning. I have neither time nor interest for so many of the things which seem to captivate other people. And so, all alone under my mosquito netting, lying in a slightly damp hammock, I fall asleep like a child, dreaming of that golden-winged insect somewhere upstream.

If you said that my life was all wrapped up in self, I would counter you with honest force of conviction. One of my greatest joys is to see delight play across the faces of the many people who discover the beauty of butterflies through my display. Mine is the quiet confidence that the world is better, richer because of what I do. I might even go one step further. Even as a non-Christian, I might insist that my efforts were bringing justifiable glory to the Creator!

The Butterfly Hunter Before God

You're right, there aren't many people around like that — unaffected by materialism, lust, or greed for glory. But even one would prove a point. Every one of us can think of some very self-less non-Christians we have encountered in our lifetime. Think about all the music, art, and science of benefit and joy to so many which have come from earnest, dedicated, unbelieving people. And certainly for the sake of the continuance of the human race on earth it is far better for mankind that you and I be civil rather than lawless, aesthetic rather than bestial.

But this is hardly new covenant righteousness. Such qualities will never commend us to God. When that butterfly hunter stands before God's throne of judgment will he be able to show off his specimen trays or cite his good deeds to society, or speak of the sins he did not commit? Will all his cultural, intellectual, moral, or social acts weigh anything at all on God's balances which determine one's eternal destiny? The answer, of course, is no. They will amount to precisely nothing. Jesus said, "I am come that you might have life, and have it more abundantly."

Life is what one needs in order to stand eternally before God—God-life. [3]

"This Too, Is Vanity"

By the way, our butterfly hunter illustrates a fundamental premise of this book: meaning in life is basic to human existence and inseparable from the nature and problem of sin. A butterfly-lover's identity is certainly adequate to give meaning to a person's life. No doubt about it. And it so happens that this particular type of meaning tends to remove a person from all sorts of immoral and socially destructive sins in contrast with a young man who develops a playboy identity. Yet even the butterfly collector, if he could only think his way through the Ecclesiastes route, would have to conclude, "This too is vanity—ultimate emptiness." By nature this "worthy citizen" is a child of wrath. He also has missed life.

But the average person doesn't "think his way through." In fact, if he has found some wholesome, socially acceptable field which challenges his capacities he may conclude that he has found where life is. He knows his identity—he is a businessman. By choice he gets up early in the morning and carefully reads his *Wall Street Journal.* In the evenings he's up late poring over charts, diagrams, and statistics. No 40-hour week for him! And though he may complain about his long hours, it's only a front. The business world is his life. To lose it would be to lose living.

The same could be said of any dedicated musician, physician, athlete, contractor, or politician.

It is also possible to say something similar about believers who have found their identity in some Christian profession. Though the product and the purpose are completely different, it is possible for even a missionary or evangelist to approach "life" precisely the same way as any hard-driving insurance salesman whose goals may be measured in terms of monthly quotas, earning gold keys, or having one's name mentioned for special commendation at the next conference.

A biblical scholar may find fulfillment in his word studies on the same mind-flesh level as the scientist who analyzes the vocabulary of a chimpanzee. Similarly, a Christian teacher may go over his books, sharpen his notes, develop stunning illustrations, utilize modern audio-visuals, and assume that if he does these things he is fulfilling life. Truthfully, he may be scarcely touching life at all—authentic life—resurrection life. To compound the loss, many Christians will put such an individual on a spiritual pedestal.

Living Straight Isn't Enough

So often we hear "victorious life" speakers say words like these: "Because the old man has been crucified, you don't have to listen to his commands any more. His power has been broken. You don't *have to* swear or lust. Before, you couldn't help it but now...."

This may sound liberating. And there is some truth in this speaker's words. But it can also be very misleading.

For you see, a non-Christian doesn't *have to* swear or lust either. Each of us knows fine non-Christian people who honestly are repelled by such things. Out of the simple, determined discipline of their own persons they have pressed themselves into other patterns of thought and behavior. They lead community battles against pornography; they are disgusted with the way other people have so degraded themselves. For the general welfare of society we can be very thankful for such non-Christians. But this is by no means new covenant righteousness! These people still are not truly alive.

A "Live" Human

What then does a "live" human look like? Who is our ultimate example? Obviously, it is Jesus. Let's take a longer look at Him. And as we look, please do not take offense that our focus will be upon His humanity rather than His deity.

Jesus was and is God. He was and is Jehovah. The Bible makes this unmistakably clear. There is no doubt, not even the slightest shadow.

> *"And the Word was God...and the Word became flesh...Before Abraham was born, I AM...while we wait for the blessed hope—the glorious appearing of our great God and Savior, Jesus Christ."*
> (John 1:1; 1:14; 8:58; Titus 2:13)

We could cite many, many passages which clearly affirm the deity of our Lord Jesus. But have you considered how much the Bible tells us about His being a real man? Our Lord's favorite title for Himself was "the Son of man."

Out of our justifiable reaction against those who have denied our Savior's deity, we Christians have tried to bulwark the Bible's already invincible evidence with "proofs" of His deity which are not really proofs at all. In fact, in our zeal we may well have cast a shadow upon the priceless truth that Jesus was fully a real man.

Is this important? *Immeasurably so!* He is the pattern for my life. If He were not a real man then someone is playing a cruel, deceptive trick on us all.

Let's think through His life. What does the Bible say about the manhood of Jesus?

The Manhood of Jesus

As a child he *"grew and became strong; he was filled with wisdom, and the grace of God was upon him."* As an overall summary of those early years Luke states that Jesus *"grew in wisdom and stature, and in favor with God and men"* (Luke 2:40, 52). That sounds human.

Next we find Him in His ministry, a ministry of wonder-filled words and deeds and miracles. How did Jesus explain His own remarkable behavior? Was he simply flexing His own divine muscles?

Let Jesus answer:

"When you have lifted up the Son of Man, then you will know who I am and that I do nothing on my own but speak just what the Father has taught me."

"Do not believe me unless I do what my Father does. But if I do it, even though you do not believe me, believe the miracles, that you may learn and understand that the Father is in me, and I in the Father."

"For I did not speak of my own accord, but the Father who sent me commanded me what to say and how to say it.... So whatever I say is just what the Father has told me to say."
(John 8:28; 10:37-38; 12:49-50; cf. 14:8-10)

There should be no question that in these passages, especially John 8 and 10, Jesus was claiming for Himself a uniqueness in His person as Messiah and the Son of God (as shown by the violent reaction of His listeners in 8:59 and 10:31-33). But this fact must not hide the significance of Jesus' own explanation of both His words and His actions as being products of a dependent relationship with the Father. By this He demonstrated the manner in which true humanness is to be lived out. Even the statement, "I and the Father are one" must be understood as having some parallel with His later statement to His Father, *"that they may be one, just as We are one: I in them and you in me. May they be brought to complete unity"* (John 17:22-23).

"In the Power of the Spirit"
In describing the amazing miracles, Luke states, *"And the power of the Lord was present for Him to heal the sick."* Earlier he says that Jesus returned to Galilee *"in the power of the Spirit."*[4]
John referring to this power says, *"For the one whom God has sent speaks the words of God; to him God gives the Spirit without limit"* (John 3:34).

A short time later on the day of Pentecost, Peter states, *"Men of Israel, listen to this: **Jesus of Nazareth was a man accredited by God to you by miracles, wonders and signs, which God did among you through him"** (Acts 2:22, emphasis mine).

Many years later Paul would write, *"(he) made himself nothing"* (Philippians 2:7). And the book of Hebrews would say, *"But we see Jesus, who was made a little lower than the angels...he had to be made like his brothers in every way...because he himself suffered when he was tempted, he is able to help those who are being tempted.... During the days of Jesus' life on earth, he offered up prayers and petitions with loud cries and tears to the one who could save him from death, and he was heard because of his reverent submission. Although he was a son, he learned obedience from what he suffered"* (Hebrews 2:9, 17, 18; 5:7-8).

What Did the Miracles Demonstrate?

When Jesus performed some supernatural act was it in demonstration of His own divine power? The answer, mysterious as it may sound, has to be "No!" Jesus manifested a totally dependent life.[5]

Moments before He called forth Lazarus from death and the grave, Jesus lifted His eyes to heaven and prayed, *"Father, I thank you that you have heard me. I knew that you always hear me, but I said this for the benefit of the people standing here, that they may believe that you sent me"* (John 11:41-42).

The works of our Lord Jesus pointed to His dependence upon the Father. That dependence pointed to the authenticity of Christ's words. Those words spoke clearly of Christ's own divine personhood. We may assume that when He commissioned His disciples with the words, *"As the Father has sent me, I am sending you,"* the dependent pattern of life that had been His was upon his mind. This very pattern empowered by their ascended Lord through the Spirit would even cause them to do "greater works" than Christ Himself had done (John 20:21; 14:12).

Certainly there are mysteries in the Trinity we will never fathom, but it would seem as though God has gone to special lengths to encourage us to appreciate His Son as a real man. A Man after whom we are to pattern our lives.

Jesus was what a truly "live" human being looked like. He is the ultimate pattern. On His own He could have spoken beautiful words. But He didn't. On His own He could have called forth the hosts of heaven to descend in a lightning bolt to His aid. He did not.[6]

Dependent Life

For Paul, the life of Jesus was a pattern and something more than a pattern. Much, much more. The life of Jesus was Paul's very life.

"I have been crucified with Christ and I no longer live, but Christ lives in me. The life I live in the body, I live by faith in the Son of God, who loved me and gave himself for me."   (Galatians 2:20)

Yes, Paul was alive. Yet it was no longer his own "flesh" life. It was Jesus. Jesus' very nature, His very life expressed itself out of Paul's innermost being through Paul's flesh by the Spirit (John 7:38).

What is a truly "live" human? Jesus put it in the simplest words:

"You in Me and I in you" (John 14:20; cf. 15:4-7; 17:21-26).

Clear. Simple. But can we begin to understand those words? Is there any illustration which might come close to its meaning? I wonder.... Since God intensely wishes that we respect our identity as His actual "born ones," His "by nature" children, perhaps there is an illustration in this.

The Umbilical Cord

Before a child is born there is a real sense in which he is in his mother and his mother is in him. It is her very life that is his life. He lives because she lives. If that tiny fellow in his mother's womb could think reflectively he would have to say with each kick of his tiny feet, "That was my Mommie's work—at least, it was her strength. An extension of her own life."

But at birth that crucial umbilical cord is severed. And though that baby will continue to draw strength from his mother, it will never be the same again. He is now on his own. He is an independent person.

There was a day God gave birth to you (*"born of God,"* 1 John 3:9). But in radical contrast, *He never severed that spiritual umbilical cord. And He never will.* Surrounded by Himself, identified with everything Jesus is, you are ever, always, "in Him."

But He is also "in you." Your life is an extension of His own life. You live because He lives. Without life from Him, you have no life. Though you may appear to be very much alive during those times when that umbilical cord is well nigh strangled and flesh has temporarily become your sphere of existence, it is only "mock" life. It is life on a sub-human level in terms of God's ultimate intention for you.

Dear Christian, can any of us imagine the full implications of these things? To wake up in the morning and declare to God, "Gracious Lord, for today, I have no life except as You give me life."[7]

Can you begin now to grasp the import of Paul's major prayer for the Ephesians?

"I pray that out of his glorious riches he may strengthen you with power through his Spirit in your inner being, so that Christ may dwell in your hearts through faith...that you may be filled to the measure of all the fullness of God."

(Ephesians 3:16-17, 19)

Eden in Reverse

In this truth, we approach the reversal of the tragedy of Eden. We were once "in Adam." We are no longer! That person has ceased to exist! We are in Christ! John the Baptist was the last prophet under the old covenant and concerning him Jesus said, *"among those born of women there has not risen anyone greater than John the Baptist; yet he who is least in the kingdom of heaven is greater than he* (Matthew 11:11).

The new covenant indeed has come![8] All that remains to fulfill our eternal destiny is the completion of God's careful facetting of His spiritual diamonds and the redemption of our bodies. *"For the perishable must clothe itself with the imperishable, and the mortal with immortality"* (1 Corinthians 15:53).

Until that day comes we have a job to do.

As Christ was the Light of the world, so we are lights in the darkness of our world. As He was the expression of the Father's love and holiness so we are to abide in love and manifest daily holiness.

"As He is, so are we in this world" (1 John 4:17, NASB).

As He was His Father's Ambassador, so are we *"ambassadors for Christ"* (2 Corinthians 5:20).

But why...why if all this is so, does it seem so easy for me to sin? No matter what you say, I have lots of problems. Why on earth if I am a "holy person" do I come across to myself and to others so much of the time as the sinner I still feel like I am?

It's time now we faced up to these most fundamental questions.

General Summary

My fundamental purpose is not to simply oppose the concept that every Christian's essential nature is sinful, but rather to emphasize an overriding issue. Every person, Christian or not, must by the very nature of being a person face up to the issue of meaning in life. If he functions in this sphere independently from God, then he is sinning whether or not he is a Christian. If he is a non-Christian, he has no alternative, and therefore his essential nature *is* sinful. If he is a Christian, the issue of meaning still incessantly confronts him. To whatever degree he fails to fulfill his truest self as one who is "from God" and totally dependent upon God for authentic life, to that degree, the "nature" he manifests by his thoughts and behavior is also sinful.

For the Christian, then, the fundamental issue is not the popular "sin nature" idea as the "catch all" explanation for the problem of sin in one's life. Instead the issue actually is, *am I aware of who I am? If so, am I aware of the resulting meaning in life which flows from that identity and the divine resources available to fulfill that destiny—and, what am I doing about it?*

We look now to those resources in Part II.

Chapter 5, Notes

1. In 1 Timothy 1:15 Paul identified himself as "the worst" of all sinners. Certainly he did not have in mind the present regenerated state of his overall moral character or the quality of his worship, but rather, Paul could think of no sin worse than persecuting Jesus and His people. This he had done even though it had been done in ignorance. Even though the present tense is used, "I *am* the worst," the focus is on the past as in 1 Corinthians 15:9. *"I am the least of the apostles. . . because I persecuted the church"* (emphasis mine). Probably this same thought is in Paul's mind in Ephesians 3:8, *"I am less than the least of all God's people."* One might wish to press the point of Philippians 2:3 as he urged believers to *"consider others better* [NASB reads "more important"] *than yourselves,"* meaning that every Christian's self image should be less than what he imagines of other people. In view of the immediate reference to the Lord Jesus and the overall emphasis on humility, would it be proper to think that Jesus too considered others as "better" than Himself? No! Since the word (Greek, *huperechontas)* commonly was used to express the idea of prominence, importance, rather than relative moral goodness (cf. Philippians 3:8; 1 Peter 2:13), the NASB rendering of "more important" seems to be not only appropriate to the passage, but also a proper parallel with the attitude of our Lord. Proper humility does not in itself demand that one hold to a fundamentally sinful concept of one's own personhood. Commonly Paul presented himself to others as an example of a godly man worthy of being copied. He clearly knew himself to be a new man who was no longer structuring his life "in the flesh."

2.   The Old Testament repeatedly anticipated the radical, inward change that someday would come. Not only is this expressed in the actual statements of the new covenant (Jeremiah 31:31-34; Isaiah 59:21; Ezekiel 36:26-27; cf. Isaiah 60:21; 62:12) but also in the deep felt agony of the prophet who realized that the day of that new covenant had not yet arrived (Isaiah 59:9-15; 64:5-7). Too often Christian communicators use old covenant descriptions of the inner nature of a believer as being proper descriptions of a new covenant believer. They either forget or misunderstand that the difference was to be so radical as to be described as the "death" of the "old man" or "old self." The new covenant was *life*.

By emphasizing this I in no way wish to cast a shadow on the profound work of the Holy Spirit under the old covenant in individual lives such as David (1 Samuel 16:13; see also Psalms 23-27). Nevertheless *regeneration* appears to be a distinctly new covenant event. See Appendix C, footnote 3.

3.   Old covenant believers needed the same. Perhaps the book of Hebrews includes this added dimension which was so necessary for eternity when it says, *"none of them received what had been promised. God had planned something better for us so that only together with us would they be made perfect."* Also in the following chapter in the description of the glorious company in heaven it includes *"the spirits of righteous men made perfect."* Could this be a reference to old covenant righteous men who since then have come to share in the resurrection life of our Lord Jesus (Hebrews 11:39-40; 12:23)?

4.   See Luke 5:17 and 4:14. See also an excellent, brief analysis of the activity of the Holy Spirit in the ministry of Christ in *Fire in the Fireplace* by Charles E. Hummell (Downers Grove, Ill.: InterVarsity Press, 1978), pp. 65-76.

5.   Some theologians criticize this point of view by pointing to such passages as Mark 2:8, John 1:48, 2:24-25, to

prove that Jesus manifested His own omniscience. The Scriptures readily counter this unjustified conclusion not only by Jesus' own statement that He did not know the time of His own return to the earth (Mark 13:32), but by telling of other men who possessed supernatural information, obviously without any claim to exercising omniscience (cf. 2 Kings 6:12; 5:6; Acts 5:1-9; 8:18-23). If the performance of a miracle proves the deity of the individual, then who were Elijah and Moses, etc.? This remarkable humanness of our Lord was also anticipated by the Old Testament (cf. Isaiah 49:4-6; 50:4-7). Even the glory that He manifested (John 1:14; 2:11) was glory which He said His Father had given Him (John 17:22), a glory which He in turn gave to His disciples.

6.   With reference to this possibility Jesus underlines His commitment to dependence with the words, *"Do you think that I cannot call on my Father, and he will at once put at my disposal more than twelve legions of angels?"* (Matthew 26:53, emphasis mine).

7.   This statement finds a direct parallel in Galatians 6:3, *"If anyone thinks he is something when he is nothing, he deceives himself."* Apart from the "umbilical cord" idea we are nothing on any divine scale of worth. As Jesus said, *"apart from me you can do nothing"* (John 15:5). Remember too that Jesus during His self-emptying on earth, said much the same thing of Himself! *"By myself I can do nothing"* and *"I live because of the Father, so the one who feeds on me will live because of me"* (John 5:30, 6:57). *"The Spirit gives life; the flesh counts for nothing"* (John 6:63).

8.   This statement should in no way cast a shadow on the future actual realization of the new covenant by God's unique covenant people, the nation Israel. See Romans 11:24-27.

Part 2

A New Lifestyle: *What Made First Generation Christians Distinctive?*

Somehow I wish it was possible to spread out all at once all the separate parts of this most crucial section of the book so that they could be seen not so much as "parts" but as one living picture. We Christians have a remarkable capacity of complicating God's truth by our long lists of rules or principles as though there were a series of individual steps a believer needs to take—one by one—in order to arrive at practical holiness. That simply isn't so.

If we could possibly identify the fundamental ingredients of those first generation Christians who "turned the world upside down," we should be able to discover in very practical terms the "how" of holiness. Your results in doing this might not come out exactly as mine. But I hope your list would at least include the distinctives that I am emphasizing.

Well, what do we find?

I am convinced certain characteristics stand out in boldest relief as explanations as to why their lives were so remarkable. Yet rather than being "steps" they took, they were ingredients which seemed to be "all stirred in" at the same time. It was as though one part was well nigh meaningless without the other parts. As though each served as a catalyst for the releasing of the flavor of all the other ingredients.

We shouldn't find it difficult to remember these distinctives, but it will be something else to keep them "all stirred in." Actually our Bible will be our biggest help because it will do the blending for us. Therefore, although we will attempt to focus on each component, we will find ourselves time and again touching all the others. First of all, let's identify the ingredients. In a list? I'm afraid so, but only so that we can get them all stirred in as soon as possible.

Functioning first generation Christians knew:

1. Who they were and why they were alive. This could not be known apart from a solid awareness of the character of God and the final authority of His written Word.
2. That holiness did not come about passively, but by the active participation of their wills.
3. That the Lordship of Christ was not an option.
4. That the Holy Spirit's presence was an *experienced* reality.
5. That the individual Christian was not an isolated pilgrim, but part of a body which could not function apart from love.

Chapter 6

A New Identity: The Knowledge of Who One Is

They knew Who they were, and Why they were alive.

*L*ike scuba divers on the floor of the sea, those first Christians were living in an alien environment. Life for them had to come from above—from their true home. Though they might look like sea creatures (with their flapping fins, masks, and wetsuits), they knew they were not of this world.

Right from the start, first generation Christians simply saw life through different eyes. Their awareness of their new identity automatically produced in them a revolutionary change as to why they were alive—as to their meaning.

No longer was meaning measured by prosperity. As needs arose they willingly sold their lands and houses to share with those who had less. Paul must have echoed the testimony of many when he said, *"I have learned to be content whatever the circumstances. I know what it is to be in need, and I know what it is to have plenty"* (Philippians 4:11-12, cf. Acts 4:34).[1]

In Hebrews 10:34 we find that remarkable statement, *"You...joyfully accepted the confiscation of your property, because you knew that you yourselves had better and lasting possessions."* (How many of us are comfortable with that statement?)

Troubles in general were not seen as essentially negative, but positive. Even the precious treasure of health was not allowed to be used as a measurement of meaning in life. They were discovering that *"power is made perfect in weakness"* (2 Corinthians 12:9). In fact, in times of suffering when the world would say they were losing life, they would respond that just the opposite was happening—life was pouring in. Who would dare question, for example, when Stephen was most fully "alive"? Suffering was like a light that shined on life! (See also James 1:2-4 and 1 Peter 1:3-9.)

To whatever degree this awareness of life is missing today, to that degree holiness will be perverted.

For instance, if I wrongly assume that holiness comes in saying "No" to all of my desires in order to say "Yes" to God (since I am primarily a sinner with sinful desires), then, on top of all the normally expected trials and disciplines and Satanic pressures, I will have to carry the added burden of my own negativism. How radically opposite to this is Paul's declaration when he said, *"I have lost all things. . . that I may gain Christ"* (Philippians 3:8). In view of the positive *(which was his desire)* he considered the "loss" but rubbish. Those early believers knew that to say "death" to the flesh was indeed saying "life" not only to the glory of God but also to themselves who were partakers of that glory as joint heirs with their Lord Jesus. *The Christian who really knows this can truly be "himself" without being selfish!*

Underlining the Positive

To focus on this first ingredient is to say that first century Christianity would be very much at home in Part I of this book. The spiritual air they breathed was fragrant with a type of liberty the world has never seen before instead of being polluted with legalism. Listen to Paul:

> *"And you have been given fullness in Christ. . . having been buried with him in baptism and raised with him through your faith in the power of God, who*

raised him from the dead...God made you alive with Christ...you died with Christ to the basic principles of this world...'Do not handle! Do not taste! Do not touch!'...you have been raised with Christ...and have put on the new self, which is being renewed in knowledge in the image of its Creator." (Colossians 2:9-3:10)

A Crucial Passage

Basic to this Colossians passage is one section of Paul's writing which is considered by many to be the most crucial of all in terms of the practical functioning of a believer, Romans 6-8. Again and again in this passage Paul emphasizes that victory is preceded by awareness of identity. Open your Bible and simply check on what he says before and after the "therefore" of 6:12 and 8:12.[2] (See footnote for a list of the "befores" and "afters.") Note the repeated contrast in 6:17-22 between who we were and who we are. Note the very first item the Holy Spirit bears witness to with your spirit in 8:16.[3]

New Places to Go, New Sights to See

Yet awareness of identity is scarcely the whole show. It rather enables you to go forward in your discovery of meaning. Once identity is a settled thing, you look no longer at self but rather at the prospect of the life in front of you.

Remember the "rabbit who was really a bird" illustration? If he simply sailed through the sky shouting "I'm a bird! I can fly!" he would be missing the very purpose for his life. There are new places to go, sights to see, and things to do that being a bird and being able to fly make possible. So also with a Christian. Though the initial focus is on identity, the lasting focus is on life.[4] *"Now this is eternal life"* Jesus said, *"that they may know you, the only true God, and Jesus Christ, whom you have sent"* (John 17:3).

Every living, intelligent being could be said to be functioning perfectly if he is fulfilling the purpose for which he exists. Often this doesn't take place because of factors totally beyond the control of the individual himself. (The watch dog that cannot chase the burglar because he is locked in the garage; the cow that can't give milk because it has had nothing to drink; the non-Christian who by nature is cut off from God's life.) On the other hand the lack of fulfillment in life may be directly due to the avoidable failure of the individual himself. (The watch dog is too busy chasing the cat; the cow is fighting the milking machine.) When this happens in the life of a Christian it is called *sin*. Sin then for the Christian is the avoidable failure of the individual to fulfill the purpose for which he exists. (It might be a good idea to compare this with the definition of sin on page 25 as it relates to the non-Christian.)[5]

A Closer Look at Common Sins

Now let's take a closer look at a few individual sins quite common among Christians and see if we can find the "why" behind them in order to underline the "how" of holiness. First of all there is that whole class of sins—jealousy, envy, pride, self-pity. Two people are nominated for deacon or senior class president or cheerleader...and you lose. Your best friend "steals" the girl you had your eye on. Your associate at work gets a promotion and raise and you don't. You got the smaller scoop of ice cream. Why do we react when things like these happen?

Is it really because of some mysterious, sinister, spiritual gland secreting wickedness within? Some vaguely described sinful nature that we Christians refer to as though it were a prominent biblical term?

Why do we react? I believe it is at that moment, consciously or unconsciously, we feel threatened in terms of whatever we thought made living significant. Meaning, even as lowly a meaning as "right this moment life for me is a stomach full of ice cream, stimulated taste buds, a delighted nose," has been hurt—someone else got the bigger scoop. But who is that "I" which feels the hurt? We don't have to look far for the answer. Paul says, *"The deeds of the flesh are evident*

...*strife, jealousy, outbursts of anger...envyings"* (Galatians 5:19-20, NASB). It is clearly the "flesh" concept of I. But just how much does "flesh" include?

Let's make a modern paraphrase of Philippians 3:4-6 because it expresses what it means to glory in the flesh. How would such a paraphrase sound? Maybe something like this:

"Born of the best family, reared in the 'members only' Olympic Estates, educated at Harvard, member of the City Club, zealous attacker of cults and subversive organizations, law abiding and untouched by scandal..."

You see, flesh includes the physical, mental, and emotional parts of me—my whole psychophysical self. Even status is part of the flesh. Yet Paul could say concerning all of this *"I consider them rubbish, that I may gain Christ"* (Philippians 3:8).

But why, Paul? Why would you call all of that rubbish?

"Because," Paul would say, *"I have found the surpassing greatness of knowing Christ Jesus my Lord."*

"Okay Paul, but aren't you going against yourself, your own desires?"

"Yes, in a way I am going against my flesh. But you see, I am not in the flesh. Life for me is in the spirit.[6] Those who belong to Christ have crucified the flesh with its passions and desires."

Whether we realized it or not, when we received the Savior we automatically moved to an entirely new sphere of finding life. From that day on, authentic life for us could never be derived from our psychophysical natures—our flesh as independent from God's life in us. Before that day, if 'life' was to be found anywhere, it *had to be found* in the flesh. Because for one who is spiritually dead that's all there is. But after that day—a miracle!—"I discovered I was alive!" (see Philippians 3:8, 20; Galatians 5:24; Romans 8:2-9).[7]

"Renewed in the Spirit of Your Mind"

The "how" of holiness in a believer's life, however, goes beyond understanding the nature of one's flesh. Compounding the whole problem is an incessant bombardment from both the world and the "prince" of this world. They call out in sounds and shapes and ideas that precisely conform to the desires of my flesh. Countless automatic, chain-reaction thought patterns have already been computerized away in my brain, ready for instant recall. It comes as no surprise at all when Paul says that if a believer is ever to know a transformed life, there must be a renewing of the mind (Romans 12:2).

Peter expresses it so clearly. He states that sin is the result of forgetting what happened to you when you were saved.

> *"But if anyone does not have them* [the qualities of godliness], *he is nearsighted and blind, and has forgotten that he has been cleansed from his past sins."*   (2 Peter 1:9)

You see, the problem is not so much a "nature" problem as it is a "knowledge" problem. But if anyone thinks that victory over sin is nothing more than an intellectual exercise, he will be terribly disappointed if he tries that route. It doesn't work. Spiritual success has never rested on a seminary education or an advanced I.Q. (Remember, at the start of this chapter we noted that one ingredient could never be put to work in isolation from the other four?)

God has carefully inserted into His Word some expressive yet mysterious phrases. Phrases like: *"the spirit of your mind,"* (Ephesians 4:23, NASB), *"the eyes of your heart," "to know this love that surpasses knowledge"* (Ephesians 1:18; 3:19). God tells us *"the man without the Spirit does not accept the things that come from the Spirit of God, for they are foolishness to him, and he cannot understand them, because they are spiritually discerned"* (1 Corinthians 2:14). Jesus encouraged His disciples to anticipate understanding certain things only after the Holy Spirit would come upon them in power (John 16:12-13).

No, it is not simply brain power. Yes, a crucial "how" of holiness *is* knowledge, but not simply a quantity of information. It is rather a participant, relational type of knowledge that in the Bible is inseparable from the ministry of the Holy Spirit. Because He is both the Spirit of truth and the Spirit of life He integrates knowledge and spiritual power. The result is life. The kind of life Jesus said He came to bring.

You and I are living in an exciting era when fresh winds of the Spirit's power are blowing across God's people. Yes, there are counterfeits. Yes, there are extremes. But only because Satan, too, feels the power of those fresh winds and he is constrained to launch a counterattack. Pity God's church if it misreads the signs of authentic Holy Spirit empowering.

Under New Management

An illustration may serve to summarize what we've been speaking of.

Imagine with me a great profit-making company whose essential purpose is to manufacture poisonous gas for the army. Department by department the company busies itself daily with this goal. In the chemistry lab they are absorbed in the search for newer, deadlier, even more destructive gases. The bookkeepers bend over the records in pursuit of profit/loss comparisons. Salesmen thumb through well-worn synonym-finders in search of positive adjectives. Quality control inspectors rush about with clipboards and sharpened number three pencils. All busy. All geared toward that one consuming goal: producing poisonous gas for profit.

And then—a remarkable thing happens to the poisonous gas company. The entire board of directors, all the top brass, the full ownership of the company—changes hands. It is actually a brand new company, not only because of a change in leadership and name, but also because of a change in its essential purpose. The new company rejects the profit-making motive. It is now committed by its very nature to be a nonprofit company. Its new product? Making livesaving oxygen for hospitals. It is more than a corporate name change. More than a simple paper shuffle. It is an actual change of identity.

Personnel Problems

Well, that solves everything! Everyone appreciates oxygen. This new company should work out just fine.

But...it isn't quite that simple. It seems that all of the company's machinery and all of those varied departments are still geared up for the same old poisonous purpose. In fact, if left to themselves, each of those departments would still measure their success as they always measured success—producing poison for profit. That's what life was all about for many of those old career poison producers. Just because the company changes doesn't mean all the departments automatically snap to attention. It's tough to teach the old hands new tasks.

So management has a clear-cut job to do. An intense indoctrination program has to take place, filtering from the top right on down.

"Listen chemists, you must change your concept of success in this department. Junk your poison formulas. Success is now to be measured by the quality of lifesaving oxygen you can produce."

"Bookkeepers—attention please! From now on you will simply have to miss the pleasure you used to derive from being the first to know the size of the company's profit. Forget profit. Management expects you to simply keep the books and keep them well. Understood?"

Understood perhaps, but not appreciated.

"Why do we have to be so different? Every other company judges its success just like we used to!"

"We've always measured ourselves against the competition. That added some spice to life!"

"You're asking us to reject most of what we've learned. It may sound easy for you up there on the top floor, but down here—that's something else!"

Reprogramming the Computer

This illustration speaks to me about what it is like to become a Christian. By nature I was a child of wrath, *"indulging in the desires of flesh and of the mind"* (Ephesians 2:3, NASB). Life for me was in the flesh, because it simply wasn't anywhere else.

But now things have changed. Deep within. God has joined me to His life. The core of my identity is a new identity. Alive to God. *"The old has gone, the new has come!"* (2 Corinthians 5:17).

Is everything new?

Not yet.

Someday.

But for now, the varied departments of my flesh are still pretty much the same, with all the programming of the past still registered on the computer of my mind. Therefore, unless a new programmer constantly inserts new instructions with new motivations, my machinery will operate just about the same as it did before.[8]

This, I believe, is what that vital yet often misunderstood sixth chapter of Romans is saying. The old board of directors, the fundamental identity of the company has died — really died. The old board does not share the boardroom with the new board. Nor is it locked up pounding on the wall next door. The old board does not exist.[9]

New Directives from the New Management

Listen again to Romans 6:6: *"For we know that our old self was crucified with Him so that the body of sin might be rendered powerless, that we should no longer be slaves to sin."*

Before the moment of our salvation, our "body of sin" (our mortal being functioning independently from God) was anything but powerless. It was, in fact, quite energetic. Everything it did, unless it did nothing (which was suicide), was self-effort, and that's *sin.* For *"everything that does not come from faith is sin"* (Romans 14:23).

But now—for the first time—it does not need to function in that way. New management is in position to issue new directives. Directives which move from the top down (or from the inner man out) to all the departments of my flesh. Directives in perfect harmony with my new identity.

"Hey listen, flesh. We're not in the business of manufacturing the poison of sin any more. We're a new company now. Life for us is somewhere else."

And my machinery—all those departments—have no authority to disobey. All that is needed now is an adequate, continuing supply of messages, underlined in red, informing the departments of the new company rules. Along with those messages I need enough power to enforce those rulings when a given department refuses to heed them. Those two words, *messages* and *power*, bring us right back again to the ministry of the Holy Spirit. (See Part II, Chapter 9)

The Last Bite of Crab Louie

Remember our earlier statement, "To say 'No' to the flesh is actually saying 'Yes' to one's deepest being?" Let's conclude this chapter with just one more analogy which may highlight this essential truth.

This time visualize yourself in the restaurant of an airline terminal eating a Crab Louie (or whatever tantalizes you the most) waiting to depart on the dream trip of your life—a trip around the world. Suddenly and joltingly, you hear the final call for your flight. There on your plate are the last choice morsels of crab legs. At that moment, however, *a far deeper level* of knowledge and power surges through your being. Shoving away the plate you run—you race—to avoid missing your dream. If there was a voice saying "Just one more delicious bite," you didn't even hear it.

Why did you push away the plate?

Because you didn't want to disappoint your rich uncle who lovingly bankrolled the thing?

Or because you were part of a very rule-conscious tour group?

Nonsense! You did it because you most deeply *wanted* to. To miss going would be to miss life.

By comparison, the "old self," the person I was before salvation, is like a person with no reservation and no ticket in a terminal where there aren't any real flights anyway. No flights. So where is "life" for that person? Life for him *is* the terminal—the curio shop, the magazine stands, the restaurant, the bar... and perhaps a coin operated flight simulator. For that person, it would make no sense at all to shove aside a Crab Louie.

That Dangerous Meaning Vacuum

Putting it in these terms makes it sound so simple. It isn't. The lust of sin often strikes with poignant, consuming force. It may be food. It may be sex. It may be one of a thousand obsessions which so captivate us that for a time we find ourselves unable to think of anything else. Why is it? Victor Frankl, who as far as I know was not a believer, was so right when he observed that the "will to meaning" is "man's most valuable asset... not only in gaining and keeping mental health, in achieving happiness, or even self-realization, but also it alone can enable man to realize the ultimate values and possibilities of which his life is capable."[10]

Usually we become gripped with an obsession to sin when some other more respectable or righteous fulfillment in life is being frustrated. Perhaps some relationship which should have been realized, some accomplishment which slipped through our fingers, some disappointment in our own ability to fulfill a task or to use our heads. Nothing opens the door to sin faster than failure. (Unless, perhaps, it is success.) Since it is simply too unthinkable to be alive without some degree of satisfaction that will bring some sense into life, I automatically reach out for whatever object or experience *is* readily obtainable. That is why physical or sensory type lusts are so especially quick to arise. My vacuum of meaninglessness can be filled so immediately! There are times when stuffing my mouth satisfies. And for those moments life is making sense. Shallow sense, but then...any sense is better than an aching vacuum.

Sometimes it takes a little more time. If the lust is sex, it may take a little while to find that person, that book or magazine, that "something" which will awaken that fantasy of meaning. I must consider my reputation of course, and my financial resources...it may require some careful planning and delay, but that's okay. For you see, from the very moment I set my mind on lust *I am moving*! My mind is alive—planning, anticipating.

And something else remarkable. Even if I cannot lay my hands on whatever object or experience lust demands, I can quite easily slide into fantasy. And for those few seductive moments, I can forget the real world. I can push aside the haunting frustration, the emptiness, the broken plans and dreams. I can even forget my lifeless, lackluster Christianity.

Then, of course, if my fantasies can be followed by actual experience, I have doubly lusted, doubly lived. Little wonder lusts are so consuming in view of such rewards! Temporary? Oh yes. And invariably followed once again by the gnawing emptiness of that "meaning" vacuum.

(Let us pause to tip our hats to this marvelous, glittering world so loaded with objects waiting to be grasped.)

This then is the first of those five distinctives.

Though it could not stand alone without the other four factors, this fundamental awareness must have been universal among those early Christians. *"How great is the love the Father has lavished on us, that we should be called children of God! And that is what we are!"* (1 John 3:1).

(Note: In my original listing of these five distinctives [see page 120] I stated that this first one "could not be known apart from a solid awareness of the character of God and the final authority of His written Word." The issue of the character of God will become central when we consider the third factor, the Lordship of Christ. The final authority of the Scriptures is seen undergirding everything in this book.)

Chapter 6, Notes

1. One may assume that since Paul said "I have learned" that he was describing an extended process. But this is to misread the early chapters of Acts. However, I do not deny that there also will be growth in contentment.

2. Let's note the context of Romans 6:12:
    6:12 *"Therefore do not let sin reign in your mortal body so that you obey its evil desires."*

BEFORE:
    6:2 *"We died to sin."*
    6:4 *"As Christ was raised from the dead...we too may live a new life."* (If the first was a historical fact, so also second! *Cf.* D. Martyn Lloyd-Jones, *Romans, The New Man* [Grand Rapids: Zondervan, 1974], pp. 52-54.)
    6:6 *"our old self was crucified with him."*
    6:7 *"anyone who has died has been freed from sin."*
    6:8 *"we will also live with him."* (Most interpreters agree that this is speaking of resurrection life now.)
    6:11 *"In the same way, count yourselves dead to sin but alive to God."* (The word "count," *logizesthe*, carries the thought that what is said is true regardless of one's acknowledgment of it.)

AFTER
    6:13 *"those who have been brought from death to life."*

Let's note the context of Romans 8:12:

8:12*"Therefore, brothers, we have an obligation—but it is not to the sinful nature* [flesh], *to live according to it."*

BEFORE:

8:9 *"You are not in the flesh, but in the Spirit."* (NASB)

8:10*"But if Christ is in you, your body is dead because of sin, yet your spirit is alive because of righteousness."*

AFTER

8:16*"The Spirit himself testifies with our spirit that we are God's children."* (The word "children" focuses on a position *by birth*, not by adoption, as is the focus of the word "sonship" in 8:15. Cf. W. E. Vine, *Expository Dictionary of New Testament Words* [Old Tappan, N.J.: Fleming H. Revell Co., 1966], p. 32.)

3.   Please note my earlier emphasis on the priority of identity awareness, pp. 52-55.

4.   This important focus is well expressed by Thomas Howard in "Who Am I? Who Am I?" *Christianity Today,* July 8, 1977, although he misrepresents the Scripture by stating that the Bible does *not* encourage us to consider self-identity as a matter for serious reflection at all. Indeed the Bible *does repeatedly* speak of the importance of a Christian being aware of his own identity. But that awareness is only a means to the greater end of occupation with *living* to the glory of God.

5.   Is sin for the Christian truly "avoidable?" Unless one has in some way been prejudiced against it, one thing comes through quite clearly in the epistles. Not only is sin avoidable, but righteousness is assumed to be the norm for every believer's behavior. *("I write this to you so that you will not sin." "No one who is born of God will continue to sin"* [1 John 2:1; 3:9]. *"So then, brethren, we are under obligation*

not to the flesh, to live according to the flesh—for if you are living according to the flesh, you must die" [Romans 8:12-13, NASB]). On the other hand, probably with a sense of personal relief, we see ample evidence in every epistle that apparently all new covenant believers do sin. Therefore in some sense sinless perfection must be seen as a theoretical possibility. Though the distinction made between willful sin and non-willful sin in the Wesleyan doctrine of perfectionism is both valid and significant, I do not believe the Bible supports the concept that only willful sin deserves the title "sin." If at this point you are raising the red flag of 1 John 1:8, I suggest you consider interacting with the thoughts in Appendix B, beginning with page 251.

6.   When Paul says *"I am of the flesh, sold under sin"* in Romans 7:14 (NASB), he is viewing himself from the perspective of one who on a flesh level is attempting to satisfy God's law, which of course a Christian is never supposed to do. This entire approach to the problem of sin (Romans 7:14-24) is soundly rejected by Paul as unworthy of the miracle of *"the Spirit of life in Christ Jesus"* (Romans 8:2, NASB) which then leads Paul into his declaration of authentic Christian personhood as one who is "not in the flesh" in direct contradiction to his statement in 7:14.

7.   See Appendix C for a consideration of the term "flesh" as it relates to Paul's statement *"They that are Christ's have crucified the flesh"* in contrast with *"For we know that our old self was crucified"* (Galatians 5:24, NASB; Romans 6:6).

8.   It is important to underline the fact that there is nothing essentially evil about the departments of one's flesh except when they function independently from a believer's essential being which in turn is inseparable from the life of God. "The part of man in which sin thus establishes itself is not his higher self, his conscience, but his lower self, the

'flesh,' which is not itself evil, but is too easily made an instrument of evil" (William Sanday and Arthur C. Headlam, *A Critical and Exegetical Commentary on the Epistle to the Romans* [Edinburgh: T & T Clark, 1952], p. 182).

9.   It should be obvious that I am making a vital distinction between the terms "old self [man]" and "flesh" as used in Romans 6-8. This distinction is commonly denied by those who hold to a "positional" view of the death of the old self. I am convinced that this denial underlies much of the confusion concerning holiness today. If my "old self" was only "positionally" crucified, then it remains a force to be reckoned with. Now since the Bible clearly teaches that I must continue to put down my flesh and anticipate future battles between my flesh and my spirit (or the Spirit), of course my "old self" could not possibly have actually died even though Romans 6 says it has. The supposed solution has been to create the "positional" concept. I can then be true to the Scripture and declare that my "old self" has been buried and yet I can speak of the necessity of "controlling" it. Time and again as I have left meetings where this approach has been presented, I've seen confused faces and wrinkled brows — those momentary glances back at the speaker. "Is what I heard what he really said? How can I be so thrilled over some positional truth that has so little bearing on my actual living? Oh well, I've always heard that Romans 6 is confusing. Maybe some day..." This fully sincere, though totally unnecessary double talk has been well corrected in several more recent books, especially by John Murray and Martyn Lloyd-Jones. See Appendix B for an extended analysis of these differing points of view and Appendix C for further consideration of the term "flesh."

10. A.J. Ungersma, *The Search for Meaning, A New Approach in Psychotherapy and Pastoral Psychology* (Philadelphia: Westminister Press, 1961), p. 23.

Chapter 7

A New Choice: The Commitment of a Person's Will

Holiness requires the active participation of one's will.

*W*hen was the last time you looked at your will? No, not your last will and testament. But that other will. That mysterious part of you that chooses, that decides what you will do. Perhaps at first you might think that your decision-making machinery is fairly simple. Your mind weighs a variety of choices before you, selects one and pushes you in that direction. Just like that.

If it were only that simple. But it isn't. To prove it to yourself, try dusting off an old systematic theology volume in your church library and look up the section "human will." I guarantee you will discover some of the most brain-twisting, tongue-tangling paragraphs you've seen in a long time.

But if we're going to get at the crucial "how" of holiness, we are going to find the issue of the will right at the center of things.

A Case Study from Romans

Let's get our bearings.

The fundamental concept of this book is that you, as a born again person, are—in your deepest self—in perfect agreement with the will of God. To whatever degree you happen to know the will of God, you agree with it. In other words, every single righteous "ought" you will ever sense will be in precise agreement with every single "want" that authentic "you" will ever have.

As a Christian, you are not and never will be at odds with God! Why? Because God gave birth to you and *"Spirit gives birth to spirit"* (John 3:6). Of necessity you possess His nature. If you sense a conflict between your "wants" and your "oughts" it is not a conflict within your truest personhood. It is rather a conflict between that true personhood and your unredeemed mortality.

The nature of this conflict is vividly expressed in Romans 7:15-20. Here Paul describes the plight of a person who wishes to do right, but finds he simply cannot produce.[1] In fact, he finds that he does exactly the opposite.

This passage does *not* say, "Sometimes I want to sin and sometimes I don't." It does *not* imply that his will was torn in two directions as though influenced by two different capacities. A Christian clearly *is not* a person who is driven at times by one will and at times by another. Neither is he a person who has two capacities (sin nature, new nature) with the will positioned somewhere in between. No! Paul could not have been clearer when he stated, *"For what I do is not the good I want to do; no, the evil I do not want to do—this I keep on doing"* and *"in my inner being I delight in God's law"* (7:19, 22).

Paul even goes so far as to say, *"it is no longer I who do it, but it is sin living in me that does it"* (7:20).

Now that was a very dangerous thing for Paul to say. It so easily could have been twisted into a neat excuse for sinning—"Don't blame me! I didn't do it, my flesh did it! I don't sin!" Paul would never agree with such an excuse. In the broadest sense of your personhood, you are fully responsible for your flesh—all that is mortal about you. Until that day when you at last experience the redemption of your body, you have the sole responsibility of presenting your members *"in slavery to righteousness"* (Romans 6:19).[2]

On the Razor's Edge

Let's take a closer look at this conflict. If it is not a conflict between two "wills" inside of us, then what is it? I would
imagine Paul himself would agree that the thoughts he was
sharing in Romans 7 were among the most difficult he ever
attempted to put into words. (Maybe this chapter is what
Peter had in mind when he said concerning some things in
Paul's letters *"(they) contain some things that are hard to
understand, which ignorant and unstable people distort!"*
2 Peter 3:16.)

In this crucial passage, Paul is walking on top of one of
the most vital, razor-edge doctrines in Scripture. Two can-
yons of error yawn on either side of a narrow ledge of truth.
On the one hand Paul is rejecting any notions of two-will,
two-person, two-capacity Christianity. On the other hand,
Paul is equally opposed to characterizing a Christian as an exclusively spiritual being.

Right on top of that razor edge of truth is a crucial warn-
ing: *A Christian can become so weak, so spiritually under-
nourished, so ignorant that the flesh level of his personhood,
which is supposed to be his slave, rises up to act as his master.*
And who is to blame? Not the slave! The slave is simply attempting to fill a vacuum in leadership.

We could take it one step further. As flesh rushes in to
fill the "meaning" vacuum we begin to conclude that we actually *want to sin.* We begin to feel that this represents what
we really are—forgiven sinners who love to sin! From that
perspective we find ourselves fighting and wrestling against
the "oughts" of Scripture because they seem so contrary to
our "wants." To do the will of God is to go against our will.
To say "Yes" to God is to say "No" to me.

Plagued with guilt, we see the Christian life and Christian service as an overwhelming sacrifice. I must lay down all
my dreams though my heart is torn inside of me and tears
stream down my cheeks. Though it is nothing short of sheer
personal torture, I must do it. God demands it! And I owe it
to Him who died for me.

I think if one were to confront Paul with this sort of reasoning, the apostle would look him straight in the eye and say, "Certainly not! Who do you think you are?"³ How few Christians today have a grasp on the fact that their inner man *delights* in the law of God!

Well Then, What About "Self-Denial"?

A very reasonable question one might raise against the emphasis of this book is, "Doesn't the Bible teach that we are to deny ourselves? Therefore isn't saying 'yes' to myself (as proposed in this book) directly opposite to self denial?

Jesus indeed said, *"If anyone would come after me, he must deny himself, and take up his cross and follow me"* (Matthew 16:24).

Paul expressed the same when he said, *"Not seeking my own good"* and *"do nothing out of selfish ambition or vain conceit"* (1 Corinthians 10:33, Philippians 2:3).

So "self-denial" is a biblical concept. But before we assume the argument is closed, we need to face the apparent fact that Jesus, too, knew "self-denial." Therefore, if we are to understand its implications we must first try to understand what it meant to Him.

Certainly for Jesus there was no "sinful self" to take "off the throne." Yet He said repeatedly *"I do not seek My own will, but the will of Him who sent Me."* Are we then to assume that Jesus' life was actually against His own wishes? No, that could not be. Speaking prophetically of Christ the psalmist wrote, *"I delight to do Thy will, O my God."* His will *was* to do the will of God His Father.⁴

Self-denial, it would seem, is exactly the same for a regenerated disciple as it was for the disciple's Lord. For Jesus to have done His own will would have been for Him to act independently from His Father (John 8:28-29). This He would not, could not do.⁵ Since my deepest motive, hence my truest will *is* God's will due to the fact that I have been born of God (1 John 3:9), it is not false pride to say, *"for to me, to live is Christ."*

The only way I could speak of *my* will as a separate will would be at the same time to think of myself as a person independent from Godlife. As a born one of God, I deny that "flesh self" any rights or fulfillment.[6]

So then, is it contradictory for me to say that delighting in the will of God means saying "Yes" to myself? No more than it is contradictory to say the same of our Lord Jesus.

Now let's see if we can tie these ideas together in one sentence.

Though it certainly is correct to speak of self-denial within the limits either of a flesh level sense of self or self as seen functioning independently from God, it is also fully biblical to say that I as a Christian, a "self," am to do the exact opposite of denial; I am to fulfill the self that I most deeply am even as our Lord Jesus fulfilled the self that He was and is. I believe that Galatians 2:20 in a very pointed way underlines these distinctives.[7]

> *"I have been crucified with Christ and I no longer live, but Christ lives in me. The life I live in the body, I live by faith in the Son of God, who loved me and gave himself for me."*

Is Knowledge the Key?

Once again we need to turn our thoughts to this second crucial issue: the action of one's will.

Remember at the beginning of Part 2 we emphasized that the five factors which bring about practical holiness must not be seen as separate steps, but as inseparable ingredients. This is so easy to say and so difficult to remember. For instance, a common assumption that pops up from time to time among evangelicals is that holiness is in some way directly proportional to the degree of knowledge one has concerning the Bible.

It *IS* important to know what God has said. But building on that, it is very easy to conclude that the more books I can outline, the more verses I can memorize, the more theology I can systematize, the more equipped I am to communicate and defend my orthodoxy...the more godly a man I will be.

Right?

Isn't that what Romans 12:2 teaches? *"Be transformed"* it says. How? *"By the renewing of your mind."* And how is it renewed? Certainly by the reprogramming of my mind with God's truth. But wait.

I remember so well when God first began to open the door of hope to me as He underlined the truth of my own spiritual personhood. All those earlier years of focus on biblical truth in college and seminary had reinforced the impression that my chief task in life was to know the Word and preach the Word (and of course to personally respond to what I knew). Therefore, it seemed to me that if only I could write indelibly, on the conscious level of my mind, the facts concerning my true identity and the resultant meaning of that identity in terms of life, then I would start experiencing practical righteousness. The prospects were exciting. I had no trouble responding to these facts. They were thrilling!

I was a saint! Well, at least I was off on the right road. I could now understand that the motivations within myself which were running counter to the will of God were not reflective of my truest personhood, but rather arose from the struggle for meaning within my members. And as such they were warring "against the soul" and therefore certainly not in my best interests.

But no matter how intensely I focused on those facts, *I soon discovered that awareness and even excitement concerning biblical truth does not produce holiness.*[8]

Well then,

Does Knowledge + the Will bring Holiness?

Maybe that's it. If I renew my mind by studying the Bible and then exercise some good old determination to obey what the Bible tells me then that ought to do the trick. Anyone who has attempted this soon discovers that he finds himself right back in the middle of frustrations quite similar to those in Romans 7.

Normally one's will is followed by action. I will to move my arm and it moves. I will to bite my tongue and "ouch!" I will to tell a lie and there it is. But I can will to live to the glory of God in perfect harmony with my growing reservoir concerning God and myself...*maybe something happens and maybe it doesn't.*

That's frustration! Why doesn't it happen? Simply because resurrection life does not flow from an educated brain and an active will; it flows from God.

Does Knowledge + the Will + Spiritual Power bring Holiness?

At last the answer is "Yes!"

A Most Remarkable Prayer

Even though we have yet to consider in any detail the final three ingredients which, when combined, produce holiness, we must see them all if we are to fully appreciate the significant place our present component has—*the will.* To do this we're going to look at one of the most amazing, comprehensive prayers in all the Bible—*the most important prayer I know to pray!* It is found in Ephesians 3:14-21. Let's spread these verses out so that we take a good look at them...

For this reason
I kneel before the Father,
        from whom his whole family
                in heaven and on earth
                    derives its name.
I pray that out of his glorious riches
      he may strengthen you with power
            through his Spirit
            in your inner being,
        so that Christ may dwell in your hearts
                      through faith.
And I pray that you, being rooted and established in love,
        may have power, together with all the saints,
            to grasp how wide
                and long
                and high
                and deep
          is the love of Christ,
          and to know this love
                  that surpasses knowledge—
    that you may be filled to the measure of all the fullness of God.
Now to him who is able to do
        immeasurably more
            than all we ask or imagine,
      according to his power that is at work within us,
  to him be glory throughout all generations, for ever and ever!
    in the church and
    in Christ Jesus,
        Amen.

Spotting the Five Ingredients

Can you imagine any better definition of holiness than to *"be filled to the measure of all the fullness of God"?* I can't. Now let's see if we can locate those five ingredients.

An awareness of one's identity and meaning in life. Paul begins his prayer with a solid awareness of truest self-identity, *"in your inner being,"* that deepest realm of human personhood which will someday grace heaven itself and which alone is equipped by God to express authentic meaning in life (which, by the way, is the essence of the entire prayer). Next, let's notice the final three ingredients.

The unconditional issue of Lordship. Paul begins with absolute submission to the Father, *"I kneel before the Father."* He then concludes his prayer with absolute commitment to the glory of God, *"to Him be the glory!"* And in between he acknowledges the fundamental necessity of Christ dwelling in our hearts. Interestingly, the word Paul chose for *"dwell"* literally means "to be at home in." In other words, there can be no practical holiness unless Christ is truly "at home" in your life. That's Lordship.

The Holy Spirit's presence and power as an experienced reality. *"Strengthen you with power through his Spirit."* Could that possibly be non-experiential? Not a chance! Why? Because the presence of that power will produce in you (1) spiritual comprehension with dimensions beyond your dreams, and (2) an awareness of the love of Christ which *"surpasses knowledge."*

A body life participation rather than an isolated pilgrim. *"Being rooted and established in love, may have power, together with all the saints. . . to him be glory in the church."* If this were not enough, the next three chapters which flow out of this prayer *are packed* with relational issues with love at the center.

Now, back to that second one. **Holiness demands the active participation of the will.** Fundamental in this prayer is *the earnest, fervent asking* by Paul. Not only for others, but certainly we should assume for himself also. One more word in this prayer spotlights the will. It's the word "faith." It is through faith that the fullness of God is received. And faith is an action word—solid commitment, firm expectation. There can be no holiness apart from the exercise of your will—in asking God and believing God!

"Above All We Ask or Imagine. . ."

That indeed is a remarkable prayer, but it doesn't stop with verse 19. As if to underline the scope and mystery of his request, Paul adds verse 20. This God to whom he prays *"is able to do immeasurably more than all we ask or imagine."*

So often this expression is used as an encouragement to trust God for big things with the knowledge that He enjoys giving us more than we ask for. We ask for a car and He gives us a Porsche. We ask for a godly wife and He also gives us a beautiful one. *But that's not the point of the passage at all.*

What is the point? As he prayed, Paul was aware of the mind-boggling scope of his prayer — *"the love of Christ... that surpasses knowledge... the fullness of God!"*

Our automatic response would be, "Paul — no! That is too much. A dream beyond any prospect of fulfillment!"

But Paul responds, "You don't know God! Our God does things beyond all we ask or imagine." And then the apostle brings us back to the proper focus, reminding us of the power that works within us. Whose power? The glorious power and Person of the indwelling Holy Spirit.

Christian, are you listening? Are you allowing yourself to be stretched as you have never been stretched before? Are you asking God for this power Paul spoke of? Daily, asking Him? Exercising your will on your knees? Remember it is not only for yourself, but it is "with all the saints." Remember too, that the end in view is not self-centered; the end is the glory of God. The glory of God *"in the church and in Christ Jesus... for ever and ever."* Oh, what an open door. *Walk through it!*

Mountain? What Mountain?

It is in this wonderful sense that we can take a new look at the commands in the Bible concerning our behavior. Not as impossible mountains, placed in front of us to break us, but rather as most reasonable expectations, well within our reach! Listen to the way D. Martin Lloyd-Jones expresses it:

> The New Testament calls upon us to take action; it does not tell us that the work of sanctification is going to be done for us. That is why it does not put us into a clinic or hospital where the patient is told 'It will be done for you,' and 'Allow the Lord Jesus to do it for you.' It calls upon us to take action, and exhorts us to do so. And it tells us and commands us to do so for this reason, that we have been given the ability to do it. If we had not been given the ability, if we had not received the new nature as the result of

the new birth, if we had not been given the new life, if the Spirit was not in us, then, of course, we should need someone to do it for us. But as we have been given the power and the ability and the capacity, the New Testament quite logically, and in perfect consistency with itself, calls upon us to do it. 'Do not let sin reign in your mortal body' it says. 'Do not present your members as instruments unto sin or unrighteousness.' Do not do it! This is something that you and I have to do; it is not going to be done for us.[9]

Knowledge + the Will + Power. God wants us to realize that these are inseparable. The "Spirit of strength" is also *"the Spirit of wisdom and understanding"* (Isaiah 11:2). The "Spirit of truth" (John 14:17; 15:26) is also the Spirit who strengthens *"with power."* This fact is so very pointed in Paul's other prayer in Ephesians 1:17. The *"Spirit of wisdom and revelation, so that you may know him better,"* is closely followed with *"his incomparably great power for us who believe."*

"Now, I See!"
Let's take the connection one step further. By the mysterious power of the Holy Spirit God transforms that which I assent to into truth that is lived. First, the truth is received and registered in my mortal brain. Then, by the Spirit, that truth moves deeper as an energizing force in my inner man (Ephesians 1:18; 4:23). In the process it becomes a part of a much larger picture that gives that single truth significance it never had before. It is almost like looking at a tiny part of a large painting. I honestly see it. I believe I can see it. I can describe what I see. But the relevance—the power of what I see—eludes me. Then suddenly the whole painting is revealed and it is as though I had never seen that one truth before.

Perhaps this is part of the explanation of the mystery of Ephesians 3:19 in which Paul speaks of knowing that which *"surpasses knowledge."*

Certainly Paul is not thinking in terms of I.Q. Let's look at it this way. I observe some biblical fact. I could pass a test on it. But then the Holy Spirit takes that same fact and, without changing it a bit, leads me in a supernatural way to see the fact from God's perspective. I cry out, "Now I see!"

It is also something like an optical illusion. Though there is absolutely no change in the object I observe, there may suddenly be a remarkable change in how I see it. If I described what I saw first I might say, "That's not much," or "It doesn't make much sense." And of course I would have little motivation to consider it any further. Yet if my perspective changed my response might be one of unrestrained awe.

So also the power of the teaching ministry of the Holy Spirit. We are moved in utter amazement that something so profound—so lifechanging—could have been in God's Word all the time and we didn't see it. (Even though we did "see it.") I think of how many times I had read Romans 6-8 and then one day...I saw the painting. And life changed.

Consider the remarkable statement in 1 John 2:27.

> *"As for you, the anointing you received from him remains in you, and you do not need anyone to teach you. But as his anointing teaches you about all things and as that anointing is real, not counterfeit—just as it has taught you, remain in him."*

The Parable of the Car

Let's see if we can summarize several of the ideas we've discussed by means of a couple of illustrations.

The first illustration takes quite a bit of imagination. You've seen, perhaps, the children's books where an automobile takes on human characteristics? The smiling grill, the blinking headlights...get the idea? We're thinking of a car as a person. And this happens to be a Christian car. His reason for existing is to glorify God. How does he do this? By *moving*. He was created to *move*.

Of course, this car can do many other things as well. There are windshield wipers to swish, a horn to honk, a radio to blare, lights to blink—all sorts of interesting gadgets and optional equipment. In fact there are so many interesting things to toy with one might get so wrapped up in the fascination of it all that he misses the main purpose, *which is to move*.

Carport Christianity

Though all of these accessories get their power from the battery, the battery is not the core of the car at all. The core is the engine.

Now for the Christian, the engine is the inner man. The battery is the will. Sadly, it is possible for a Christian to become so involved in all the varied potentialities of his flesh—his mortal being—that he may begin to think that life is right there...in the accessories. But that isn't really life for him at all. His radio may be blaring, his horn honking, wipers swishing, lights blinking—he may have everyone thinking he's a productive person. But he hasn't moved. He's still in the carport.

On the other hand, this Christian might honestly realize the reason for which God saved him. Therefore he exerts his will to roll forward. (At this point his will would be expressing the earnest desire or motivation of his inner man. See Romans 7:18,22.) Of course he finds it very difficult. He presses on the starter with the gears meshed and—ah!—that good ol' battery comes through. The car lurches forward. About two inches. Somehow he knows that moving must involve something more significant than that. An inch here, a lurch there. And before long the battery's worn down anyway.

Hmmm. Well, it's back to the turn signals or eight-track—something that isn't quite so hard on the battery.

Maybe...someday...he'll get the hang of this "moving" idea. But then, none of the other cars around him seem to be moving, so why should he? Everyone else seems satisfied with the gadgets and accessories. No one seems to disapprove of his lifestyle. Maybe this "moving" idea is something you are to just "take by faith." One thing for sure...the scenery hasn't changed a bit.

Distinctive "Honks" and Fine-Focused Fog Lights

Ah, thank goodness for the books and seminars that specialize on personality types and individual gifts. This Christian can now focus on his personhood in terms of the distinctive "honk" of his horn or the fidelity of his tape deck. He finds his identity as a "high fidelity" person in contrast with someone else who happens to be a unique "fog light" person or "variable, intermittent-speed windshield wiper" person. And of course that makes each person very special and of unique worth.

Yet, even with all that, the whole thing is somewhat depressing because the battery (his will) keeps running down and he has to find someone to charge it up again. Happily, there always seems to be some new thing going on in town that provides the necessary "jump" to keep him going.

Of course all these variables between individual cars opens a very disturbing potential: he may start comparing himself with someone else and either become quite depressed or jealous or both if he senses that he is not nearly the car they are. Or he may become very proud because he decides that it is just the opposite. No matter how he feels it always hurts when some new model comes out which automatically dates him.

"Oh God, I Want to Move!"

And then one day he stops and thinks—really thinks. "Just what am I doing? Something inside me—way down deep—is crying out for action. Real action—moving action! Who am I? What is my identity? I am a person created by

God to express the very life of Jesus in the world. I was
created to move! Oh God, I want to move!"

Quickly he turns to his Bible and begins to read and
diligently study. "Maybe," he thinks, "if I knew more of what
this book says, that would make me move." So with his will
he sets his alarm to go off half an hour earlier in the morning.
With his will he rejects the urge to tap the "snooze" button on
his alarm. With his will he opens the Bible, reads the verses—
even takes notes and memorizes a verse or two. He closes
with a prayer and his day begins.

But is he moving?

We all know that our simple wills *cannot produce
holiness* any more than a battery can make a car go. No, he
isn't moving.

"Well, what next? I've tried Bible study and prayer...
maybe if I volunteered to take an evangelism class or opened
my home for a group Bible study? Maybe..."

What then *can* produce holiness? What does it take to
get the car moving? How about the fuel tank? Can we, with
all respect and reverence, make the fuel the Holy Spirit?
Finally our illustration begins to fit. How does a car move? In
layman's terms, I think it happens like this: Drawing initially
on the resources of my battery, I turn the ignition key to the
"ON" position and, holding it there, turn the engine over. In
so doing, fuel is drawn into the carburetor where it is
prepared to join a spark from the battery. A series of inner
explosions begin, the gears are meshed...I move!

Ignition!

Consider the similarities in our lives as Christians. A
Christian's will in itself *does not* produce holiness. But it does
initiate the circumstances in which holiness can be realized.
That most important act of turning the ignition key to "ON"
and holding it there also parallels an essential spiritual act:
the conscious openness, dependency, and expectation of
receiving the necessary energy in the Person of the Holy
Spirit. *That openness to Him and His supernatural empower-*

ing must be an attitude of the mind, not simply a passing thought. I resolve not to resist *anything* He might wish to do in my life—He is sovereign. It is then that I find myself moving into an entirely new dimension of living. The scenery *is* changing. I *am* moving. Jesus is being seen through me!

Yes, my will does set the alarm to go off. And that will continues to function as I open my Bible and read words and sentences using my intellect. But I find that I cannot credit my will (battery) with the adequate power to move even though it is fundamentally part of the power system by being wired to the engine (my inner man). The credit goes to God the Holy Spirit. He is the fuel! He is my life! He is my strength... *"the help given by the Spirit of Jesus Christ"* (Philippians 1:19).

I believe that in a most tangible way this is the essence of those paradoxical words of Paul,

> *"Therefore, my dear friends, as you have always obeyed—not only in my presence, but now much more in my absence—continue to work out your salvation with fear and trembling, for it is God who works in you to will and to act according to his good purpose."*   (Philippians 2:12-13)

In our illustration there is one most important and wonderful difference. That difference parallels the thought of Paul, "Though our outward man (all those things which work off the battery) is perishing, our inward man is renewed day by day." The capacity for my engine to work more effectively in enabling me to move seems to improve with age! In fact, it never wears out!

Happily, too, since the measure of true worth is most fundamentally the effectiveness in fulfilling the "moving" idea, it really doesn't make much difference whether my car is a clunker or a Cadillac! Of course, it is nice to move in style, but if my focus is not simply on moving, but on what moving can accomplish, then the style of that moving needs scarcely to be considered; it really isn't relevant, no matter how much other "cars" appear to make so much out of it and also measure me by it.

One final note might be added to this illustration. Sometimes a person discovers that he is a terribly weak-willed individual. He feels helpless to even begin the process. What does he need? He needs a "jumper cable" linked to some strong-willed person to temporarily support his weak will. Oh how good of God to place us in local bodies of believers. *"And we urge you, brothers, warn those who are idle, encourage the timid, help the weak, be patient with everyone"* (1 Thessalonians 5:14).

"Oughts" vs. "Wants"

Since the "how" of holiness in terms of your actual birthright is the most crucial issue of this whole book, I can think of only one other way to underline what is so much on my heart, and that is to take one more brief look at an opposing view that seems to be so common today. This view appears to be built on the idea that whenever you are feeling sinful desires you are actually encountering your fundamental nature—a sinner. At those times of pressure you either follow through with that sin and do what you want, or you by God's strength stand against it and end up doing what you ought.

Now, whenever you end up on one of those "interior cabinet meetings" by deciding to go against what you want in order to do what you should, you discover quite a variety of emotional responses. On one hand you may feel quite good because you know you have pleased God by responding to His urgings. But you may also feel a little bit miffed by your decision because you know that you have missed out on what you really wanted to do. (Remember the illustration of watching TV?)

Yet whether or not one obeys the "oughts" he still must reckon with the true nature of the kind of person he assumes himself to be. Is there no answer? Let's first look at two answers which must be rejected.

"Somehow I must get 'self' off the throne—better still, I wish it could just die. I do indeed hate myself, because I know full well that God's law is holy and I am so sinful. If I could only die to self, then the 'oughts' would no longer be in conflict with the 'wants' because the 'wants' wouldn't be there anymore!" Now there are two huge problems with this popular approach. First, I find that I can't kill this sense of self. I simply am an "I." Second, if somehow God does the killing and He fills the void with Himself, then when I die, He will go to heaven; I won't, because I, the "self," am not alive to go. This most certainly is not what the Bible teaches!

Another common approach is to say quite boldly that according to Romans 6, our "old self" (falsely equated with the word "flesh") has in fact suffered violent death. God has done this for me. He not only has overcome the penalty of sin for me, but He has overcome the power of sin for me. I am to simply thank God that "self" has died on the basis of the Word of God taken by faith. But soon I sadly discover that "self" is still very much around as a quite active corpse, and I am either led to conclude that I haven't "believed" well enough or else I have been reading too much into this "dead old man" idea. If I choose the latter, I then simply modify my previous bold statement by saying, "the power of the old self has been broken."

In making this revision I sincerely hope no one presses me to explain how something that is dead can still exert its "broken power." If they do press me, I will have to remind them that of course this death is judicial or positional (or some such word), which is another way of saying that this death is not really actual at all, but rather true only in God's divine bookkeeping. Remember the filter illustration (see page 46). One writer goes so far in pressing this judicial idea that he makes a direct parallel between Satan's judgment at the cross (yet he continues being very active) and the crucifixion of our old self (yet it too continues very active). This parallel has no scriptural base at all since the Bible in no way states that Satan has been crucified, but it does say that our "old self" has been crucified in the same absolute sense as Christ's own crucifixion.

How tremendously important it is for every Christian to be taught quickly that when he was regenerated, not only was he forgiven, but God did indeed change his essential personhood. His deepest self, his truest self, never desires to sin. He is always in perfect agreement with the "oughts" of God's moral law. Tragically if in his early years as a Christian he has been sincerely brainwashed with well-meaning "positional truth," he may struggle for years before he realizes that the "oughts" which so often seemed to be contrary to his "wants" were not some exterior voice of conscience or God, but rather the very things that were his true "wants" in light of who he has become in actual fact. He simply needed to stop and look deep enough beyond those shallow levels of personhood to finally encounter a fundamental identity that was in harmony with God! I fear that the voices of well-meaning teachers have drowned out the voice of the Spirit Who *"testifies with our spirit that we are God's children* (born ones)" (Romans 8:16).

Filling the Vacuum

Strangely enough, I have found that my own need of responding to this truth is greatest during those times when my life is least structured—when the pressures are off!

Look out for vacations!

I haven't the slightest doubt that God is pleased to program into our lives an ample supply of lazy afternoons and even a few vacation trips out of which dreams are made. But what is it about us that so easily corrupts "rest" into "restlessness" and well deserved vacations into struggles with guilt and boredom? What is it? Simply that none of us were ever made to endure a state of meaninglessness very long. How often we sin simply out of boredom as to meaning in life![10]

I'm afraid that sometimes we Christians deceive ourselves into thinking that we are handling this problem fairly well by packing our spare times so full of one thing or another that we are not even aware that we have completely lost touch with authentic life. But if we stop and attempt to get our bearings as to our true identity, we may end up no better off as we struggle with guilt because we aren't witnessing or reading our Bibles. Could it really be that the prayer of Ephesians 3:14-21 (to "be filled to the measure of all the fullness of God") is *not* compatible with a fantastic week in Hawaii or an evening of doing nothing more than sitting on the porch and watching the sky until the last of the sun's rays fade away and the first evening star glimmers its way into existence? I don't believe that. I hope you don't either!

Well then, if these things *can* be in harmony with our birthright, why the difficulties? The answer takes us right back to the focus of this chapter. There can be no practical holiness apart from *the active* participation of our wills. God never intended for our "wills" to take vacations! The joining of our wills to the power of the Holy Spirit is just as needed on our days off as any other time. *That's so easy to forget!*

It still embarrasses me to think about it, but I remember a lazy afternoon a few years ago when I went with my children to a motel swimming pool. All was well until a couple of very attractive girls joined us. Having nothing else to do, I found myself staring. Time and again I determined not to look, only to look again (that law "in the members of my body" was working overtime!). In my determination I went so far as to think through the fact that I was indeed God's new creation; that I was not "in the flesh." But somehow even this was not enough to override the desires that I felt.

I remember thinking as we left the pool, "David, you simply cannot go back to that pool again and still glorify God!" But that hurt because it was an admittance of defeat.

And then I thought, "Could Jesus have been at that pool?" Sure he could have. But He would have had a good reason for being there. Peter tells us that Jesus, empowered with the Spirit, always *"went around doing good"* (Acts 10:38). And I knew that same Spirit was also mine.

"But at that pool, Lord?"

"Yes, David."

"But how?"

"David, with My power, why don't you *plan* next time to simply wrap your life around those two children of yours that you love so much."

That's it! I could then have a reason for going to that pool that was in full harmony with who I was.

"Thank you, Holy Spirit, for an answer to the vacuum my flesh was so ready to satisfy!"

And sure enough, the next time we went, it worked. The problem was gone because *life* had filled the vacuum.

I'm sure this same principle is equally effective whenever we unexpectedly find ourselves with time on our hands. I remember one time when I became very impatient waiting for a friend who was to meet me in a restaurant. What right did he have to mess up my schedule? After a few minutes of steaming inside I was stopped short by the question,

"David, what is the most important thing in your life right now?"

"Oh, I guess as usual it would be to express the fruit of the Spirit — to be that container for the fragrance of Christ."

"Well then, is this delay really a frustration as to life for you? Remember, *patience* is part of the fruit I produce."

"When you put it that way, I guess I really don't have any reason for being upset."

"Wake up to it, David, you're free! Free to simply wait and in waiting know that you are fulfilling life."

Oh, that felt so good to be free! And in that atmosphere of freedom it was amazing to discover how readily the Holy Spirit filled those minutes with significance.

But the Spirit must be an active participant. Otherwise, we will fall prey to those extremely subtle counterfeits of righteousness that can unknowingly slip in to fill the void. By exerting our wills all by ourselves we may reject whatever clearly sinful behavior we might do and instead come up with some high quality alternative. By all appearances the alternative looks quite wholesome and befitting of resurrection life when it isn't at all. For instance, we reject the sin of gossiping by getting all caught up in baking a cake; we turn away from some type of lust by giving ourselves to athletics. Any non-Christian can do exactly the same thing! Remember the butterfly hunter illustration (page 104)? It is so hard to keep in mind that eternally significant living is not found in simply rejecting sinful things nor is it found in coming up with wholesome alternatives; it is found only as God's life is actually received and displayed through us as a prism reflects light and produces all the varied colors of the rainbow. Jesus' life was not holy simply because He was an honest carpenter or a boy who respected His parents. He was holy because as He said, *"I can do nothing from myself."* Christianity is not simply living that ideal, "eagle scout" type of life; *it is dependent resurrection life.* It is not simply discipline; it is the discipline of the Spirit. It is not simply the biblical instruction to the brain; it is the instruction of the inner man. It is not as though Jesus said, "the words I have spoken to you are a behavior manual," but rather, *"the words I have spoken to you are the spirit and they are life"* (John 6:63). No matter how we look at it we can't get away from the fact that spiritual life is exactly that: "spiritual." And as such it is mysterious and beyond the reach of the human will alone.

Even when one comes across the numerous commands in the epistles concerning behavior, we must understand that the simple response to the command to be loving does not in itself produce the "fruit of the Spirit." I may not only *know* that I should love someone that appears to be unloveable but I may actually *want* to love them. In fact I may push myself to perform a "loving act," yet still miss expressing the "fruit of the Spirit." It is at this point that the simplest and yet most mysterious of all statements must be seen in sharp focus, *"you are in me, and I am in you"* (John 14:20). Only out of the Spirit-empowered motives of one's inner man, death is declared upon all other motives. And as one single will arises to God, unconditionally open to His Lordship, the Spirit of life places His royal impress upon our words and actions and the divine dimension of resurrection life occurs — Jesus is seen in human flesh, our flesh!

The Impossible Trip

I think one final illustration may serve as an anchor for these crucial issues.

There is a most remarkable bird called the arctic tern. Once a year it travels on the longest migratory journey of any bird known on earth; all the way from one pole to the other. The bird soars across trackless oceans, thousands of miles to its own particular nesting place. That alone would make it a very unusual bird indeed. But there is something even more remarkable about it.

After the tiny terns are hatched and old enough to feed and care for themselves, the parent birds leave for the South Pole. Weeks pass by and the young birds grow and exercise their wings, enjoying all the games that seagulls seem to play in the sky. But finally a time comes when the young terns take one last look at the only place they have ever known, and begin a journey to a place they have never been!

Somehow, deep within them, they know they cannot stay. They must go; they *want* to go. But which way? Did Mamma and Papa Tern leave a set of directions propped up in the nest? "Follow the star Arcturcus until you see the Southern Cross, then, going south by southeast...." No! The trip is buried deep in their natures. No, the terns do not resist leaving, no matter how tantalizing those seagull games may have been — catching the updrafts, playing tag over cliffs above the sea.... Oh yes, they waited, for no matter how strong their desire was they knew they could not leave without *the power* to make that remarkable journey.

Written on Our Hearts

Is it clear, oh is it clear? God's purpose in the new birth is *not* a matter of merely learning His will and trying to do it. It is rather a matter of becoming a living, God-empowered expression of His will which He, by the new birth, has *already* implanted in your deepest self. You are living in the age of the new covenant; God has written His law on your heart (Jeremiah 31:31-34; cf. 2 Corinthians 3:3)! You and I "are from God." Our nature is His!

And the power? The pattern for us is the same as it was for our Lord Jesus.

> *"Just as the living Father sent me and I live because of the Father, so the one who feeds on me will live because of me."*
>
> *"I in them and you in me. May they be brought to complete unity...."*
>
> *"As the Father has sent me, I am sending you."*
> (John 6:57; 17:23; 20:21)

God's Special Catalyst

Well then, is it that simple? Not quite. It would appear that God has chosen a catalyst, a particular environment in which the joining of **Knowledge** + **the Will** + **Spiritual Power** takes place.

And what is that?

Trouble times—stress times.

Perhaps it is because at those times we see most clearly the fragile nature of our earth-oriented, time-bound relationships, dreams, and securities. In our intense awareness of our weakness and our inadequacy, we cry out for holiness. And Jesus said, "Blessed are those who hunger and thirst for righteousness, for they shall be satisfied" (Matthew 5:6)

I have come to believe that *there is no growth in holiness apart from trials.*

> *"For those whom the Lord loves He disciplines, and scourges every son whom He receives...but He disciplines us for our good, that we may share His holiness."*   (Hebrews 12:6, 10, NASB)

"Consider it pure joy, my brothers, whenever you face trials of many kinds, because you know that the testing of your faith develops perseverance. Perseverance must finish its work so that you may be mature and complete, not lacking anything."

"Not only so, but we also rejoice in our sufferings, because we know that suffering produces perseverance; perseverance, character; and character, hope. And hope does not disappoint us, because God has poured out his love into our hearts by the Holy Spirit, whom he has given us."

(James 1:2-4; Romans 5:3-4)

Oh Christian friend, could it be that the day might come, even a few minutes of the day, that you and I could say, "He that has seen me has seen Jesus?"

Chapter 7, Notes

1. Because Paul's concept of himself as expressed in Romans 7:14, *"but I am of flesh, sold in bondage to sin,"* is in direct contradiction with Romans 8:5-13, it certainly is not a description of Paul's present state as he is writing, but rather he is standing in the shoes of a man who is struggling with the demands of God's moral law without a personal awareness of what Paul is going to say in Romans 8. (See D. Martin Lloyd-Jones, *Romans, the Law: Its Functions and Limits, Exposition of Chapters 7:1-8:4* [Grand Rapids: Zondervan, 1974]).

2. "It would appear to be that the apostle is using the word 'will' throughout this passage, when he speaks both of what he does will and of what he does not will, in the highly restricted sense of that determinate will to do good, in accordance with the will of God, which is characteristic of his deepest and inmost self, the will of 'the inward man' (vs. 22). It is that will that is frustrated by the flesh and indwelling sin. And when he does the evil he does what is not the will of his deepest and truest self, the inward man. This explains both types of expression, namely, that what *he wills* he does not do and what *he does not will* he does. If we appreciate this restricted, specialized use of the word 'will,' then it does not mean and the apostle is not to be understood as meaning that will in our psychological sense of the term was not present in that practice and performance which he upbraids as evil and which was in contravention of his determinate will in the more specialized sense." (John Murray, *The Epistle to the Romans* [Grand Rapids: Eerdmans, 1968], p. 272)

3.   Paul's apprehension of his union with Christ "was so ab-
      sorbing; it was such a dominant element in the life of the
apostle that by degrees it came to mean little less than an actual identification of will." (William Sanday and Arthur C.
Headlam, *A Critical and Exegetical Commentary on the
Epistle to the Romans* [Edinburgh: T & T Clark, 1952], p.
162.)

4.   The one Scripture section around which there is a special
      mystery is the record of Christ's struggle in Gethsemane.
There it would appear that He expressed a wish contrary to
the will of His Father. *"My Father, if it is possible, may this
cup be taken from me. Yet not as I will, but as you will"* (Matthew 26:39; cf. Mark 14:36, Luke 22:42). Some have suggested that this is simply an expression of His human will
which naturally would draw back from the cross. I wonder.
Could the repulsion that He felt be rather the expression of
His essential will as a person, of absolute righteousness,
spotless purity, that most properly reacts not so much against
the impending suffering as against the impending reality of
being "made sin" (2 Corinthians 5:21)?

      The "will" of holiness would normally stand against per-
sonal contamination. How could it ever properly be the will
of a holy person to become unholy? Only the overriding purpose of His Father which encompassed not only holiness but
love, grace, and the necessary satisfaction of His own
righteousness would be adequate for the Savior to say, *"Thy
will be done!"*

5.   This raises the standard question, "Could Jesus have
      sinned?" "Could He have gone against the will of His
Father?" His answer was clearly "No!" (John 8:28). The Bible
does not tell us why. Theologians simply say that Deity cannot sin, therefore Jesus could not have sinned. Though obviously that is true, the clues the Bible gives us point to other
answers which allow for a more realistic appreciation of
Hebrews 2:18 and 4:15. First of all Scripture states that God

gave Jesus *"the Spirit without limit"* (John 3:34). A second
clue which is probably inseparable from the first is that Jesus
expressed an irresistable commitment to the fact that life for
Him was in fulfilling the will of His Father. Those facts forbid the possibility of sin committed even apart from the fact
of His Deity. By contrast, the fullness of the Spirit, though
offered every believer, has never been guaranteed. I would
think it reasonable to assume that at whatever moment a
believer is truly "full of the Spirit" he is at that moment also
without sin. But since there is not residing in him that un-
shakable awareness of his own personhood and consequent
meaning in life, lapses in memory lead to lapses in the free
flow of the Spirit and sin results (Cf. 2 Peter 1:9, *"he who
lacks these things is blind or shortsighted, having forgotten his
purification from his former sins"* [emphasis mine]).

6.   Concerning self-denial, 2 Corinthians 5:15 needs to be
      evaluated. It is important to see that the statement
"those who live should no longer live for themselves," comes
right in the middle of an important progression of thought.
Paul begins the chapter by making a clear distinction between
one's deepest self and his mortal house. This follows with a
contrast between those who take pride in appearance, who
recognize people according to the flesh, over against the fundamental fact that a Christian is God's "new creation," God's
ambassador. To make the "oneself" concept of 5:15 a
reference to one's deepest self would be to go against the entire flow of thought. Paul would say "sad is the Christian who
lives as though we were still out to fulfill life as though he had
not died with Christ, as though he were not 'a new creation'."
Paul is saying essentially the same thing as in Galatians 2:20.
      This distinction is most important to see. The Bible
repeatedly asserts as sinful anything that is selfish, in other
words, anything that manifest's one's concern or interest in
oneself without regard for others. Thus Paul stated *"for
Christ's love compels us"* with the result that *"those who live
should no longer live for **themselves**, but for him who died for*

them and was raised again." Jesus expressed words quite similar when He spoke not only of the proper self-denial of His followers, but also of His own self-denial (see Mark 8:34; Mark 10:45; John 8:28).

7. In Galatians 2:20 Paul is not declaring that he has lost his own distinct selfhood because he pointedly says "I live." But the self that he now *is* lives only because it is inseparably linked to the will and life of Christ. The "self" that he once was, the "old self" of Romans 6, no longer has any existence. Happily, and for very practical reasons, this risen, new covenant life that he lived was "in the flesh."

8. "Knowledge alone can never solve this problem, it has already failed to do so. What man needs is not knowledge; it is power. The problem of sin is not a problem of knowledge, of instruction or information." (D. Martyn Lloyd-Jones: *Romans, The Law,* p. 206.)

9. D. Martyn Lloyd-Jones, *Romans, The New Man* (Grand Rapids: Zondervan, 1972), p. 179.

10. Psychiatrist Henry Ward states "Most of my patients come to me simply because they are bored." Parallelling this thought is an observation by Dr. Robert Heath of Tulane Medical School: "Man is a passionate being, in need of stimulation; he tolerates boredom and monotony badly, and if he cannot take a genuine interest in life, his boredom will force to seek it in a perverted way of destruction or violence." (Quoted in *Discern the Times*, by James Reapsome, Issue No. 3.) This fundamental need for meaning is also well expressed in the following: "one rarely reads a contemporary novel, sees a serious movie or play, or listens to the lyrics of popular music without confronting blatant or symbolized reference to the human need for meaning...Science and technology are handily providing the answers to the who-and-what questions, but answers to the why questions and the who-am-I-

and-where-am-I-going questions continue to be disturbingly elusive.... Little wonder that existentialism has captured the imaginations of so many people in recent years.... Most defense mechanisms, adjustment-to-need conflicts, are attempts to maintain self-equilibrium. This urge for balance expresses itself most fundamentally in the universal human need for meaning in life, without which some measure of the person will cease to exist. The organization of personality around some focal center designates the locus of meaning— reason for being" (C. Carl Leninger, "Man's Basic Need for Meaning," *Church Administration,* January 1972, pp. 12-13).

Chapter 8

A New Master:
The Lordship of
Christ is Central

The Lordship of Christ was not an option.

*T*he book of Acts is very clear. The new birth normally
produced an immediate and radical change in behavior
(cf. Acts 2:37-47; 4:32-35; 10:44-46; 16:31-34. Note especially
1 Thessalonians 1:9 within the broader context of 1:2-10.)
*"They tell how you turned to God from idols to serve the liv-
ing and true God."*
So often this does not occur today.
Why is that?
I believe a major reason is because in many Christian
circles, months and often many years will pass by in the lives
of new Christians before they respond to the Lordship of
Christ. In fact those involved in witnessing are warned
against making any connection between Jesus being Savior
and Jesus being Master. The expectation is that eventually the
convert might hopefully decide to dedicate his life to Christ. I
am absolutely sure this was not so in the early church. And
because this was not so, the radical change in behavior was
the norm rather than the exception.
Well then, is the solution simply to add the word "Lord"
to whatever plan of salvation we might follow? Hardly. The
real issue is not the word; the issue is the character of God.

It is very easy for us to forget that those first Jewish Christians did not begin at ground zero as so many converts do today. Through their Jewish background they already had a solid concept of the character of God. They already realized that He was a Person of absolute, transcendent holiness, authority, and majesty—they knew their Bibles! If, therefore, they were forgiven they saw that forgiveness over against the holiness of God. If Jesus was Lord—Deity—then He could be nothing less than Master in the most unconditional sense.[1]

Little Truth; Little Response

By contrast, many individuals who are converted today may know next to nothing about God. Therefore, the Holy Spirit is to that degree limited in leading them into those experiential realities which are the by-products of truth. As Jesus said, *"You shall know the truth and the truth shall make you free."* Scanty truth may well produce a scanty sense of deliverance, worship, and joy.

Can we even begin to imagine the instant, spontaneous joy of someone converted to Christ from a life under the old covenant? The endless remembrance of sin, the absence of a clean conscience, the impenetrable barrier between the God of Mt. Sinai and sinful man and then—*then it was all gone! All of it!* And in that context of *truth* the Holy Spirit was free to lead them to look vertically and cry "Abba! Father!" and "Jesus is Lord!" And then to look horizontally at their brothers and say, "I love you!" They were filled with the Spirit! Their spiritual eyes were opened to understand the Scriptures *because they already knew the Scriptures.*

Savior and Lord

Without any question, the New Testament expectation of a regenerated individual is one to whom Jesus is not only Savior, but also Lord. Lord not only in the sense of His Deity, but Lord in the relational sense of being one's Master, one's Sovereign, one's absolute Despot.[2] In view of their Old

Testament frame of reference, no early Christian would have ever thought of separating those two aspects of Lordship. Only demons would do that and they shudder at the horror of the implication. *"You believe that there is one God. Good! Even the demons believe that—and shudder"* (James 2:19).

The very name JEHOVAH (YAHWEH) underlined the fact that a man must always view his God as a relational Being. He is the God of the covenant; He is the God who would be to His people everything He was. Any question concerning this should have been settled once and for all by Jesus' statement of the greatest commandment:

> *"Love the Lord your God with all your heart and with all your soul and with all your mind."*
> (Matthew 22:37)

At last some little mysteries fall into place. We can understand why with little children their act of receiving the Savior is almost humdrum. What do they know of the holiness of God and the utter despicable nature of sin? What do they know of the implications of Deity?

On the other hand, it is reasonable for someone who has groveled in his own depravity to experience a momentous conversion. Though he may know little of the Scriptures, he knows much about sin! And it is truth the Spirit uses as a catalyst. If all that a man knows is that God loves him, while knowing next to nothing about the nature of sin as seen over against the righteousness of God, what truth does the Holy Spirit have to work with? Can he understand what God's love really means? Can he even begin to appreciate the wonder of the grace of God? Spiritual understanding will not grow in a vacuum!

I believe that in view of the phenomenal ignorance and misconceptions concerning God that most people have today we should take far more seriously Paul's pattern of evangelism before the pagans in Athens. They had no education in the Old Testament at all. Therefore he first built a foundation of facts concerning God (Acts 17:24-29) before he encouraged his listeners to make any commitment to the Gospel.[3]

What is the average non-Christian's mental image of the word "God" when you say, "God has a wonderful plan for your life"?[4] Is it not strange that we so readily can talk of their need of a "personal relationship with Christ" when we have utterly failed to fill them in on even the elementary facts about God? It was only in light of Paul's description of God that he could speak to the Athenians of the need of repentance. This God was "Lord of heaven and earth," the One to whom they owed their very existence and the One before whom someday they would stand in judgment. It was He who commanded repentance!

The Bent Knee

A Christian is a person to whom Jesus is Lord—God *and* Master. To mistakenly read something less than that into Romans 10:9 is to ignore the inseparable demands of "Lordship."

It is simply impossible, unless one has lost his rationality, to say "Abba! Father!" and at the same time reject the Lordship of Christ. John Stott stated it so clearly:

> The bent knee is as much a part of saving faith as the open hand... Faith is commitment to Him as a whole Person, not a particular role. Faith may not choose to be committed to Him in the role of Savior and not in the role of Lord.[5]

I am absolutely baffled by the resistance to this truth among Christians today. We are warned by some that if Lordship is made a part of the message of salvation we are adding works to the gospel of grace. It is perplexing. On the one hand we respond to the Holy Spirit's convicting work which leads us to trust Christ as Savior. And we call that *grace.* On the other hand, we respond to that same Holy

Spirit in the same context concerning God's exclusive, holy demand of allegiance. And we call that *works*?

The Unavoidable Issue

To become a Christian is to become part of the kingdom of God. And remember, it was the "kingdom of God" that Christians preached throughout the entire book of Acts.[6] How can one assume he is entering the kingdom of God and at the same time reject the King—the rule of Christ? If Jesus is not Lord, then the new believer has no prayer to pray. Out of his humanism, he might as well call his God "Santa Claus." To whom will he speak? To God? *A God before whom he will not bow?*

You may be satisfied with an intellectual assent to the deity of Christ. You may agree with the fact that He died for you and that God loves you and has accepted you. But the moment you pray to Him you are assuming a relationship. At that point the issue of Lordship is unavoidable, unless we are simply playing a game with words.

Groping for a Pole

Every year I plant a row of pole string beans in our backyard. Soon after a seed sprouts in the damp spring soil, its tendril begins to reach upward. Moving back and forth. Searching. Groping for something that will direct its climb. Eventually, if it finds nothing, it will collapse to the dirt. Continuing to twist and turn it will often grab hold of itself in a desperate attempt to find some support for climbing. Ultimately it will become a tangled confusion with a pittance of the harvest it might have had.

But if it finds a pole...it will become artistry in motion. Climbing higher and higher. Lush foliage, blossoms. And long, crisp string beans.

Biblical truth concerning God—His Lordship—is that pole, that object around which the Spirit will entwine God's child. By nature he reaches upward; by the Word of God he finds direction.

But because so many converts begin at ground zero as to God's truth, they may for years know only the depression and frustration of attempting to reach upward (for "reaching upward" is characteristic of their truest nature, cf. Romans 7:18-22), only to fall back in defeat and introspection. After a few stabs at reaching out for whatever comes along, they may out of sheer desperation attempt to climb upon themselves through legalism or self-created experience. And then one day—perhaps very suddenly—they at last grasp those things they should have known long before—the precious things from God. And they cry "Jesus *is* Lord!"[7]

With this cry comes such a release of the Spirit it is as though they had never lived before! Sincerely looking for some scriptural title to their new-found jubilation, they might call this "the baptism," or "the filling," or "the anointing." Or any number of other titles which may or may not stand the test of the Scriptures. But something did happen and life would never be the same again. Christ is Lord.[8]

"Salesmanship Evangelism"

I think you have a right to ask why I am making such a point of this.

Consider for a moment where we are in much of today's evangelism. It seems as though we are so eager not only to convert people but to give them assurance of their salvation that they end up with a very self-centered, humanistic package that is really a perversion of the gospel. I am afraid that due to the guilt feelings most of us have had for not witnessing and our dread fear of the whole business, that "good old American ingenuity" has come to our rescue. Loaded with our well-memorized, super salesmanship pitch—"easy open," "snap in place," "instant this or that" philosophy—we venture forth with our product, convinced that it beats all the other religious products on the market. Loaded with well-rehearsed answers to every possible question and a neat way to "close the sale" we at last discover we have found deliverance from our guilt—our customer signed on the dotted line! And why shouldn't he sign? Hell's no fun. If Jesus had used this approach you can be sure the rich young ruler never would have gone away sorrowing, would he? (Luke 18:18-23)

(Certainly I know it would be wrong to conclude that this type of evangelism never produces truly regenerate people. In fact, I would imagine that some of you who are reading this date your salvation from such an encounter. We worship a wonderfully merciful God who sometimes brings about His regenerating miracle in spite of our methodology.)

Unless somehow our witness leads to repentance in view of an awareness of the holiness of God, we have failed to provide a truly biblical, *informational* basis for the convicting work of the Spirit. And unless we share in some way the prospect of a *relationship* with Jesus as Savior *and* Lord, regeneration may not take place at all. And if it doesn't then there is no corresponding gift of the Spirit and no Spirit-produced witness of assurance, "Jesus is Lord!" "Abba! Father!" Apart from the gift of the Spirit no one is regenerated no matter what a person may say he believes — *"If anyone does not have the Spirit of Christ, he does not belong to Christ"* (Romans 8:9). This fact is fundamental to new covenant conversion.

Sadly in our sincere zeal for converts we have made assurance a very academic, non-experiential thing totally in contrast with the repeated biblical explanations as to how assurance is realized.

How *is* it realized?

Assurance and Experience

The greatest little book on assurance is 1 John. And what does John say? He begins by emphasizing that salvation is not primarily a product or a proposition but an institution of a relationship — "fellowship with God." We may be confident we have this fellowship by the presence of several things: by keeping *"his commands"* (2:3), which include loving one's brother (2:9-10; 3:14, 18-19), walking in the *"same manner"* as Jesus walked (2:6), plus a radical change in one's attitude toward sin in general (2:15; 3:4-9). Not only that, but we can enjoy assurance because *we are aware* that God *"has given us of his Spirit"* by Whom we confess that *"Jesus is the Son of God"* (4:13-15) and that *"we remain in him"* (that last phrase certainly underlines that the gospel points to *a relationship* which in turn affects behavior).

In view of the varying shades of gray concerning evangelistic methods today, how thankful to God we should be that those who are most prominent in mass evangelism— men such as Billy Graham and Luis Palau—are bold in speaking of repentance and the Lordship of Christ.[9]

Security vs. Assurance

Though I am tempted to put this in a footnote since it is a digression, it's simply too important to miss: it is absolutely necessary for Christians to distinquish between *security* and *assurance*. The Bible is clear that one is eternally secure *if* he is truly born again (Hebrews 10:39, etc.) even though at various times one's experience may provide him with no basis for assurance. But I am convinced that the personal pleasure of having assurance *was never given by God to gently soothe the anxieties of an individual who is at odds with the Lordship of Christ.*[10] Tragically I have encountered professing believers who were in willful rebellion against the holiness of God and knew it. Yet they would say they were not concerned too much because, after all, they had been saved and at least heaven was a certainty even though admittedly they would have to pay a price for what they had chosen to do. In such cases the shoddy teaching of the doctrine of assurance became like grease on the skids of their spiritual rebellion! The doctrine of security is an objective theological fact; the doctrine of assurance is something else!

Remember, Simon the sorcerer "believed" and was baptized just like the rest of the Samaritans. But there was something critically wrong with his belief. To him, believing in the fact of the gospel was a nifty gimmick to get what he wanted for himself—a new act he could put together that was better than the one he had. Certainly with him there was no response to the convicting work of the Spirit leading to repentance and saving faith which would in turn be manifested by the fact that he had received the Spirit.[11]

Who knows how many "Simons" are "believers" and members of our churches who are either watching out for their own skins (with the attitude, "who wants to go to hell, anyway?") or who are seeking some new experience that will put some zest into life. *Such sincere though crass humanism is not what regeneration is all about! And evangelism which leads to such products is not worthy of the name.* All one needs to do to stand corrected is to honestly evaluate how Jesus handled the rich young ruler who sincerely desired eternal life. Jesus told him that before he could have eternal life there had to be a radical change of mind (repentance) involving a rejecting of where he thought meaning in life was to be found—riches—in order to be open to discover where meaning truly was—in Jesus (Mark 10:17-21).

I am sure that right now someone is saying that to hold such a view of evangelism is to insert "works" into the gospel of grace. Please think for a moment; if one assumes that saving faith is a work of the Spirit and therefore not a human self effort, why should one cry "Works!" if the same Spirit brings conviction which leads to repentance?[12]

The Tragedy of Missing Reality

Of all the troubles which humans encounter there is one that I think is the most pitiable of all. There are diseases so dreaded that the mere mentioning of one of their names causes instantaneous fear. There are physical losses such as paralysis, blindness, or deafness that are in themselves true tragedies. But one—the loss of one's sanity—is the saddest. To be unable to distinguish the real from the unreal or to be unable to function in reality even if one knew where it was, is a type of darkness only those who have been there can describe. Strangely enough, some who are truly insane are the least worried about it because they have concluded that they are the only ones who are sane.

I am convinced that a samilar insanity with far more serious implications is epidemic in evangelicalism today. There are only two explanations the Bible gives us for the absence of an active commitment to Jesus' Lordship on the part of professing believers: either they are not true believers, or they are out of touch with reality.

The first reason is expressed in 2 Corinthians 13:5.

"Examine yourselves to see whether you are in the faith; test yourselves. Do you not realize that Jesus Christ is in you—unless, of course, you fail the test?"

The second reason (being out of touch with reality) can happen to any true believer whenever he either loses sight of the majesty and heart of God or his own spiritual identity. The repeated expression "do you not know" in 1 Corinthians illustrates this reason. For example,

"Do you not know that your body is the temple of the Holy Spirit, who is in you, whom you have received from God?"
(1 Corinthians 6:19; cf. 6:2, 3, 9, 15, 16; 9:24 and James 4:4)

Ignorance or rejection of Christ's Lordship by any Christian demonstrates that he is really living in a fantasy world, an irrational world. He desperately needs someone to point him back in the direction where living actually happens in the real world of the kingdom of God and its Most High King.

It is absolutely appalling that we have so broadened the limits of Christian sanity so as to make the Lordship of Christ an option! As though I could still enjoy fellowship with my God and say "No!" to the call of Romans 12:1-2.

Because it is so easy for us to forget His Lordship, in a very practical sense many of us find ourselves repeatedly shifting from real to counterfeit life. Time and again after failing in holiness we say, "If I had only remembered, I never would have done that!" or "Sorry, Lord, I simply forgot," or "Lord, won't I ever learn?" But to realize this is quite different from saying that God has given us an option. *There is no option.* A Christian is a person to whom Jesus is Lord whether he is always aware of it or not! Though we have the *power* to ignore His Lordship, and by so doing, exist (not live) outside of reality, *we do not have the right!* (Read 1 John again.)

It is also true that even after our commitment there will come times when we see the implications of Lordship in such fresh light that we might wonder whether we had ever truly faced Lordship before. Those are momentous times. And afterward life is never quite the same again.

Chapter 8, Notes

1. It is without justification to assume that Peter's statement "Surely not, Lord" (Acts 10:14) was in any way a rejection of his commitment to Christ as Master as though Lordship was not that crucial of an issue to Peter. In fact if anything, it was just the opposite. It was Peter's deep-seated commitment to holiness in light of the Word of God (the Old Testament Scriptures) that led to this automatic response. (See a somewhat similar situation in Ezekiel 4:12-15 in which no shadow should be cast upon the dedication of Ezekiel.) In like manner there is no hint that either Paul or Barnabas were rebelling against Christ by their falling out in Acts 15:36-39. Rather it would be far more reasonable to assume there was a disagreement as to what was the will of God. It is also presumptuous to conclude that the Christians in Ephesus lived non-dedicated lives for up to two years before they submitted to Christ's Lordship. (See Acts 19:10, 18-19.) The passage simply does not tell us how long before the burning of the articles of witchcraft that the believing took place. We only know the believing preceded the action. Also, because the text states "many of those who believed...openly confessed their evil deeds" does not imply that the rest of the believers remained in their supposed rebellion. Some could have rid themselves of witchcraft long before, while others may never have been involved at all. (See Charles C. Ryrie, *Balancing the Christian Life,* [Chicago: Moody Press, 1969], pp. 170-72.)

2. Only five times in the New Testament is the Greek word properly translated "despot" and used as a title for God. It conveys the idea of "unrestricted power and absolute

domination" (R.C. Trench, *Synonyms of the New Testament* [Grand Rapids: Eerdmans, 1948], p. 96). It was said by Simeon as he held the baby Jesus in his arms as a fitting title for the covenant-keeping God of the Old Testament (Luke 2:29). It was used by the early Christians as they felt the first sting of persecution (Acts 4:24). Twice it was used to describe false teachers who deny God as their Despot (2 Peter 2:1 and Jude 4). And finally, it is used by the spirits of martyred saints in heaven (Revelation 6:10). It is nothing less than confusion to hold the view that a person can receive Christ as Savior and yet be in agreement with apostates who reject God as their Despot. A gospel devoid of repentance will lead to a "salvation" without Lordship. And if that is absent there is no ground for assurance that the Holy Spirit has been given.

3.   A similar problem is encountered when someone is encouraged to find security and affection in God's title "Father," when the only image that word brings to his mind is his own cruel and unreliable father whom he learned to hate.

4.   See J.B. Phillips, *Your God is Too Small* (New York: Macmillan Co., 1969), pp. 15-59.

5.   Cf. John R. Stott, "Must Jesus be Lord to be Savior? — Yes," *Eternity,* September 1959, p. 17.

6.   Cf. Acts 8:12; 19:8; 20:25; 28:23, 31.

7.   I tend to think that it is this distinction more than anything else that explains the marvelous, transforming, and often profoundly emotional "second work of grace" in the lives of many believers. Even though perhaps they had grown up in a Bible-believing church, their conversion was still essentially in a vacuum concerning Lordship. Assuming their conversion was actual, then it was at that time they received the gift of the Holy Spirit. But there finally came a time when this truth and the encouragement of others as to the

sovereignty of the Spirit would set them experientially free.

In view of the division in the body of Christ today over the issue of the baptism of the Spirit, it might be a major step in dissolving the barriers if we could first realize the common ground that there can be no regeneration apart from receiving the Holy Spirit (Romans 8:9) and that second, the apostles used the term "baptism in the Spirit" and "receiving the Spirit" (or the "gift of the Spirit") *as describing the same event* (cf. Acts 1:5; 8:15-17; 10:44-45 and especially 11:15-17). Hopefully on that basis we might be able together to look more objectively at the multitude of examples of previously regenerated believers who later on experienced a realization of the Spirit's presence and power and to assume that they were not only valid, but of major significance as to their future life for God. A remarkable record of the radical, life-changing effect of the Holy Spirit in the lives of 20 well-known Christians is well described by V. Raymond Edman, *They Found the Secret* (Grand Rapids: Zondervan, 1960).

8.   Switching to a completely different analogy, in our well-meant zeal we may be like overzealous obstetricians who promote premature births. Yes, the child indeed has been "born," but for the time being it must be confined within an incubator, scarcely functioning in anything that could be called the real world. Unless we are alert to his condition, he may be left there for years in the carefully controlled, sterile atmosphere provided by well-meaning spiritual nurses.

9.   I would imagine that this last mentioned basis for assurance is the most foundational. Assurance is realized through one's awareness and response to the Lordship of Christ. That is a fact that any believer must acknowledge unless he is either very ignorant or irrational. If he is either of these, what he needs is not experience; he needs knowledge in order to get a proper perspective and to break out of either his ignorance or his temporary insanity. Nevertheless, the awareness of Lordship eventually brings experience—Philip-

pians 4:6-7 cannot properly be prayed from the heart of one who is at odds with total dedication of life (or Lordship).

10. It is quite popular to use 2 Timothy 2:13 as a source of comfort for one who claims to be a Christian and yet is at odds with his Savior. *"If we are faithless, he will remain faithful, for he cannot disown himself."* It is as though the "good Lord" will always keep His loving promise to me no matter how much I go against Him. The following quotation from Lange's commentary should at least give such a person a second thought: "It is a gross misunderstanding to interpret this last reminder as *a word of consolation* in any such sense as this: if we, from weakness, are unfaithful, we must calm ourselves with the thought that He will not break His word; and that, notwithstanding it, His faithfulness to us will be forever confirmed. In a certain sound sense this thought is certainly true; but the connection of the discourse here plainly shows that the apostle will warn with emphasis, and, in other words, will say "Fancy not, if thou are unfaithful, that the Lord's punishment will fail. He is just as faithful in His threatenings as in His promises. He remains ever like Himself, and can also just as little endure the unfaithful, as He can allow the faithful to go unrewarded" (comp. Hebrews 2:3; John 3:20). (J.J. Van Oosterzee, "The Two Epistles of Paul to Timothy" in *Commentary on the Holy Scriptures,* ed. by John Peter Lange, 24 vols. [Grand Rapids: Zondervan, 1960], 21:95. [Note this is page 95 of the section on 1-2 Timothy, not the entire volume].)

11. The reading of Acts 8 alone might lead a person to con-
     clude that the event of receiving the Holy Spirit took place sometime *after* the Samaritans had been born again. This then would support the possibility that there is indeed a crucial "second blessing" or "baptism" or "receiving" after conversion. Yet if one draws this conclusion he clouds the most fundamental issue of all—the fact that it is *in the receiving of the Holy Spirit that an individual becomes a Christian,*

a regenerated person (Romans 8:9), and apart from that he is not saved (in any new covenant sense).

Were the Samaritans saved before they received the Holy Spirit by the laying on of hands, before Peter and John came down from Jerusalem? To this query a negative answer must be given. They were *not* saved. . . their faith was evidently not saving faith, but merely intellectual assent, for it is impossible to distinguish between them and Simon Magus, who is also said to have believed and to have been baptized (8:3). (Merrill F. Unger, *The Baptizing Work of the Holy Spirit* [Wheaton: Van Kampen Press, 1953], p. 66.)

Perhaps God withheld the true regenerating ministry of the Holy Spirit for two reasons, the latter of which I would consider the more important. (1) This guaranteed that there would be no schism between Jerusalem Christians and the mixed blooded, non-accepted Samaritans. A schism might have happened had not the apostles been present to bear witness to the reception of the Spirit. (2) The immediate circumstances surrounding the Samaritan's belief warranted the withholding of the regenerating ministry. Prior to Philip's coming, the Samaritans had been astounded by the magic of Simon to the degree that they were calling him "the Great Power of God." Then along comes Philip who also is a miracle worker to the degree that even Simon was impressed. If they had immediately been born again (receiving the Spirit), they might have begun their Christian lives with a very warped concept of the nature of Christianity as "the better among several." Therefore the delay could have allowed for some reflective thinking plus whatever added instruction may have been given both by Philip and the apostles prior to their regeneration. (It is much to be regretted that some have so misused Acts 16:31 as to teach that all one needs to get from a prospective convert are the magic words "I believe," as though the Philippian jailor spoke those words out of a repentance and commitment vacuum. Cf. John 2:23-25.)

Certainly a mystery remains concerning this event. Though I do not believe we are justified in questioning the sincerity of the Samaritans' faith (as inferred by Unger above), nor the validity of their water baptism, these people did not become part of the body of Christ until they had received the Spirit. Resurrection life could not have been theirs until they had received the "Spirit of life."

Other passages used to support the supposed norm of a "second work" must be evaluated in a similar manner in light of their contexts; cf. Acts 19:1-7 and possibly Acts 9:1-19 in light of Acts 22:16.

In defending a separation between salvation and the baptism of the Spirit, some have relied heavily on John 20:22, identifying that as the point in time when the disciples received the Spirit thus distinguishing it from their later "baptism." Even without a clear understanding of the significance of the John passage, it is exceptionally clear that whenever the apostles had opportunity to draw a parallel between their own experience and that of new converts concerning the event of receiving the Spirit, they went back to the Day of Pentecost, not to the John 20:22 event. See Acts 11:15-17; 15:8. Thus the receiving of the Holy Spirit and the baptism of the Holy Spirit are seen to be synonymous.

Also any evaluation of first generation Christians must include the assumption that some of them already enjoyed an acceptable old covenant relationship with God prior to their receiving the Spirit to the same degree as any Old Testament believer or any of those who shared the perspective of John the Baptist. Certainly we should not be comfortable with the idea that old covenant believers became "unsaved" the moment the new covenant became fully operative (this would include both the finished work of Christ and the coming of the Holy Spirit). In applying this to Acts 19:1-7, the issue then is not whether they were "lost" or "saved," but whether they had personally entered into the revolutionary new life brought about by the promise of the Spirit resulting from the glorification of the Savior.

Having raised the "second work of grace" issue, I do not wish for a moment to cast even the slightest shadow on the remarkable, life-changing encounters with the power of the Spirit which so many individuals have known. Please see page 172 and footnote 7 concerning my understanding of that event. Rather than to focus on criticism and argue over terminology, the entire body of Christ should be grateful for the renewed focus on the gift of the Holy Spirit as being distinct and in addition to the forgiveness of sins, though both occur at salvation. I feel this debt very personally.

One final note: even among those who allow for a separation in time between conversion and the reception of the Spirit, there is an openness to the simultaneous event of both forgiveness and the gift of the Spirit. See J. Rodman Williams, "Pentecostal Theology: A New-Pentecostal Viewpoint," *Perspectives on the New Pentecostalism,* ed. Russell P. Spittler (Grand Rapids: Baker Book House, 1976), pp. 84-85.

12. Cf. Harry Ironside, *Except Ye Repent,* American Tract Society, 1937.

Chapter 9

A New Power:
The Experience of the
Holy Spirit's Presence

*The Holy Spirit's presence was an experienced
reality.*

O ne fact we cannot miss. As we read through Acts and
the Epistles we find that the possession of the Holy
Spirit was of unsurpassed importance to that first generation
of believers.[1] It was not only important to that huge group on
the Day of Pentecost, it was also important to each individual
who received this gift in the days and years which followed.

Somehow, in my past thinking about the Holy Spirit, I
found myself caught up with all the fine lines of distinction in
the terminology. "Baptized in the Spirit," "filled with the
Spirit," "anointed by the Spirit". . .all of those hotly debated
theological words and phrases. I now realized that the overall
emphasis is simply that the Holy Spirit had been *received*. In
fact, this matter of receiving the Holy Spirit was characterized by Peter on the Day of Pentecost as being, if that were
possible, even more climactic than the forgiveness of sins!

*"Repent, and be baptized every one of you, in the name
of Jesus Christ so that your sins may be forgiven. **And you
will receive the gift of the Holy Spirit**"* (Acts 2:38, emphasis
mine).

It was as though receiving the Holy Spirit was the core of
the whole salvation package.[2] In order to remove any doubt

185

as to the centrality of this event, let's take a quick look at a variety of passages which magnify this fact.

> *"And if anyone does not have the Spirit of Christ, he does not belong to Christ."*   (Romans 8:9)

> *"Did you receive the Spirit by observing the law, or by believing what you heard?"*
> (Galatians 3:2, cf. 3:14)

> *"Can anyone keep these people from being baptized with water? They have received the Holy Spirit just as we have."*
> (Peter's response to the falling of the Holy Spirit upon Cornelius and his house, Acts 10:47)

> *"So if God gave them the same gift as he gave us, who believed in the Lord Jesus Christ, who was I to think that I could oppose God?"*   (Acts 11:17)

> *"God, who knows the heart, showed that he accepted them by giving the Holy Spirit to them, just as he did to us."*   (Acts 15:8)

> *"Paul took the road through the interior and arrived at Ephesus. There he found some disciples and asked them, 'Did you receive the Holy Spirit when you believed?'"*   (Acts 19:21-22)

> *"These are the men who divide you, who follow mere natural instincts and do not have the Spirit."*
> (Jude 19)

Two Key Questions

We need to answer two questions. First, what led these early Christians to place so much importance on receiving the Holy Spirit? Second, in what way was His presence and power an experiential, observable reality to them? (Or indeed was it experiential?)

Ready? Question one: **Why was so much emphasis placed on receiving the Holy Spirit?** First of all, receiving the Holy Spirit was the central dream and desire of every believing Jew who looked for and longed for the coming of the new covenant.

> *"And I will put my Spirit in you and move you to follow my decrees and be careful to keep my laws."*
> (Ezekiel 36:27; cf. Isaiah 59:21; Jeremiah 31:31-34
> in light of 2 Corinthians 3:3-6)

> *"I will put my Spirit in you, and you will live."*
> (Ezekiel 37:14)[3]

> *"Until the Spirit is poured out upon us from on high."* (Isaiah 32:15)

> *"And afterward, I will pour out my Spirit on all people...And everyone who calls on the name of the Lord will be saved."* (Joel 2:28-32)[4]

Second, it was central in the teaching of the last Old Testament prophet, John the Baptist.

> *"I baptize you with water, but he will baptize you with the Holy Spirit."*
> (Mark 1:8; cf. each of the gospels)[5]

Third, the Lord Jesus gave His followers abundant basis for a vivid expectation of receiving the Holy Spirit.

> *"And I will ask the Father, and he will give you another Counselor to be with you forever—the Spirit of truth."*
> (John 14:16-17; cf. John 14:26; 15:26; 16:7, 13)

"I am going to send you what my Father has prom-
ised; but stay in the city until you have been clothed
with power from on high."
                                   (Luke 24:49; cf. Acts 1:4-5; 11:16)

"'Whoever believes in me, as the Scripture has said,
streams of living water will flow from within him.'
By this he meant the Spirit, whom those who be-
lieved in him were later to receive. Up to that time
the Spirit had not been given, since Jesus had not
yet been glorified."   (John 7:38-39)

If this were not enough to cause those early believers to
view the receiving of the Spirit almost as an obsession, certainly the dramatic, life-changing effects upon those who first
received the Spirit would have filled any remaining lack of interest. Little wonder that Peter said, *"Repent and be bap-*
tized. . .and you will receive the gift of the Holy Spirit" (Acts
2:38).

Now for the second question: **In what way was His**
presence and power an experiential, observable reality to
them? First, I hope it is possible right now, once for all, to
settle in our minds that *an experienced awareness of the*
possession of the Holy Spirit by a new believer was con-
sidered to be the norm in early, new covenant Christianity.
I do not believe the New Testament gives us any justification for the idea that the new believers knew they had
received the Holy Spirit simply because someone *informed*
them of the fact. As if they wouldn't have known it unless
someone had come along and told them. No! Such a view
hardly parallels such statements as these:

"Did you receive the Spirit by observing the law, or
by believing what you heard?"   (Galatians 3:2)

"Did you receive the Holy Spirit when you
believed?"   (Acts 19:2)

*"And if anyone does not have the Spirit of Christ,
he does not belong to Christ."*   (Romans 8:9)

*"And this is how we know he lives in us: We know it
by the Spirit he gave us."*
(1 John 3:24; cf. 1 John 4:13)

Not to mention the experiential emphasis of Acts
11:15-17 or Acts 15:8. Of course it was an experienced thing!
They knew a radical event had taken place! In that
miraculous event of receiving the Spirit, new covenant life
poured into their deepest beings. They had been "born of the
Spirit." Out of their innermost being "streams of living
water" were flowing.

Jesus was Lord! They understood God's truth as they
had never understood it before. There was joy and spiritual
power. They loved and cared for one another as they never
had loved and cared before. They witnessed with conviction
and boldness. And in many cases, there were very special
manifestations of the fact that the spiritual flow between
themselves and God was open and active: they spoke in
tongues and prophesied.

Listen again—really listen—to the words of our Lord
Jesus:

*"If a man is thirsty, let him come to me and drink.
Whoever believes in me, as the Scripture has said,
streams of living water will flow from within him
("from his innermost being" NASB). By this he
meant the Spirit, whom those who believed in him
were later to receive."*   (John 7:37-38)

In view of these most expressive words, who would wish
to question the normal expectation of *an experienced
awareness* of the reception and presence of the Holy Spirit? It
was to be as tangible a reality as when a thirsty man has at last
slaked a burning thirst. Now that's experiential!

Reality of Holiness

Let's move in for a closer look. *Our Bible gives us several revealing titles for this third Person of the Trinity.* Of course, most obvious of all, He is the *Holy* Spirit. Not only in His being, but in everything He does. He is separated from everything that is not in harmony with the absolute perfection of God. He is a Being of loftiness and splendor and utter purity. He is *holy.* In view of this, little wonder that the "fruit of the Spirit" is what it is! Therefore, regardless of the reality of someone's "spiritual" experience, if it is not in harmony with biblical holiness then it is not a product of the Holy Spirit.[6]

Holiness is beautiful. Beautiful things are meant to be appreciated, enjoyed, and respected. This first title for the Spirit at least opens the door to the possibility of a connection between experience and the Spirit.

Reality of Grace

The next title points us to that initial *experienced* work of the Spirit in bringing that first sense of conviction of sin and the necessity of repentance. It is He who confronts us with the issue of meaninglessness and who points us toward life. He is the *"Spirit of grace"* (Hebrews 10:29, cf. Romans 2:4; John 16:7-11; Acts 16:14).

Reality of Life

He is also called the *"Spirit of life"* (Romans 8:2). It takes quite a stretch of the imagination to exclude experience from Titus 3:5-6; *"He saved us through the washing of rebirth and renewal by the Holy Spirit, whom he poured out on us generously through Jesus Christ our Savior."* (cf. John 3:3-7; 10:10; Galatians 3:21-22).

Would anyone choose to deny experience in the joyous cry of a new-born child of God, "Abba! Father!"?[7] Little wonder those first Christians were marked by joy—they knew they were alive to God! The old covenant barriers were gone!

Reality of Truth

Another title for the Holy Spirit is the *"Spirit of truth"* (John 14:17; 15:26; 1 John 2:27; 1 Corinthians 2:4-10).[8] I cannot imagine a more significant ministry of the Spirit to a believer than this. Jesus said, "He will guide you into all truth" (John 16:13).

Do you remember our proposition?

Knowledge + the Will + Power brings Holiness

Remember too, that we found that spiritual power is inseparable from Spirit-taught truth. Certainly this teaching ministry was central in our Lord's mind when He promised that the "Helper" or the "Comforter" would come. First, He would teach by convicting men of *"sin, and righteousness, and judgment"* (John 16:8). As repentance and faith are awakened, there follows that fresh, clean awareness of sins forgiven. It is the Spirit of truth who bears witness with our spirit and we cry "Abba! Father!" All is well (Galatians 4:6). This fact is fundamental to new covenant conversion.

Extra Dimension

But there is an added dimension to this particular title for the Holy Spirit which carries us way beyond any initial awareness that He has been given to us. As long as we live it is this wonderful Person who awakens in us fresh responses to God as we listen to the actual voice of God speaking to us in the words of the Bible. In a truly mysterious way He "testifies with our spirit" (not simply with our intellect), over and over again. And in those moments, propositional truth is transformed into praise, love, patience, and hope.

Maybe it would be possible right this moment to see this in action by listening to the flow of thought which follows the happy "Abba, Father" in Romans 8:15-39. (Though the next few paragraphs will take but a few minutes to read, what I really have in mind is that you will stop and take the time to actually listen for the witness of the Spirit to your spirit as you ponder what God is saying personally to you. This may take more than a few minutes!) Let's look at these verses:

> First He tells me that I am to think of myself not only as his adopted son but as *His begotten child.*[9] A "born one" of God. (Cf. 1 John 3:9-10. What amazing implications are wrapped up in that statement *"God's seed remains in him!")*

> Next, the Spirit teaches me that I am an "heir," a "fellow heir with Christ." (Verse 17. Could that possibly be?) Because of this, He tells me of an entirely new way to evaluate the hard times of my life: *"Our present sufferings are not worth comparing with the glory that will be revealed in us."*

> But He doesn't stop there. I then learn how to understand my own mortality, the groaning and corruption of my flesh—the slavery of the world in which I now live. He tells me that the day will come when *"creation itself also will be liberated from its bondage to decay and brought into the glorious freedom of the children of God."*

Now please—think for a moment, Christian. Right now as you are listening to God's personal voice to you. If the Holy Spirit's teaching presence is not producing some response from you it is because you are *not thinking*—meditating. The voice of God is certainly worthy of exclusive focus.[10]

No, you can't push any button marked "Experience." Nor are *feelings* the central issue. But it is true that the conscious, experienced response to Spirit-taught truth is a tangible trademark of His presence. Even as the awareness that you love your brother is another trademark of Spirit-begotten life (1 John 3:10). The Spirit of truth does produce experience!

Taught by the Spirit

But Romans 8 is not finished yet.

Next, this Divine Teacher guides me through an understanding of my mortal weakness. Those times when I do not even know how to put the cry of my heart into words. Those times when neither my lips nor my mind seem capable of shaping prayer to the Father.

The Spirit tells me that He intercedes for me *when I come to the end of my mind.* And His intercession is always *"in accordance with God's will"* (verse 27). Since that is true, then Romans 8:28 is understandably true. And yes...I *do* love Him.

Then from His mind through my mind all the way into my inner man He teaches me of the glorious *sovereignty* of my God (verses 29-30). He teaches me the infinite *giving* of my God (verses 31-32). He teaches me of the *glory* of my dying, rising, living Savior who also intercedes—for me! And finally (verses 34-39), as though I could absorb any more, He tells me how much, how very much He loves me. *And that He will never stop loving me!* (Oh God! *My* God! My *God!*) All this from only 24 verses.

To receive the Spirit is to receive the *Spirit of truth.* To come under His tutelage is to walk through doors of truth leading to experience unknown before.

Now let's stop for a moment and get our bearings.

Over the years I have earnestly—time and again—read and studied and outlined Scripture. Yet for all of that, I still sensed an emptiness in my heart and an embarassing lack of reality in my life.

Looking back, I am afraid that although I was exercising my brain, I was only in a very limited sense being taught by the Spirit. I am sure that part of the reason was that I was after *feelings* rather than after Spirit-taught truth. It was as though the Bible was some sort of Aladdin's lamp to be rubbed by my mind in order to satisfy my experiential whims, rather than a supernatural treasure which answers only to the Holy Spirit Whose intention is to bring me into the light of the glory of God. I was failing to appreciate the fact that experience is a by-product of the Spirit's teaching work in the context of faith.

Another reason was a failure to realize that His teaching is most fully realized within the expressed motive of the prayers of Ephesians 1:16-23 and 3:14-21. We simply cannot forget that His teaching is a mysterious, supernatural event.

More and Much More

So much more could be said.

To receive Him is to receive the *"Spirit of promise"* (Ephesians 1:13, NASB) who leads me to change my definition of "hope" from something I *wish* would happen to something I *know* will happen.

> *"May the God of hope fill you with all joy and peace as you trust in him, so that you may overflow with hope by the power of the Holy Spirit."*
>
> (Romans 15:13)

He also is the One who gives fruit—behavioral fruit. And gifts—spiritual gifts. And then the power to manifest them both!

A Difficult Question

In view of all these things, we are compelled to ask a difficult question. Why isn't the experienced reality of the presence and power of the Holy Spirit the norm for Christians today?

It is quite obvious that the early church had not yet been conditioned against the Holy Spirit's sovereign right to manifest His presence and power. In fact, they expected it.

Sometimes, in radical, life-changing ways. Both at the moment of salvation and afterward. Remember, the first observers concluded that those first Christians were drunk!

The Holy Spirit could be quenched, too. Through their sin, certainly, but also in other, more sophisticated, "orthodox" ways. Only today we don't call it "quenching the Spirit."

The Lordship of the Spirit

To receive the Holy Spirit as a Gift Who dwells in my body (1 Corinthians 6:19) should certainly imply an acceptance of His absolute right to bring about all He wants to accomplish inside of me. In view of who we now are as born ones of God, it is insanity to offer Him anything less than unlimited freedom of operation in our lives. No strings attached. We have no scriptural right to build restraining fences around God's Spirit. Do we dare dictate terms, saying, "This far and no farther?" Do we dare say to Him, "You may produce the fruit of the Spirit in my life, but You are not allowed to express and empower through me any spiritual gift You might desire to give me?"

How tragically we have quenched this gracious Spirit through our shabby half-truths! Using our supposedly biblical arguments, we have roped off the manifestations of the Spirit to whatever limits our particular "Christian" culture deems sufficiently respectable. We have maintained rigid standards to "protect" the body from anything which might appear strange or mystical even though it is biblically sound. *What have we done?*[11]

"Please Don't Rock the Boat!"

Of course we fervently believe in all those remarkable stories of the Spirit's work in the Acts and the epistles. But that was a long time ago. So please don't rock the boat! Who wants to be classed with those "other Christians"? Things might get out of hand. And yet by saying those very things we are expressing a lack of confidence in the Lord of the Church.

We are casting aspersions on the protective quality of His Holy Word which we hold in our hands and which speaks to those very concerns!

We talk much today about "Spirit control." *Yet it would appear that we are much more concerned about controlling the Spirit.* We are like David's wife, Michal, who could not reconcile the king's "leaping and dancing before the Lord" out of sheer joy before God with the prescribed dignity of a monarch. We would prefer to shut our windows and stay safely within our controlled environment. And like Michal, we may remain barren to our death. [12]

There is a glorious freedom in the safety of the Lordship of Father, Son, and Holy Spirit who have given us not only their Word, but also themselves.

I am afraid in our day, in some circles at least, if someone came up to me and asked, "Are you saved?" And I responded by saying, "Yes, I received the Spirit when I was eight years old," they would not be pleased with that answer even though it is in perfect harmony with the New Testament emphasis. It would be far more "orthodox" for me to say "I received Christ!" (Which indeed would *also* be a correct response. Cf. John 1:12; Colossians 2:6; 1 John 5:12.) Now, of course, it is impossible to receive the Spirit apart from repentance and faith related to the gospel concerning Jesus Christ, but it *is* in that event of receiving the Spirit that Jesus' risen life and all that is the outflow of that life comes to me. How many brand new believers have ever been told, much less were aware of the fact, that in believing the gospel they would receive the Holy Spirit?

The reason that I mention this is because so many of us have been disturbed by what may well have been Pentecostal extremism to the degree that we have remained "Spirit shy." Until we reckon with this, we may very well quench much of His life-producing work in us.

When was the last time you heard a brand new child of God say "Praise God! I have received the Spirit"? Yet we can be very sure those first Christians said exactly that. [13] But of course, that was not all they said. They spoke of forgiveness, of joy, of the Lordship of Christ — of being alive toward God.

Spirit-taught truth cannot help but form a wide, deep channel for the flow of the Spirit's power. (Remember the umbilical cord illustration?) But such truth left either unknown or misunderstood will choke one's capacity to function as a lover of God or a displayer of Jesus in the real world even as it did for some in Corinth or Galatia or Colosse. Actually, I suppose we can be thankful that there were some Christians even in the early church who were confused or ignorant. Otherwise those corrective epistles might never have been written!

Chapter 9, Notes

1. Like any fact, it [the gift of the Spirit] could be warped out of its original shape. This certainly was true in Corinth. On one hand, they were quite impressed with the gifts of the Spirit, but on the other hand they had to be reminded that they possessed the Giver of the gifts in the special sense that their bodies were the temples of the Holy Spirit. In their fascination with one of the results of the Spirit's presence—gifts—they had forgotten the holy, sovereign character of both the Person and His purposes (1 Corinthians 14; cf. 6:19).

2. "In 2:38 [Acts] it is the climax of conversion-initiation: of the two things offered—forgiveness of sins and the Holy Spirit—it is the positive gift which Peter emphasizes, that which first attracted the crowd, and that which is the essence of the new age and covenant" (Acts 2:39). "In the last analysis the only thing that matters in deciding whether a man is a Christian or not is whether he has received the Spirit or not." (James D.G. Dunn, *Baptism in the Holy Spirit* [Philadelphia: Westminster Press, 1970], pp. 91-93.)

3. Ezekiel 37:14. Note, the context of this passage is the familiar "Vision of the Valley of Dry Bones." In the vision the "bones represented Israel in captivity and the 'graves' represented the places where they were held captive." Therefore the expression "you will come to life" had nothing to do with physical life because they had that; it had reference to an entirely new dimension of life—spiritual life—which they did not receive in the days which followed although God did restore many of them to their homeland once again.

4. Joel 2:28-32. Peter had no doubt that the miraculous reception and demonstration of the presence of the Holy Spirit on the Day of Pentecost was the actual fulfillment of this prophecy. Though the promised signs in the heavens and the consequent arrival of the Day of the Lord did not appear in his day, we have no justification in assuming that Peter used the Joel passage as "an illustration...not as a fulfillment" (Charles Lee Feinberg, *Major Messages of the Minor Prophets, Joel, Amos and Obadiah* [New York: American Board of Missions to the Jews, 1948], p. 29), or "as a foretaste of what it will be like when Jesus returns" (Joseph Dillow, *Speaking In Tongues, Seven Crucial Questions,* [Grand Rapids: Zondervan, 1975], p. 104). The fact that Peter did not use the standard formula, "that it might be fulfilled," is best understood as expressed by Everett F. Harrison: "[That] Peter said 'this is what was spoken' rather than the more common 'that it might be fulfilled,' is better explained by noting that Peter's response immediately followed the question 'What does this mean?' (Acts 2:12). Peter simply used the 'this' in his answer." (See Everett F. Harrison, *Acts: The Expanding Church* [Chicago: Moody Press, 1975], pp. 57-58.)

Since Peter gives us a general outline of what would have happened had the nation Israel responded to the grace of God (see Acts 3:19-21), the lack of that response appears to be the primary reason for the failure of fulfillment of the remainder of Joel's prophecy. In God's eternal purposes, this rejection by Israel opened the door for the promised activity of the Holy Spirit related to the new covenant to the entire world. As a *"wild olive...grafted in"* anyone who responds to God's grace may receive the blessings of the *"rich root of the olive tree"* (Romans 11:17). (See F.F. Bruce, *The Book of Acts,* [Grand Rapids: Eerdmans, 1954], p. 92.)

Are we then still living in the age of Pentecost? I find no biblical reason for even the slightest negative answer. This opinion is well stated by G. Campbell Morgan,

You and I are living in this Day of Pentecost. This is the day of the Holy Spirit, when sons and daughters prophesy; when the Spirit is poured out upon the servants as well as the masters, the handmaidens as well as their mistresses. The day when, by the Spirit, old men dream dreams and young men see visions. This day is still proceeding, the darkness is ahead. But even that darkness will be the darkness that presages the dawn of God's day that never wanes, but remains eternal noon in His great victory. (*The Birth of the Church,* [Old Tappan, N.J.: Fleming H. Revell Co., 1968], p. 98.)

In opposition, Joseph Dillow argues that the "signs and wonders are related to the era in which Israel is in belief in her kingdom" (*Speaking in Tongues,* p. 105). Therefore, according to him, the ultimate fulfillment of tongues, prophecy, etc., will take place in the Millennium. Nevertheless, since Dillow considers that "the gift of tongues was primarily a judicial sign against Jewish unbelief as a nation" (ibid., p. 106), I find it very difficult to understand how he sees such a gift as he defines it as appropriate in that future age of Jewish belief. It would appear that he also ignores the fact that Joel places these miraculous events *"before the great and awesome day of the Lord comes"* (Joel 2:31). (See Gotthard V. Lechler, "The Acts of the Apostles," in *Commentary on the Holy Scriptures,* ed. by John Peter Lange, 24 vols. [Grand Rapids: Zondervan, 1960], 9:40.) Note: To assume, as does Dillow, that *"the powers of the coming age"* (Hebrews 6:5) is a reference to gifts such as tongues, thus making them parallel with Joel 2:28-32, is without any contextual basis in light of both the sequence of the Joel prophecy and Peter's use of that prophecy.

5.   Though the term "spirit baptism" as used by Paul in 1 Corinthians 12:13, *"For we were all baptized by one Spirit into one body,"* places the emphasis upon that act by

which a person is placed in the body of Christ, it would be a totally false conclusion to assume that the term is not also directly referring to the event of receiving the Spirit. Cf. Acts 11:15-17, *"As I began to speak, the Holy Spirit came on them as he had come on us at the beginning. Then I remembered what the Lord had said, 'John baptized with water, but you will be baptized with the Holy Spirit.' So if God gave them the same gift as he gave us, who believed in the Lord Jesus Christ, who was I to think that I could oppose God!"* Certainly the "baptism of the Holy Spirit" encompasses both the receiving of the Spirit and the placement of a person in Christ's body. I fear that theologians all too readily latch on to an exclusive technical definition of a biblical term by its usage in one passage and thereby exclude from it the obvious meanings as demanded by other passages. In their sincere effort to be theologically precise, they create for themselves interpretative problems which then require unique creativity in explaining passages which will not bend to their theological precision.

6.   An apparent contradiction with this statement appears in the unholy handling of certain spiritual gifts in 1 Corinthians 14. Since we have every reason to conclude that these gifts indeed were manifestations of the Spirit, how could such a paradox exist? Clearly 1 Corinthians 13:1-3 declares that it is never God's intention to separate the fruit of the Spirit from the gifts of the Spirit. Therefore a gift such as speaking in tongues (that is, the act of one's spirit speaking to God apart from one's intellectual control of the action, the mind shaping both the thoughts and the word forms differnt from the language known to the individual) was truly "by the Spirit," and therefore a holy expression. The communication itself will always be in harmony with the character of God. If it is not, it is not of God no matter how much an individual may claim it is. Nevertheless the individual's attitude toward his gift and the timing of that expression might be quite contrary to holiness.

7.   "'Abba,' is the familiar title Jewish children used of their
       earthly father. The precise Aramaic form 'abba,' was
avoided in both synagogue and private prayers out of
reverential motives, some alternative form (e.g., 'Abinu,' 'our
Father') being substituted.... The cry under intellectual or
spiritual emotion reveals the naked soul of the believer and is
spontaneously accompanied by the corroborating testimony
of the Holy Spirit to real sonship." (Davidson, F., Ralph P.
Martin, "Romans," in *New Bible Commentary, Revised*, ed.
D. Guthrie and J.A. Motyer [Grand Rapids: Eerdmans,
1970], p. 1031.)

8.   It would be possible to assume that 1 Corinthians
       2:12-13 has reference *only* to the Spirit's teaching of the
apostles in fulfilling their unique prophetic authority, were it
not for the parallel that Paul makes between the "spiritual
man" who perceives the things of the Spirit and the Corinthians who were not spiritual and therefore limited in receiving the teaching of the Spirit (in this case, through the apostle). Cf. 12:15 and 3:1-2.

9.   "Begotten son" seems to be a term exclusively reserved
       by the Father for only one individual, His divine Son,
Jesus. We are often called His "begotten children," but never
His "begotten sons." The nearest the New Testament comes
to this usage is in Romans 8:14-17. Preceding the statement
"and by him we cry, 'Abba! Father,'" Paul describes believers
as *"sons of God"* by reason of the fact that they have received
"a spirit of sonship [by adoption].*"* Yet following this he
speaks of the fact that the Spirit bears witness to the truth
that we are the *"children* [born ones] *of God."* In a most
general and universal sense Paul spoke of all men as being
God's "offspring," certainly radically removed from the concept of Romans 8. (See Acts 17:28.) Though Israel in the old
covenant could speak of God as their Father (Isaiah 64:8),
this certainly was a far cry from the exhilaration of John's exclamation in 1 John 3:1-3.

10. I believe that one of the major hindrances in experiencing the truth of God as one studies the Bible is that we
tend to divorce Bible reading from prayer. It is strange that
we who are so emphatic concerning the Bible being God's
Word, are so passive to the personal voice of God to us! Isn't
it true that when we read the Bible God is indeed speaking to
us? Really speaking? Imagine how rude you would be if
someone were talking to you and you not only never looked
at them, you never even acknowledged they were talking—
even to simply nod your head from time to time. I am sure
that much of Scripture was given to us to be used as one side
of a two way conversation. Even as the disciples interacted
with Jesus when He spoke to them, we too should do the
same. I would like to illustrate this at length, but I hope you
get the idea. Start asking God questions as you read. Pause to
thank Him for what He is saying. Confess the difficulties you
sense in wrapping your mind around His amazing words.
And then listen to His answers as you read again and then
read on. God is having a talk with you—as tangible a talk as
anyone could have. In fact it is more tangible than most conversations, because what He is saying is written down in black
and white! Can any human truly have a personal audience
with the Most High God and then walk away as though
nothing had happened? He can, if he is unaware of it!

11. I sincerely empathize with any of you who, like myself,
have at some particular time either formulated or accepted someone else's particular interpretation of 1 Corinthians 13:8-13, Hebrews 2:3-4, 1 Corinthians 14:21-22, or any
one of several varieties of dispensational or "transitional"
arguments which are then used to support the limitations of
the work of the Spirit today. Having passed through some
very painful struggles in attempting to be objective and ac-
countable before God Who will be my Judge, may I urge you
to look once more.

Are you absolutely confident that the logic of those interpretations adequately overrides those passages which without any question encourage the acknowledgment of all the spiritual gifts? Is your confidence so solid that you not only would forbid their exercise by God's people in their local assemblies within the limitations of 1 Corinthians 14:23-40 and 1 Thessalonians 5:19-22, but also would ostracize those who "pray in the spirit" in private? Are you sure of your biblical base for redefining the gift of prophecy so as to remove from it any hint of its being a *revelatory* gift? (By raising this question, I am not equating the product of such a gift with the inerrant Scriptures.) Before God I urge us all to tremble as we handle God's inerrant Word. Could it possibly be that we have suppressed the precious ministry of the Spirit, sincerely believing that the corrective instructions to the church at Corinth are either not adequate or are not relevant for our times? Though it most certainly is true that the expression of any particular spiritual gift is no mark or guarantee of godliness, it may well be true that forbidding their exercise may stifle the overall ministry of the Spirit and weaken the godly character of a local body of believers. Oh may God protect us from those curious, fascinating eddies of peripheral debate in which we happily go round and round, all the while missing the mainstream of God's work in the world! (See Donald Bridges and David Phypers, *Spiritual Gifts and the Church* [Downers Grove, Ill.: InterVarsity Press, 1973]; Michael Green, *I Believe in the Holy Spirit* [Grand Rapids: Eerdmans, 1975]; David Howard, *By the Power of the Holy Spirit* [Downers Grove, Ill.: InterVarsity Press, 1973]; Kenneth Cain Kinghorn, *Gifts of the Spirit* [Nashville: Abingdon Press, 1976]; Edward Murphy, *Spiritual Gifts and the Great Commission* [Pasadena, Calif.: Mandate Press, 1973]. Though none of these books were written within the historical Pentecostal frame of reference, they have in common the view that all the spiritual gifts are the Holy Spirit's prerogative to give to His church today.)

12. See John White, "David's Style of Dance," *Eternity,*
     February, 1978, pp. 60-61, or his book *Daring to Draw
Near* (Downers Grove, Ill.: InterVarsity Press, 1977), from
which this article is a condensation of one chapter.

13. In view of the dominant emphasis upon Christ in Gala-
     tians 1-2 we would assume that in 3:2 Paul would have
said, *"Did you receive Christ by observing the law...?"* The
fact that he did not should carry some significance. The terminology "receive the Spirit" is underlined in 3:5 by *"gives
you his Spirit"* and in 3:14 (cf. 3:22) *"so that by faith we
might receive the promise of the Spirit."*

Chapter 10

A New Community: The Membership in a Body Bonded by Love*

The individual Christian was not an isolated pilgrim, but part of a body which could not function apart from love.

*F*irst generation Christianity did not see the local church as merely a classroom where believers were taught the Scriptures or a hospital to care for God's hurting children. In fact, it was seen not so much as a place as it was an environment. It was an environment in which the saints could fulfill a most remarkable destiny as being valued parts of the visible body of Christ on earth.

> *"From him the whole body, joined and held together by every supporting ligament, grows and builds itself up in love, as each part does its work."*
> (Ephesians 4:16)

---

*NOTE: This certainly will be our shortest chapter, but not because it is least important. There simply is no point in attempting to duplicate the excellent materials which are now available that focus on this crucial distinctive. See *Body Life* by Ray Stedman, and *A New Face for the Church* and *Three Churches in Renewal* by Larry Richards. Also consider such organizations as *Dynamic Church Ministries*.[1]

God never intended holiness to thrive in isolation.
Everywhere believers went they bore the common mark of
Jesus' words, *"All men will know that you are my disciples if
you love one another."*

In an age when catchy words and slogans come and go so
quickly, it is remarkable whenever one comes and stays.
"Body life" has done just that. And with it has come a
freshness to local churches which has revolutionized the lives
of thousands of believers. It is almost as though certain long
lost chapters of the Bible have suddenly been rediscovered —
1 Corinthians 12-14, Ephesians 4-5, and, most especially,
Romans 12:3-15; 13.

In place of the believer who returns home for Sunday
dinner with the singular satisfaction that he has worshipped
God because he heard the choir and took good notes on a fine
expository sermon is that growing band of saints who have
found that life-transforming added dimension of the
fellowship of the body in worship and in love. This, combined with a fresh awareness of the ministry and power of the
Holy Spirit, has allowed God's people to taste once again of
first generation Christianity.

The results too have been the same. *Commitment to the
authority of the Scriptures* has been strengthened by a
deepening conviction that truth must be related to life.
Separation from the world has shed its negative shroud and
put on its much better fitting garments of light in the midst of
darkness — genuine joy, genuine love, genuine purity.
Evangelism has come alive because the saints are no longer
ashamed of the gospel. They have found it to be what it
is — the power of God. *Submission to authority* is losing its
legalistic sound as the concept of multiple spiritual eldership
increases the opportunity for first name relationships in
which the truth is shared "in love." The gradually developing,
distinctive lifestyle which marked early Christianity is becoming easier to accept when believers begin to realize that not
only are they "not of this world," but also that they are "not
alone." Finally, *worship* is once again becoming truly *God-*

centered when, for example, I find myself in a local fellowship where no one gets too upset whether or not I raise my hands toward heaven when I pray. Of course the issue is not the raising of my hands. The issue is the focus of my worship.

If this fifth distinctive of first generation Christianity is allowed to flourish, we may be sure that increasingly we will encounter another common result: *Satanic counterfeit.* It just so happens that spiritual blessing and spiritual warfare occupy the same dimension—"in heavenly realms" (cf. Ephesians 1:3; 6:12).

Whenever God's truth begins to affect one's behavior—and it must—at that moment Satan has a brand new area in which to work. Up to that point, he could divide and weaken God's people by corrupting truth, but now he can further his cause by counterfeiting experience. And since authentic Christian experience is a very wonderful thing, it is terribly easy to develop an "experience menu" mentality in which we attempt to satisfy our hunger by whatever "spiritual" experience might happen to catch our fancy. God simply will not be our waiter, but Satan gladly will play that role and he is a master at it.[2]

In these days of greater openness to spiritual realities among the children of God, how desperately we need true undershepherds who not only know the Scriptures and their God, but who deeply love and guard their flocks!

These five distinctives of first generation Christianity scarcely tell it all. But I think they tell enough to at least get us on our way as to the "how" of holiness. And there is no time to waste. The glory of God demands it *now.*

Chapter 10, Notes

1. Dynamic Church Ministries, a non-profit mission, Box 1788, Annapolis, Maryland 21404.

2. One of the finest corrective works dealing with this danger is the unabridged edition of the book by Jessie Penn-Lewis, *War on the Saints* (New York: Thomas E. Lowe, Ltd., 1973).

Conclusion

Where is the Joy?

*I*t's the last chapter. Can we afford a little melodrama? Imagine the most horrible prison you can. Now put yourself in its blackest, slimiest cell. Are you there?

You have no hope of release. None. You have long since given up scratch marks on the wall to record the passing of the days and years. So you sit in a dark, damp corner waiting for death.

And then...

The cell door swings open. Blinding light floods the cell. Sweet, fresh air rushes in. And someone gives you the message. PARDON! A complete, unexpected, bonafide pardon. You are *free!* Your entire past record has been erased. One by one, the locks click open and the gates open wide. Before you lies the open, fenceless countryside. A fragrant summer breeze touches your hair. You *are* free.

Cautiously at first you repeat those impossible words. "I am free."

Climbing higher past lush meadows and rocky crags, breathing that cool, clean air, you stand on the highest rock that tops out a vast mountain range. Again you shout until you have no breath left at all, "I am free!" Later on, you stretch out on your back in the sun, watching a great hawk soar lazily high in the afternoon sky. And you say it again! You sing it, you whisper it, you laugh it, you weep it. You cannot stop. You tell it to everyone you meet even though you know they cannot really understand.

Yet Christian, this is what has happened to us—and so much more. *"Because through Christ Jesus the law of the Spirit of life set me free from the law of sin and death"* (Romans 8:2).

You Are Safe

Now, let's think again. This time our imagination sinks us down among huge, cold, dark, cresting waves with nothing but a soggy life jacket in the midst of a terribly lonely, endless sea. You are sure that it will only be a matter of time. There is no reason to swim for you are as good as dead. Instinctively you curl your toes and pull your feet up as close as you can — you can't just let them hang straight down into those dark fathoms below. And then, out of nowhere, a ship! And moments later you are safe on board! You were dead and now you are alive. You are SAFE.

Yet Christian, you and I are *eternally* alive and safe! *"But when the kindness and love of God our Savior appeared, he saved us"* (Titus 3:4-5).

You Are Loved

Let's use our imaginations one more time. And for some of you, this exercise will be especially easy to do. Picture yourself for years, perhaps for all of your years, as being totally unloved, ignored, rejected, avoided, alone. Even when in a crowd, you are alone. You find that you cannot even love yourself. And why should you? Then one day, the most loving and loveable individual you could ever imagine — even in your most private fantasies — singles you out and says, "I love you! You mean more to me than I can put into words. You are important to me. I choose you as my friend from this moment on." And then this person backs up every word he says with uncontestable evidence. He even goes so far as to bring out an attractiveness, a loveableness about yourself. Even as one might gradually remove crude paint from a canvas in order to reveal an artist's priceless masterpiece underneath.

Just how would you respond to someone like that? Yes, you would be very cautious at first. But finally, at last, you believe. Barriers fall and you begin to rest in the pleasure of loving and being loved.

But Christian, we *were* loved while we *were* yet sinners, and not only that, we *are* loved by the One who invented love — who dreamed up every type of pure love anyone has ever experienced! In fact, He *is* love! (1 John 4:8). *"To him who loves us and has freed us from our sins by his blood, and has made us to be a kingdom, and priests to serve his God and Father — to him be glory and power for ever and ever! Amen"* (Revelation 1:5-6).

Free. Alive.

Eternally safe.

Eternally loved with an infinite love.

All this. And yet...

A Strange Silence

Have you ever stopped to wonder why there seem to be so few shouts of joy from God's children? Where are they? Where are those spontaneous shouts of sheer delight in God?

And what must God think about this strange silence? Or if not actual silence, what does He think of those carefully timed, sometimes even pleasant sounds that drift from churches full of unfeeling hearts and wandering minds? Do we really know what those unrestrained shouts of joy sound like? Would we recognize them if we heard them?

"You who bring good tidings to Zion,
go up on a high mountain.
You who bring good tidings to Jerusalem,
lift up your voice with a shout,

lift it up, do not be afraid;
say to the towns of Judah,
'Here is your God!'"

"Rejoice in the Lord always.
I will say it again: Rejoice!"

"Speak to one another with psalms, hymns
And spiritual songs.
Sing and make music
In your heart to the Lord."
                (Isaiah 40:9; Philippians 4:4; Ephesians 5:19)

What Does Joy Sound Like?

Spend a few minutes reading Exodus 15:1-21. Then try painting a mental and emotional picture of the children of Israel when, after 400 years of slavery, they found themselves on the safe side of the Red Sea. Can you visualize that glorious day? Moses and the sons of Israel singing to God. Miriam and all the women dancing with timbrels in their hands. Can you see them? Can you hear their song as it ascends toward heaven?

What do joyful Christians sound like? (Read Romans 11:33-36 and Revelation 4, 5, and 19.) Have you heard them—those spontaneous yet most appropriate sounds? No, not some emotional noise stirred up by external stimulus or electronic gadgetry, but the joy that rises out of one's innermost being—stirred by the Spirit of God. Even as Elizabeth, filled with the Spirit, *"cried out with a loud voice"* as the unborn John the Baptist leaped in her womb for joy! Even as Paul, who said, *"we cry out 'Abba! Father!'"* Or Peter, who could not even find words but said, *"(you) are filled with an inexpressible and glorious joy."*

Have you heard it?

Have you known it?

Not the sounds or music which try to make us joyful, but the sounds which rise from our spirits because we are joyful!

We *do* know what God thinks about the absence of such sounds among His people. And what we know should jolt us. Remember what Jesus said to the Pharisees who took offense at the joyful singing of His disciples as He rode into Jerusalem on that little donkey?

"I tell you, if they keep quiet, the stones will cry out!" (Luke 19:40). We all agree that Jesus came to bring us life. We teach it; we talk about it. We may even think we know *about* it, but what is that life actually like?

> *"For the kingdom of God is not a matter of eating and drinking, but of righteousness, peace and joy in the Holy Spirit, because anyone who serves Christ in this way is pleasing to God and approved by men."*

> *"'However, do not rejoice that the spirits submit to you, but rejoice that your names are written in heaven.' At that time Jesus, full of joy through the Holy Spirit, said, 'I praise you, Father, Lord of heaven and earth, because you have hidden these things from the wise and learned, and revealed them to little children.'"*   (Romans 14:17; Luke 10:20-21)

"But That's Just the Way I Am"

Why then is joy so often the missing ingredient in our lives? Even as I write these words I can remember those times when I could hear within my own mind those terse, tense words: "Stop it! Don't manipulate me. Don't get too close. If I want to be unhappy, that's my right. If I want to feel lonely, don't interfere. That's just the way I am and don't you change me. I have my inhibitions. When I want to be happy, I'll do it. Just don't meddle."

Such words were coming either from my fleshly mind or from the devil himself. They simply are unfit for a Christian to say. Why? Because, *first* of all, they reflect the false concept that I belong to myself. I do not! I am God's property and it is His right to do as He pleases with His property. And He wishes His children to be joyful. I have no right to say no.

Second, to say "that's just the way I am" is displaying a remarkable lack of insight. Even though through various psychological tests I may be able to discover my fleshly makeup, I have no right to limit God to that shallow level. God took a cowardly Gideon who "from weakness was made strong." If Jesus could make "even the stones" to cry out, dare you or I limit the workings of our God by such shallow "personality" classifications? Remember, Ephesians 5:19 was not written "to the choir only."

"But What Will People Think?"

And *finally,* inhibitions. What right does a perfume bottle have to keep its lid on? What right does a flute or a trumpet have to be silent on the lips of their owners?

"But what will people think?"

Paul answers that. *"If we are out of our mind, it is for the sake of God"* (2 Corinthians 5:13).[1]

Why then is God's joy so often missing among His children? To answer this, we find ourselves looking one final time at the implications of the new birth and the nature of sin. Out of our struggle with meaning and our fleshly capacity to search for it independently, we have gone about creating our own shallow identities, securities, and love objects. So also we have taken it upon ourselves to create our own joys. Over and over we discover that on the far side of our expensive, emotionally-draining efforts there is only more emptiness. Yet somehow we find renewed strength to set out once more in our illusive search for happiness. (Note Isaiah 57:10 and especially 2 Corinthians 11:2-3.)

The Way Back to Joy

How then do we find our way back? How are we to rediscover the joy that is our very birthright as born ones of God? Let's look at four helps in "finding our way back."

(1) We need to take a long look at the fact that the entire Trinity is very pleased to have us.

Did you know that? Perhaps we've been assuming that our God is not truly happy to have us at all. Instead, we are only objects He uses to show how patient and forgiving He is. For some of us, it will take a while to look long enough into the face of God to see His smile. To hear His shouts of joy. To become aware of the sheer pleasure which is His in having each one of us as a part of His new creation. Listen to God:

"Rejoice with me;
I have found my lost sheep."

But while he was still a long way off,
his father saw him,
and was filled with compassion for him;
he ran to his son,
threw his arms around him
and kissed him.

But the father said to his servants,
'Let's have a feast and celebrate.
For this son of mine was dead
and is alive again;
he was lost and is found.'"

(Luke 15:6, 20, 23-24)

O how far God has gone to bring us back! Out of that initial joy that was His when He laid the foundations of the earth,

"while the morning stars sang together, and all the
angels shouted for joy."   (Job 38:7)

which was tragically interrupted by both angelic and human sin, there came at last that expectant message above Bethlehem,

> *"I bring you good news of great joy that will be for*
> *all the people."*   (Luke 2:10)

Then with face set "as a flint," God's beloved Son moved toward the impenetrable darkness of Calvary and the piercing cry was heard,

> *"My God, my God,*
> *Why have you forsaken me?"*   (Matthew 27:46)

All that way—that long way—our Savior went. Infinite distance! And yet Hebrews 12:2 says *"for the joy set before Him"* He *"endured the cross, scorning its shame."* And He completed the journey. *From heaven to earth to hell and all the way back from the far side of eternal judgment to His Father's side in glory!*
And for what reason?

> *"In bringing many sons to glory it was fitting that*
> *God, for whom and through whom everything ex-*
> *ists, should make the Pioneer of their salvation*
> *perfect through suffering. Both the One who makes*
> *men holy and those who are made holy are of the*
> *same family. So Jesus is not ashamed to call them*
> *brothers."*   (Hebrews 2:10-11)

How Can We Keep From Smiling Back?
Yes, it is true that God is very pleased to have us. And that is true even though we may temporarily grieve the Spirit. He is still pleased to have us. You see, even though you do not know who you really are, He does! How can we look into the face of Someone so loving and so loveable who is smiling at us and delighted with having us—and not smile back? Could it be that we feel terribly out of place or unworthy or guilty?
Are you out of place? God says that He has *"seated us with him in the heavenly realms in Christ Jesus."*

Are you unworthy? How can any believer cast a shadow over God's creative masterpiece which will hang eternally in the art gallery of His own glory with such false shame? God has said that He *"has qualified you to share in the inheritance of the saints in the kingdom of light."*

Are you guilty? This same God tells us that He *"forgave us all our sins."*

I think that if you and I had just one tenth of the joy in having God that He has in having us as His children we would explode with joy! (Ephesians 2:6-7; Colossians 1:13; 2:13).

> *"The Lord your God is in your midst,*
> *A victorious warrior.*
> *He will exult over you with joy,*
> *He will be quiet in His love,*
> *He will rejoice over you*
> *With shouts of joy!"*
>
> (Zephaniah 3:17, NASB)

Imagine—if God brought the universe into being with simply a word, can we even begin to grasp what God's shouts of joy over us must be like? But you cannot know God's joy *until you see God's joy.* Oh Christian, look! And look again!

(2) God's gift of joy comes to us wrapped in a package. That package is Holy Spirit-taught truth. We must give the Spirit a chance.

Listen to God for a moment as He tells us of the intimate relationship there is between the Holy Spirit and joy in the lives of God's children.

> *"You became imitators of us and of the Lord; in spite of severe suffering, you welcomed the message with the joy given by the Holy Spirit."*
>
> (1 Thessalonians 1:6)

> *"We also rejoice in our sufferings...because God*
> *has poured out his love into our hearts by the Holy*
> *Spirit, whom he has given us."*   (Romans 5:3, 5)

> *"May the God of hope fill you with all joy and*
> *peace as you trust in him, so that you may overflow*
> *with hope by the power of the Holy Spirit."*
> (Romans 15:13;
> see also Romans 14:17 noted earlier).

The fact that two of these three passages are in a context of trouble only serves to underline the remarkable, supernatural nature of Holy Spirit-given joy.

Well then let's assume that we are committed to the "Spirit-taught truth" concept. And we pack up and head off for three years or so of intensive Bible study at the best school we can find. Intensive? You bet! Are we open to the Spirit's teaching? Absolutely! But what is it like when it is all over? How will we feel? Relieved, that's for sure. But will there be that free flow of joy in the Holy Spirit? Perhaps, but maybe not. Why not?

Memorize and Outline the Louvre, Please

Imagine you are an art student who has been given a huge assignment. In a very limited amount of time you are to digest all of the works of art in the Louvre in Paris. You are expected to memorize all the names of the artists, their styles, their historical periods, number of works, types of art, materials and instruments used, comparisons between artists, plus much, much more. Now if you were sharp enough, if you possessed a faultless memory, you might be able to do it. You could analyze, memorize, criticize, categorize, synthesize, and then pass a test on it all and pull off an "A." *But you would flunk in terms of the intent of the artists!* And we all know why, don't we? How does one appreciate a painting? It is only as we pause before a single painting, look and then look again, that we can begin to appreciate it. And then go away only to return and look once more until we find ourselves walking right into that work of art. We begin to think and feel and respond with the artist, as the artist. Only then have we fulfilled the full desire of that artist. Only then do we know anything about true response.

Looking Until We See

And so it is with God's truth. The Spirit Who *is* the Artist invites us to follow Him as He walks with us among God's masterpieces of truth. Truths concerning Himself and His ways. And as He invites us to pause, to look long enough — to look until we truly see, only then is He able to fulfill in us His teaching ministry. The only possible value in running through an art gallery is to motivate us to go back again... very slowly. And until we do, God's gift of joy will remain neatly packaged, but unopened.

A.W. Tozer was one of those rare individuals who knew much about that almost forgotten practice of meditation. In his own literary masterpiece, *Knowledge of the Holy*, he included the following quotation by Frederick W. Faber:

> Only to sit and think of God,
>   Oh what a joy it is!
> To think the thought, to breathe the Name;
>   Earth has no higher bliss.

On my office wall is a very treasured motto by George MacDonald:

> To exist is to be a child of God;
> And to know it,
>   to feel it,
> Is to rejoice evermore.

Please Don't Run Through the Gallery

Many of us are ready to ascribe to the authority of the Scriptures as a product of the Holy Spirit. But are we just as

ready to look long enough at His single masterpieces so that
He might have time to produce in us the depth of appreciation He intended?

Suppose I asked you, "Are you saved? Do you believe
that God has set you free? Do you believe that you are loved
by God?" I imagine that you would have little difficulty
answering. But it is another thing to have allowed the light of
God to so shine on those facts that you would actually shout
with uninhibited joy, "I am loved! I am free! I am safe!
Hallelujah!"

I really don't think God has made us in such a way that
we could endure one constant, emotional "high."

*But I am equally sure that God never intended His truth
to remain merely academic.* Zephaniah 3:17 tells us that
within the scope of God's experience, He both rejoices over
us *"with shouts of joy"* and is *"quiet in His love."* I would
assume He desires a parallel expression from His children.

Don't rush through God's gallery.

Let Him speak to you.

The next time you are singing one of the standard hymns
of your church, take note of how many overwhelming facts
about God and life you are required to focus on in the space
of two or three minutes. In some hymns we will quickly travel
past a dozen divine works of art, each one worthy of a clear
focus. Most of us are simply not equipped to do that.
Therefore, although we may sing well enough and pronounce
all the words correctly, we might as well have not sung them
at all. Thoughtlessly mouthing deep, dramatic truths of God
does more harm than good. It makes us immune or calloused
toward truth that demands a heart response.

Perhaps this is the reason why the hymn, "When I
Survey the Wondrous Cross," has so properly captivated
God's people. It's one of those rare, special hymns which give
us time to meditate, to follow the Holy Spirit on a spiritual
journey past but one section of one wall of the central gallery
in God's halls of glory.

Bringing Truth into Focus

I used to be offended by repetitive songs such as the chorus "Alleluia, alleluia, alleluia, alleluia" or by people who repeat the names of Jesus over and over again in prayer. But then I had to admit to myself that I could say that word or that name just once and scarcely give it another thought! Repetition doesn't have to be "vain." (Read Psalm 136.) Most of our minds are already saturated with more information than we know how to handle. To buck the pressure all around us to stuff in even more, will demand that we set aside some of the standard measurements of Christian success. Only then will those priceless words and concepts be seen in depth. Dear Christian, please give God's truth a fighting chance to do its work in you!

(3) God's joy can only function when we are honestly resting in the adequacy of Christ.

"For though we live in the world, we do not wage war as the world does. The weapons we fight with are not the weapons of the world. On the contrary, they have divine power to demolish strongholds. We demolish arguments [logismous, "reasonings"] *and every pretension that sets itself up against the knowledge of God, and we take captive every thought to make it obedient to Christ."*

(2 Corinthians 10:3-5)

Though Paul first had in mind the reasonings of those in Corinth who were opposed to his apostolic message, the principle certainly is the same when one reckons with his own reasonings which for all practical purposes leave God out of the picture. And certainly the solution is the same.

A "Reasoning" Sampler

About the fastest way I know to bring this principle into focus is to allow two groups of vivid Bible stories to flash through our minds. The first set are positive ones; the second, negative. Ready? (By the way, if any of these stories are unfamiliar to you, please take the time right now to look them up.)

First: **Moses before the Red Sea**
          Joshua before the walls of Jericho
          Gideon before the Midianites
          **The disciples before two weary, hungry
              multitudes**
          **Peter and John before the lame man at
              the gate**
          **Paul before the philosophically elite in
              Corinth**

          (Exodus 14:10-21; Joshua 6:1-20; Judges
          7:2-9, 19-22; Matthew 14:14-21; 15:32-38;
          Acts 3:1-10; 1 Corinthians 1:20-29, 2
          Corinthians 11:1-4, 13-15.)

Second: **Elijah sulking in his own self pity**
          Josiah before Pharoah Necho
          **The disciples waking Jesus during the
              storm at sea**
          **Peter observing the waves as he walked
              toward Jesus**
          **Martha's anxiety over fixing dinner while
              Mary sat at Jesus' feet**
          **Christians who went to court against
              each other in Corinth**

          (1 Kings 19:3-10; 2 Chronicles 35:20-24;
          Mark 4:38-41; Matthew 14:29-30; Luke
          10:39-42; 1 Corinthians 6:1-8.)

Just imagine, if you can, what if "reasonings" *had* ruled the day in the first set of stories, and what if they *had not* ruled the day in the second set! Is the principle in focus now? I hope it is.

Now, let's bring it up to date.

The doctor says it's cancer.   **What will you do?**
Your "impossible situation" simply won't go away.
What will you do?
You sense a growing distance between you and your wife.   **What will you do?**
Someone is scheming behind your back to get your job.   **What will you do?**
Someone you love resents your love for Christ.
What will you do?

Perpetual Motion Computer

Well, what do we usually do? I can answer that, because I'm an expert in the field. The computers of my mind begin to work double time, overtime, all the time! Figuring, creating, anticipating, planning, scheming. I carry on a thousand imagined conversations and arguments. I memorize how I will fend off each verbal lunge, how I will conquer each blind alley, or if all else fails, how I will make a quick escape and still save face.

Let's take a closer look at our fleshly imaginations even though they're not pretty.

First of all, I give my mind full freedom to repaint whatever my existing situation is in wild, three-dimensional, thoroughly frightening color. Not that I leave it with that. Next I probe into the dark future, imagining what is most likely going to happen...the worst. All the horrible details. And finally, unless by then my emotions have finished me off, I put my brain on emergency status to do all that figuring, planning, plotting, and scheming in order to somehow extricate myself from the present and future difficulties.

"Now if only that new drug is approved by the FDA soon enough there might still be time to...."

"If only I can remember to say 'this' then they would say 'that' and I would come back at them with 'there!' Ah, maybe then, just maybe, things would all smooth out."

Over and over and over my battle-weary brain rehearses its neat strategies. (It's smart to have several plans just in case the first one fizzles.)

And what is the practical result of all these "reasonings?" Well, it's exciting if one likes anxiety or suspense. But let's call it what it really is — *worry*. Consuming, corrosive worry.

And where is my joy in God?

What's that?

I really think I've forgotten what it's like.

But How Do I Handle These Thoughts?

Ah, but you see, I am a Christian. Therefore, somewhere along the line I remember to pray. But all I probably do is bring my anxiety-ridden strategies to God and ask Him to initial them! I even begin to tell myself that if only I could work out solutions to all my problems then I could start resting in the Lord. That's sheer insanity! Since when did God need me for an advisor? Well then, how do I handle these forceful, intrusive thoughts? Let's go back to 2 Corinthians 10.

Paul knew that he was coming against attitudes and factions in Corinth that would be very difficult to handle. And so he begins by clearing the air as to what a believer is to do when he is facing something impossible for mere flesh to handle.

Equipment Check

First of all he tells us to take a good look at our equipment. What equipment? Our intellectual reserves, our emotional make-up? No. Our *real* equipment. *"The weapons we fight with are not the weapons of the world."* So we take inventory of our spiritual arsenal. Ephesians 6:10-18 has a lot to say about that, as does Revelation 12:11. (This inventory we should know by heart!)

And don't forget that most unusual weapon King Jehoshaphat placed in front of his army in 2 Chronicles 20:21-22.

> *"Jehoshaphat appointed men to sing to the Lord and to praise him for the splendor of his holiness as they went out at the head of the army, saying:*
>
> *'Give thanks to the Lord,*
> *for his love endures forever.'*
>
> *As they began to sing and praise, the Lord set ambushes against the men of Ammon and Moab and Mount Seir who were invading Judah, and they were defeated."* (2 Chronicles 20:21-22)

It was probably the first time in history a choir had marched before the army as first-line warriors. Strange indeed that an essential part of the equipment to lead us into God's joyous victory is praise. It's something to think about.[2]

Finally, the simple declaration of the name of Jesus is divinely powerful for the destruction of fortresses. (See Acts 3:6 in view of the repeated emphasis Jesus had placed on praying and acting "in his name.")

No, it is not as though God asks a Christian to reject his mind when facing a difficult situation. Quite the opposite. God simply asks us to join our minds with His—to think His thoughts. Of course in the flesh this would be impossible, but because they are His thoughts and we are "in the Spirit" and "praying in the Spirit," we can and we must.

Body Life and Spiritual Warfare

Another weapon against our own imaginations is something we have already referred to in chapter 10. Every believer must see himself as a functioning part of a local body.

"Frightening" is too mild a word to express how we should feel about the flood of moral troubles plaguing Christians today. Just when everything seems to be going so well, suddenly some Christian husband and father runs off with someone else's Christian wife and mother. Of course, it really wasn't "suddenly" at all. Long before both individuals had quietly isolated themselves from the body and the openness that such a relationship requires. They came to see themselves as *individuals* who had a right to create a little world of their own happiness. Oh, they knew the Word, they knew it well, but that was not enough. It has never been enough!

If only there could have been some brother or sister — some spiritual elder with whom they could have been fully open. With whom they could have shared those first feelings — those initial frustrations. Together they could have seen the healing graces of God! (Remember the "jumper cable" illustration, p. 153?)

Spiritual accountability within a local body and under spiritual elders who actively demonstrate caring love is one of the most powerful weapons against this well camouflaged, satanic fortress — immorality. (See 2 Corinthians 6:11-13; 7:2-3; Galatians 6:1-2; James 5:16.)

Thinking God-Thoughts

Now let's look back over those two groups of Bible stories listed earlier. Did Moses, Joshua, and Gideon turn off their minds when crises came? Of course not. But the thoughts inside their minds were "God-thoughts." *"Apart from me you can do nothing,"* Jesus said.

That's the way it was.

It still is. Praise God! The joy of the Lord is not dependent on the quality of your intellect. A simple little child who is enjoying the security of the word "trust" probably knows far more about "God-thoughts" than many a scholar. It's just plain wonderful that the knowledge of God can be both marvelously simple and yet infinite. He says to me, "Trust me." That's simple. That's infinite!

And so we raise our rod over the Red Sea. We bring our tiny five loaves and two fishes to Jesus.

To Jesus?

"For from him and through him and to him are all things. To him be the glory forever! Amen."

(Romans 11:36)

That is the knowledge of God!

A Higher Reality

In so doing we literally destroy all those quite logical reasonings of the flesh, whether they are reasonings which come against us or those we create ourselves. We do not deny that they are real. They *are* real. Instead, we simply assert a higher reality!

Before we leave this issue let's take note of the remarkable way the Holy Spirit illustrates this principle in relation to experiencing God's joy. Both James and Peter tell us to expect and experience "pure joy," "inexpressible joy" right in the middle of our suffering.[3] Now really, does that make sense? Does it make any sense to someone who is missing out on so much that this life has to offer for any one of a thousand reasons which plague so many of God's children? No! Unless God looms big in the picture it makes no sense at all!

Some of you who are reading these words right now are hurting in ways that perhaps no one but God knows anything about. But if Jesus is Lord, your *Lord*, He still is committed *to give Himself to you.* "Trust Me, to be to you all that I am!" Be tough on your mind. Bring into captivity—to sword point—every thought that leaves out God and the promises of God.

Time and again you will need to repudiate those rushing, worrisome, squirrel-cage thoughts and replace them with the knowledge of God. Step over the line and let God's mind be yours. Give Him a chance to lift you high enough to at last see just a tiny bit from His eternal vantage point. Yes, the fortresses are real and mighty. But you will find yourself singing as you march around them when God is the biggest thing on your mind!

> *"No, in all these things we are more than conquerors through him who loved us. For I am convinced that neither death nor life, neither angels nor demons, neither the present nor the future, nor any powers, neither height nor depth, nor anything else in all creation, will be able to separate us from the love of God that is in Christ Jesus our Lord."*
>
> (Romans 8:37-39)

(4) God's joy is inseparable from unconditional discipleship with all its costs.

The last "way back" to joy—that trademark of holiness—is almost a paradox.

Jesus said, *"Any of you who does not give up everything he has cannot be my disciple."* But to His disciples He also said, *"I have told you this so that my joy may be in you and that your joy may be complete"* (Luke 14:33; John 15:11).

"Everything He Has..."

It is so very difficult for any of us to face up to the implications of those words *"everything he has...."* Even when we have a proper perspective. Even when we remember that in view of who we are, to forsake what we "have" is to fulfill what we are. Even then, those words of Jesus seem heavy. So very heavy.

Oh, we might bring ourselves to sing:

"All those vain things which charm me most,
    I sacrifice them to His blood."

But what about those not-so-vain things? What about my dream of finding that one special person to love and to be loved by? What about the joy and pride in the successful outcome of my children? What about the worthy results of my life work? And being well-received by those closest to me—my wife, my parents, my special friend?

What about those things?

Just how well would I handle being rejected by those I love?

Especially when I need them the most?

Yet my Lord Jesus, even as He anticipated that very type of rejection, could talk so freely about His joy! How could He do that?

To Him there was *one thing* above all else.

One measurement of life which superseded all measurements.

He was His Father's Son, committed to do His Father's will.

To please His Father, to finish His work was His highest joy!

"Everything he has . . ."

We can say the words. Memorize them. Repeat them. But to embrace them—to face up to their meaning in the real flesh and blood world in which we live—that is something else.

To actually experience joy while grieving for someone you love who is floundering. To experience joy when someone with more talent steps into the very spot that would have been the climax of all that you had worked to complete. To experience joy after you have fallen flat on your face. To experience joy when you realize that something which could have been (and in a most wholesome sense, should have been) will never be—that's reality. Reality that bites into the flesh and numbs the heart.

It's easy enough to rattle off our stock answer, "This is God's perfect will for your life." Certainly, in an ultimate sense, this is true. But there *are* real tragedies. There *are* things which "might have been" and "should have been" which often never are.

Remember, Jesus did weep over Jerusalem.[4] Life has its "Demas's" and its "Judas's." Not every godly parent ends up with godly children.[5] Not every godly wife enjoys a godly husband.

Choosing the Joy

In those agonizing moments of crisis, we have several choices as to how we may respond. But only one fully harmonizes with the joy of the Lord—the kind of joy Jesus knew.

First, we can simply lock out all other thoughts and with a cold, fatalistic commitment say, "give thanks in all circumstances" through our clenched teeth.

Or we may move to the opposite extreme and waste away in our grief.

Or we can charge straight ahead, empowered by our growing bitterness.

Or we can approach those crisis times the only way God ever intended: as indeed "sorrowful, yet always rejoicing." God would have us to face reality, to honestly admit to grief and pain and pity; to sorrow in what others have suffered or in what might have been. But God would have us know beyond that the higher reality of who He is and who we are.

He would have us know that we are our Father's son or daughter, committed to do our Father's will.

He would have us know that our highest joy is His "well done."

"But Lord, I have failed you so often!"

Oh Christian—face up to it. You know what to do. So do it!

There is a world that needs to see the invisible God through the prism called "you." Don't waste another minute missing life.

There is a God Who has chosen you to be the object of His love—*the displayer of His person.* Why waste another second frustrating the very reason Jesus came?

What Do You See?

Look up into His face. Remember, He is Lord! Right now...what do you see? An angry God? No, you do not see an angry God. Yes, He may have been grieved because you temporarily lost perspective and missed living for a while. But now, right now, you are looking into His face and saying "Abba! Father!" What do you see?

Be tough on those fleshly imaginations that so easily distort your sight of God. He is there on His throne in all His majesty...exalted, holy, and loving. And you...*you* are destined to grace His holy heaven forever.

O dear Christian, rejoice! Live!

Do you know who you *are*?

Conclusion, Notes

1. Of course such expressions of praise to God must be seen within the context of 1 Corinthians 14:33, 40. See also Acts 4:24.

2. See Joy Ridderhof, *Count It All Joy* (Los Angeles: Recordings, Inc., 1978).

3. James 1:1-12; 1 Peter 1:3-9. See also 2 Corinthians 4:6-18; 6:1-10; Romans 8:14-30.

4. See Luke 19:41, 42. Cf. Matthew 23:37; Ezekiel 33:11; Jeremiah 18:6-12; Deuteronomy 30:10-20. We have no right to weaken the obvious intent of these passages in order to force them to conform to any view of God's eternal purpose which does not have room for "things as they might have been."

5. In our interpretation of individual Scripture passages we so much need to maintain balance. In this case, our theological statements must harmonize both Proverbs 22:6 and Titus 1:6 on the one hand, and Matthew 10:35-36 and Luke 15:11-24 on the other hand.

Appendix A

A Summary of the Practical Values of a Biblical Perspective on Spiritual Identity and Meaning in Life

1. This perspective delivers me from the frustration of believing that if I am to do the will of God and live for Him, I must go against myself and all I desire in life. True, I must go against my flesh, but I am never called upon to go against my authentic personhood, myself as God's newly created child.

2. Obviously it allows me to have a positive, wholesome sense of self worth and yet protects me from pride due to the fact that the fundamental nature of my true personhood is one of absolute dependence upon life which flows from God. It delivers me from the morbidity of some of the "crucified life" approaches to spirituality.

3. It protects me from a variety of extremes, such as believing that my flesh in itself is essentially evil, or that I am really two persons—a good one and a bad one—or that my ultimate deliverance is when at last "self" is forever eliminated (when I get to heaven) and I become a non-self in a limitless infinity full of Jesus.

4. It liberates the biblical concept of Christian liberty. If my basic nature is righteous even as Christ is righteous, then I am totally free to fulfill life. I am truly free to do what I want to do! As Paul says, "for me to live is Christ." Because of this a delightfully positive tone is added to the entire picture of the Christian life.

5. Through understanding why I sin, I can retrace my way back to the cause and really do something about it.

6. Due to the fact that by the new birth all the "equipment" is present for a God-oriented, meaningful life, it directs my attention to the fundamental necessity of the energizing power of the Holy Spirit. Ephesians 3:14-21 becomes overwhelmingly significant.

7. It opens the door to a much fuller appreciation of every believer I meet realizing that he, too, whether it is outwardly apparent or not, is God's inner workmanship, His pure creation. Since there is no evidence that would lead us to think that there are varying degrees of quality or value in God's individual creations, it allows me to show the fullest respect for *every* child of God.

8. It frees me from a warped emphasis on the values of various aspects of my mortality. I am not less of a person if I am not married, if I cannot walk, or if my mental faculties are not in the best shape.

9. It encourages me to enlarge my concept of my spirit (used here as a synonym for "inner man") so as to see myself fundamentally as a spiritual being, regardless of what might happen to my physical brain or any other part of my mortality.

10. It brings new sense into Paul's statement "my spirit prays" (1 Corinthians 14:14-15; cf. 14:2, 4, 28). Regardless of one's particular view concerning present-day tongues speaking, at least the *concept* of private praying in tongues can be understood as being a means by which one's spirit, the deepest level of his personhood, may communicate with God. The resulting edification occurs, then, apart from the management by one's mortal brain of the nature of the communication.

11. Because I am aware of being most essentially a spiritual being, it adds a new seriousness to the fact of spiritual warfare and my direct involvement in that warfare.

12. In a simple manner it replaces the very complicated approaches to spirituality which are often marketed today. In so doing it corresponds to the obvious simplicity of operation of the first generation believers.

13. It enables me to appreciate by direct parallel how the earthly life of my Lord Jesus can be an actual working example for me.

14. It certainly frees me from having to believe in the well meant "double talk" of so many popular explanations of Romans 6 which teach that victory comes only when a dead man is being controlled, or that by some mysterious exercise of faith a positional truth becomes actual, but only as long as you are believing it to be so. (I am referring here to the view that "reckoning" makes the crucifixion of the old man a reality.) It therefore allows a variety of Scripture passages to speak with fresh authority rather than being bridled by the well meant rationalizations of some Bible teachers.

15. It encourages me to greatly value the facetting process which God is undertaking in my life. And even though it is painful at times, I can truly rejoice because I know that the process only increases the potential of meaning, of glorifying God—which *is* ultimate meaning—both in time and eternity.

16. It tremendously heightens my vision of the prospects of manifesting holiness.

17. It increases my appreciation of the continuity between my life here on earth and my life in heaven. Since the Bible does not teach that there will be any change in one's authentic, deep personality between the moment he dies and his arrival in heaven, it then logically underlines the sacredness of my present union with Christ. Naturally it also causes me to joyfully anticipate the time I will receive a redeemed body to match my presently redeemed spirit.

Appendix B

The Relationship Between the Christian and the Terms "Old Man" and "Flesh"

Introduction

The purpose of this appendix is to provide some basis for comparison of the perspective of this book with what would appear to be the most common alternate point of view. In brief, this alternate view holds (1) that the terms "old man," "old self," "sin nature," and "flesh" are synonyms. Consequently, since the New Testament clearly teaches that a Christian still has the flesh, he still has the old man. (2) And since this is so, the "crucifixion" of the old man in Romans 6 cannot be accepted as actual, but rather positional or judicial. We will contrast quotations reflecting these statements with those which are in harmony with this book and then conclude with comments concerning several supporting arguments which are used by some to justify the alternate view.

NOTE: In writing this section I face what is to me an unavoidable dilemma. Since it will be necessary to include a considerable number of quotations, it is fitting that I identify the source of each statement. This then brings to the front the names of the individuals who produced these statements. But I have no wish whatsoever to do this. The important issue is that these statements have been taught and believed among those in the body of Christ. It is not particularly important who has made the statements. The issue is the ideas, not the individuals. In fact it could well be that some quotations no longer represent the present view of the person quoted. (I would be quite embarrassed to be required to defend some statements I made ten years ago!) It also could be true that they did not mean to say what those who read them thought they meant. Some individuals I quote are respected personal friends of mine with whom I find far more to agree with than to call into question. I am eternally indebted to them for their ministry in my life. Therefore, may I urge you, the reader, to respect my concern and to focus on the statements rather than on the individuals. For the sake of the oneness and love within the body of Christ, I will thank you sincerely.

(1) *Are the terms "old man," "flesh," and "sin nature" essentially synonyms?*

YES: "The Scriptures reveal that every child of Adam possesses Adam's nature, with all its predisposition to sin. Whether designated as the sin nature (Romans 5:21; 1 John 1:8), the Adamic nature, the *flesh* (Romans 13:14; 1 Corinthians 5:5; 2 Corinthians 7:1; 10:2-3; Galatians 5:16-24; 6:8; Ephesians 2:3; etc.), the *old man* (Romans 6:6; Ephesians 4:22; Colossians 3:9-10), or any other term, the reference is to the human nature, including soul, spirit and body."[1]

"What is here called 'the old man' Paul elsewhere calls himself, as in Romans 7:14, 'I am carnal,' 'In me there dwelleth no good thing,' verse 18; or, 'law in my members,' verse 23; or 'the flesh' as opposed to the spirit, as in Galatians 5:16-17. This evil principle or nature is called old because it precedes what is new, and because it is corrupt. And it is called 'man,' because it is ourselves."[2]

"We have inherited a basic temperament from our parents that contains both strengths and weaknesses.

This temperament is called several things in the Bible, 'the natural man,' 'the flesh,' 'the old man,' and 'corruptible flesh,' to name but a few. It is the basic impulse of our being that seeks to satisfy our wants."[3]

NO: "What then is this 'old man'? First, it does not mean the carnal nature and all its propensities. Paul is not teaching that our carnal nature with all its propensities was crucified together with Christ. Neither does it mean our moral being previous to our rebirth. Neither does it mean the flesh with its affections and lusts. Neither does it mean 'old' simply in the sense of 'former,' whereas now I am something different. Why am I so concerned with these negatives? It is because I want to show that if you will identify the 'old man' with any one of these ideas you will of necessity be in hopeless confusion in the light of other Scriptures which we have to consider. What then does Paul mean by 'old man?' It seems to me to be quite plain if we look at the context of the entire passage which begins in chapter 5 verse 12 [Romans]. The 'old man' is the man I used to be in Adam. . . . It is the man I once was, but which I am no longer."[4]

"The Heidelberg Catechism rightly draws a distinction between 'the old man' and 'the flesh.' 'The old man is crucified and buried with Him, so that the corrupt inclinations of the flesh may no more reign in us.' The 'old man' is not 'the flesh,' he is not the 'corrupt nature;' the old man is the Adamic nature, the old humanity. The 'flesh' is 'the body of sin,' the body in which sin tends to tyrannize still, the body in which sin yet remains."[5]

"The term 'old man' does not lend itself to the same kind of usage which we have in the case of 'sin' and 'flesh.' 'Old man' is a designation of the person in his unity, as dominated by the flesh and sin. Though Paul, indeed, identifies himself, his ego, with sin (Romans 7:14, 20a, 25b) and then also with righteousness (Romans 7:17a, 20b, 25a), yet he does not call the former his 'old ego' and the latter his 'new ego.' In like manner he does not call the 'sin' and 'the flesh' in him the 'old man.'"[6]

"This is an important verse [Romans 6:6], and we must clearly distinguish between 'our old man,' 'the body of sin,' and 'we.' The first of these, 'our old man,' means 'our old self;' what we were as unregenerate sons of Adam. It must not be identified with 'the flesh,' or 'our sinful nature.'"[7]

(2) *Is the crucifixion of the old man in Romans six judicial or positional rather than actual?*

YES: *"Positionally,* the 'old man' has been put off forever. Experimentally, the 'old man' remains as an active force in the life which can be controlled only by the power of God."[8]

"There is no Biblical ground for distinction between the Adamic nature and a 'human nature.' The unregenerate have but one nature, while the regenerate have two.... The 'old man,' then, is the Adamic nature which has been judged in the death of Christ. It still abides with us as an active principle in our lives, and our *experimental* victory over it will be realized through a definite reliance upon the indwelling Spirit."[9]

"The judicial crucifixion of the 'old man' took place centuries ago.... The old 'I' in you and me was judicially crucified with Christ. 'Ye died' and your death dates from the death of Christ. 'The old man,' the 'old self' in God's reckoning was taken to the cross with Christ and crucified and taken into the tomb with Christ and buried."[10]

"Our former master still lives and works hard at his task but Christ, our new Master, makes us deaf to sin's appeals by making us dead to sin itself..."[11]

"We must consent to the crucifixion of the old man. He [God] has declared 'the old man' worthy of crucifixion, in fact, he has already accomplished his crucifixion with Christ. Now God asks the believer to give his hearty consent to this transaction and to consider it an accomplished fact in his experience. Again this would seem like an extremely easy thing to do. In theory it is, in practice it is not, for the 'old man' will fight like a tiger for his life."[12]

"We must cooperate with the Holy Spirit in keeping the old man crucified."[13]

"The Scriptural explanation of this duality in Christian experience is found in the co-existence of two natures within the believer: the old, sinful Adamic nature and the new, spiritual Christ nature."[14]

"The old nature is to be regarded as having been sentenced to death. God refuses to acknowledge it, and it has no right to obstruct the Christian's progress."[15]

"First, just as the judgment upon Satan does not mean Satan is inactive and the judgment on sins does not mean that one can no longer sin, so the judgment on the sin nature does not mean that the sin nature can no longer operate."[16]

"The Bible says that in the present Christian life we are in practice to live by faith *as though we are dead* now. 'For in that he died, he died unto sin once for all: but in that he liveth he liveth unto God. Likewise 'reckon (this is an act of faith) ye also yourselves to be dead indeed unto sin' (Romans 6:10, 11a).[17] [Note: This statement is followed by ten "as though's" on the next two pages. The significance of this terminology is to be understood in light of his later statement: "judicially we are already dead and raised.... Judicially this is a reality."][18]

"Our old life is finished. 'You have died, and your life is hid with Christ in God'" (Colossians 3:3).

"But exactly what does this mean? Some claim that something inside of us as believers actually changes or a part of our person, 'the spirit,' which before was dead is made alive, and so we can look inside ourselves and see 'new life' there. Paul does say that we are a new creation, that we have new life, but he does not mean by this that a dramatic change, observable internally, has taken place in some part of us. He is referring, primarily to our new status before God: because Christ is our representative and is alive, we too, being *in* Christ by faith, have life."[19]

(Though elsewhere in the book quoted above the writers refer repeatedly to one's "true identity," and in so doing endeavor to underline a positive sense of self worth, they nevertheless appear to deny any fundamental interior change in regeneration.)

NO: "The old man is the unregenerate man; the new man is the regenerate man created in Christ Jesus unto good works. It is no more feasible to call a believer a new man and an old man, than it is to call him a regenerate man and an unregenerate. And neither is it warranted to speak of the believer as having in him the old man and the new man. This kind of terminolgy is without warrant and it is but another method of doing prejudice to the doctrine which Paul was so jealous to establish when he said, 'our old man has been crucified.'"[20]

"Paul is dealing with the believer's death to sin. 'We died to sin'—this is Paul's thesis. He is dealing with death to sin as an actual and practical fact, shall we not say existential fact? He brings within the scope of this statement not merely the guarantee or the promise of death to sin, but its realization in the life-history of the believer."[21]

"The contrast between the old man and the new man has frequently been interpreted as the contrast between that which is new in the believer and that which is old, the contrast between that which the believer is as recreated after the image of God and that which he is as not yet perfect. Hence the antithesis which exists in the believer between holiness and sin, between the Holy Spirit and the flesh, is the antithesis between the new man and the old man in him. The believer is both old man and new man; when he does well he is acting in terms of the old man which he also still is. This interpretation does not find support in Paul's teaching; Paul points to something different."[22]

"The term 'crucified' is that of being crucified with Christ, and therefore indicates that the old man has been put to death just as decisively as Christ died upon the accursed tree. To suppose that the old man has been crucified and still lives or has been raised again from this death is to contradict the obvious force of the import of crucifixion. And to interject the idea that crucifixion is a slow death and therefore to be conceived of as a process by which the old man is progressively mortified until he is finally put to death is to go flatly counter to Paul's terms.... Exegetically speaking, it is no easier to think of the old man as in process of crucifixion or mortification than it is to think of the resurrected Lord as being still in process of crucifixion."[23]

"...the figure which Paul is using, namely, that of having put off and of having put on, does not agree with the idea of being both an old man and a new man at the same time."[24]

" 'Our old man' is the old self or ego, the unregenerate man in his entirety in contrast with the new man as the regenerate man in his entirety. It is a mistake to think of the believer as both an old man and new man or as having in him both the old man and the new man, the latter in view of the regeneration and the former because of remaining corruption."[25]

"Understand that the 'old man' is not there. The only way to stop living as if he were still there is to realize that he is not there. That is the New Testament method of teaching sanctification. The whole trouble with us, says the New Testament, is that we do not realize what we are, that we still go on thinking we are the old man, and go on trying to do things to the old man. That has been done; the old man was crucified with Christ. He is non-existent, he is no longer there. . . . If we but saw this as we should, we would really begin to live as Christians in this world."[26]

"We say again, this is. . .a real fact; not something real in Christ 'positionally' in the heavenlies, but real actually on earth. When Paul said, 'Then were all dead,' 'Ye are dead' and 'We that are dead to sin' and 'your old man is crucified with him,' he meant exactly what he said."[27]

"The 'old man' ceased to exist at our regeneration, when it was 'put off.' "[28]

(3) *An analysis of the arguments used to support the positional or judicial concept of the death of the old man.*

Before considering some of the common arguments, I think it would be helpful to illustrate the well meaning double talk that this "judicial death" concept of the old self produces. The following quotations are taken from what I would imagine is the most complete recent book which deals exclusively with describing and supporting the judicial death concept of the old man.

> "God gave up the old nature and killed it" (p. 58). "Consider that the old nature is dead indeed, and keep it in its coffin" (p. 59).

> "How can the new nature cope with the old nature? The Lord has not left us without answers. The first step, of course, is to be aware that the old nature is present and eager to take over. We must be vigilant. Then the believer should study the personality and characteristics of his old nature and understand how it operates" (p. 49).

> "The discerning Christian will recognize the awesome power of the old nature in his daily life" (p. 84).

> "A Christian either must learn to live with his old nature and control it, or it will dominate him. He must adjust—or self-destruct" (p. 121). [NOTE: The entire second chapter of this book deals with the various titles for the old nature. Massey considers "old man," "flesh," "natural man," and "carnal" as synonyms for "the old nature."][29]

Now we will turn to the arguments.

A. The death cannot be considered actual because Paul states that the sin nature—the "body of sin" (synonymous with the old man) has been made "powerless" or "inactive," according to Romans 6:6, and that is something short of the full "death" idea.

This argument is illustrated by the following quotation:

"This same truth is presented in Romans 6:6, where Paul says, 'Knowing this, that our old man (you could substi-

tute the words "the sin nature" for "old man" in this
verse and do no violence to the text) is (has been)
crucified with him, that the body of sin might be
destroyed (disannulled).' The sin nature is not destroyed,
as the English text suggests. But the sin nature has been
rendered inoperative; it has been disannulled."[30]

Lloyd-Jones responds to this view by saying,

"There are those who teach in their commentaries that
this simply means 'the old man' again [reference to 'body
of sin']. They say, 'the body of sin;' in other words 'the
old man.' So it amounts to this, that the apostle's
teaching is that 'the old man was crucified with Christ in
order that the old man might be rendered ineffective, or
null and void, or inert.' This exposition is due to one
thing only, namely, that the writers have gone astray in
their interpretation of the 'old man.'"[31]

"I trust that the distinction between 'the old man' and
'the body of sin' is clear. It is most important. That is
why I have contended so much against the idea that the
'old man' means the 'old nature,' and that the 'old man'
and 'the body of sin' are one and the same thing. If you
believe that, you will still be in bondage."[32]

"What then does the term 'the body of sin' mean? It
means the body, our physical body, of which sin has
taken possession. . . . Here is the vital distinction as I see
it, the distinction between 'I myself as a personality' and
'my body.'"[33]

". . . sin still remains and is left in our bodies; not in us,
but in our bodies. As persons, as souls, we have already
finished with it, but not so the body. This body of
sin—this body which sin inhabits and tries to use—still
remains. . . sin not only remains in our bodies; but if it is
not checked, if it is not kept under, it will even reign in
our bodies, and it will dominate our bodies."[34]

Murray appears to be in full agreement with Lloyd-Jones by stating, "The expression 'the body of sin' would mean the body as conditioned and controlled by sin, the sinful body."[35] By this he clearly meant the physical body.

> "'Body' can well refer in this case to the physical organism. 'Body' is certainly used in this sense in verse 12 in the expression 'your mortal body.' The same is true in 8:10, 11, 13, 23; 12:1 (cf. 1 Corinthians 6:13, 15, 16, 20; 2 Corinthians 4:10; Philippians 1:20; 3:21; Colossians 2:11; 1 Thessalonians 5:23). These references suffice to show the extent to which the apostle thought of sin and sanctification as associated with the body."[36]

Commenting on the "deeds of the body" of Romans 8:13, he adds,

> "The physical entity which we call the body is un-doubtedly intended (cf. vv. 10, 11) and implies, therefore, that the apostle is thinking of those sins associated with and registered by the body.... 'The deeds of the body' are those practices characteristic of the body of sin (cf. 6:6), practices which the believer must put to death if he is to live (cf. Colossians 3:5)."[37]

Lloyd-Jones expresses,

> "The teaching of verse 6, then, is that my 'old man' was crucified in order that the remaining use of my body by sin might be disannulled, might be rendered ineffective."[38]

One final comment by Murray should be added in which he equates the "body of sin" with "body of this death" of Romans 7:24.

> "'Body' in Paul's usage, as was noted at 6:6, refers to the physical body and there is not evidence to support the view that it is used figuratively. Hence we are con-strained to think in this instance of the physical body."[39]

Finally W.H. Griffith Thomas states,

> "The 'body of sin' does not mean in our modern ter-
> minology, 'the mass of sin,' or that sin has its source in
> the body. It simply means that the body is the seat, or in-
> strument of sin. The 'we' of this verse means our real self
> as united to Christ."[40]

At this point you are encouraged to note the degree of
emphasis Paul places on the physical body in Romans 6-8,
observing especially Romans 6:11-13, 19; 8:10-11, 13, 23. In
view of this it would be completely inconsistent of Paul to
make Romans 6:6 an exception. Not only is this so, but it
would force upon Paul a redundant literary style, quite out of
character if the verse were translated, "Knowing this, that our
old self was crucified with Him that our old self might be
made powerless."

Three final quotations quite clearly express what I
believe to be a proper view. Lloyd-Jones, in commenting on
the phrase, "your members" of Romans 6:13, says,

> "The various activities of our bodies, our physical bodies
> as such, come into this category of 'members.' It does
> not stop at that. The term also includes the mental
> powers, the power of thought, the power of reason, the
> power of imagination. It seems to me that in this
> teaching it is quite clear that the apostle puts all such
> things under this general heading of 'the mortal body.'
> The natural man has brains, he has understanding, he
> has mental powers which he can use, he has imagination.
> All these belong in a sense to the physical man and are
> parts, therefore, or members of this mortal body. But
> the term also included the emotions. In other words, the
> term 'members' is a way of describing the functioning of
> man."[41]

"My old self, that self that was in Adam, was an utter
slave to sin. That self has gone; I have a new self, I am a

new man. The moment I realize that I am a new man I am in a better position to deal with this old nature that remains in my body, in what Paul calls my 'mortal flesh.' We shall find the apostle saying in chapter 7, 'It is no more I that do it but sin that dwelleth in me' (verse 20). Is not that a marvelous thing to be able to say? I am not doing this or that, it is this sin that remains in my members that does so. Sin is no longer in me, it is in my members only. That is the most liberating thing you have ever heard!"[42]

"What I am asserting is that sin which formerly governed the whole of my personality is now only governing — or trying to govern — the bodily part of me. I in spirit, I as a soul, I as a personality am delivered; I am dead to sin."[43]

What a wonderful fact Paul gives to us! Since the old self has died, that is, the person I was in the truest sense, now the members of my body can be presented as instruments of righteousness to God in complete harmony with who I am now as they become the channels through which divine life — dependent life — is flowing!

B. *The death of the old man cannot be considered actual because to do so would be to contradict 1 John 1:8.*

The reasoning which leads to this conclusion is hardly simple. It goes something like this: When the word "sin" occurs in the singular it commonly can be translated "sin nature" and "sin nature" is a synonym for the "old man." Therefore since John states "If we say that we have no sin, we are deceiving ourselves," he is really saying, "If we say we have no 'old man' we are deceiving ourselves."

A statement of this view follows:

"But the word *sin* also refers to the basic nature which men have as sinful human beings. The sixth chapter of

Romans uses this word a number of times to refer to the quality of a man's nature, to the kind of person he is apart from the saving work of Jesus Christ...(in Romans 6:6) he is talking about the *essential nature* [emphasis mine] that is within us, and he uses the word *sin* to describe the quality, or kind, of nature we possess.... In 1 John 1:8, the Apostle John says, 'If we say that we have no sin, we deceive ourselves, and the truth is not in us.' John is using the word *sin* as Paul uses it in the sixth chapter of Romans, to emphasize the fact that we have a sin nature within us that God calls sin, which we can refer to as 'the sin nature.'" (Note: in this particular work the "sin nature" has previously been defined as "the old man." Note also that the old man is referred to as one's "essential nature.")[44]

If this argument can stand, then of course Romans 6 must be interpreted judicially and I must conclude that my essential nature is sinful. Thus, the person I was before I was born again, I still am (of course, with the addition of a new nature).

Perhaps this apparent problem might best be reconciled by observing the unique way in which the writer John uses the phrase "to have sin." The following quotation from Robert Law's comments concerning 1 John 1:8 clarifies a distinctive usage,

"The phrase 'to have sin' (*echein hamartian*) is peculiar to St. John, and has quite a definite sense. Thus in John 15:22 our Lord says, 'If I had not come and spoken to them, they had not had sin; but now they have no excuse for their sin.' Here, beyond question, 'to have sin' specifically denotes the guiltiness of the agent. In John 9:41, 15:24, 19:11 the sense is equally clear; and those parallels must be held as decisive for the meaning here."[45]

For those who are not at rest with this interpretation I suggest that they carefully evaluate what they actually understand by the term "nature." What is really meant when someone says "all Christians have a sin nature"? If those who use this terminology meant by it that in a general way Christians because they have not yet received the "redemption of their bodies" have a tendency to produce fleshly sinful behavior out of harmony with their innermost being, I would find no fault with the terminology.[46] But is that the way the term is used? Very pointedly Paul in Ephesians 2:3 considered it to refer to one's *essential nature* as descriptive of a non-Christian. This usage would appear to be in agreement with at least two of the following dictionary definitions, (1) the intrinsic characteristics and qualities of a person; (2) an individual disposition, "She had a gentle disposition;" (3) the aggregate of a person's instincts, penchants, preferences.[47] In other words, the idea of "nature" seems to be the essence which most adequately describes a person. One's "nature" in this sense is then not simply something a person "has," but rather that which a person most deeply "is." Therefore many who use this term would agree that one's sin nature is one's essential nature.

Well then, in view of this, can it be defended that John in his epistle is saying "if we say that our essential nature is not sinful, we are deceiving ourselves?" If that is what he is saying then it is in direct opposition to the overall thrust of 1 John in which the focus is on the righteous nature of the children of God. (See especially 1 John 3:1-9.) In order to get this idea one has to make a major distinction between the "we have no sin" of verse 8 and "we have not sinned" of verse 10, a distinction big enough to make the first passage refer to one's essential nature and the second to individual sins. There *is* a difference in the same way there is a difference between saying "I have no cough" and "I haven't coughed." But in neither case is one saying anything about his deepest self as a "cougher." (By using this comparison I by no means am minimizing the seriousness of sin, but rather I wish only to underline that to say "I have something" instead of saying "I have done something" does not require the essential nature idea of the former.) Probably the major distinction in these two verses is not seen in the first half of each, but in the second half anyway.[48] (For other occurrences of the singular "sin" which would be inappropriate to relate to one's nature, see James 1:15; Hebrews 3:15; 1 Peter 4:1; and certainly Romans 6.) To use the singular noun argument either in 1 John or anywhere else as even secondary support of a "judicial" interpretation of Romans 6 is weak deduction at best and is unworthy of consideration in an issue of such major importance.

The practical result of this "judicial" type of terminology is that it tends to produce a strange double talk. On one hand Christians are encouraged as to the importance of having a proper positive self image. Yet in the same context they are reminded of their essentially sinful nature. That's like describing all the positive qualities of a shark, its skin, sense of a smell, agility, etc., as it dashes around your swimming pool while all the time you are trying to shoot it because of its essential nature. But rather than ridiculing this very popular approach, it is constructive for us to ask why this concept is being pressed upon Christians today. Certainly it is not out of a willful wrong, but rather it is due to the sincere effort of Bible teachers to explain why believers sin without seeing the relationship between sin and the fundamental issue of meaning which grows out of an awareness of identity.

C. *The death, even if considered actual rather than judicial, does not mean extinction or cessation, but only separation.*

Therefore, even though the Bible states that one's old self has died, one must adjust to the fact that it has not ceased to exist. That old self is still very much "there," but happily the Christian is "separated from its power." One writer illustrates this by a comparison with physical death. "Physical death is a separation of the immaterial part of man from the material part. It does not mean that the person has become extinct or that he has ceased to function."[49]

At first glance this line of thought sounds reasonable until one asks the question, What died at the point of physical death? The answer, the body dies. Does that which actually dies cease to function? The answer, "Yes." Indeed, the person as a spiritual being continues to live, but that is not what dies in the first place. It seems to me that one may rightly call death "separation," but it doesn't change *the fact that death in some sense does involve a cessation of function of whatever dies.* What then about the "spiritual death" of the unbeliever? Certainly there is no cessation of activity here is there? There certainly is. Spiritual death involves a separation from the life that is in God; therefore, in the unbeliever there is a total *cessation* of the one entity that is dead—one's life in relation to God. This is also true of the biblical "second death." By illustration, one may still react to a dead snake with considerable alarm as though that snake were still alive, but the snake is dead and has indeed ceased to function no matter what one's reaction may be; so also the old man. A Christian may still think himself to be the old man, or to have the old man, thus reacting as though this is who he is. This happens even though the old man has ceased to exist. A prince may continue to act like a pauper because this is who he thinks he is even though in no sense is he a pauper, though perhaps he once was.

One additional proof of the cessation of activity is the parallel Paul draws between Christ's death and the death of the old man in Romans 6. There should be no question that there is no continuing activity of sin with Him.

Indeed it is correct to say that when a person has passed through the awesome death and resurrection described in Romans 6, the person he used to be has ceased to be and the person he now most deeply is will be forever (even though that person remains housed in unredeemed flesh which may at times provide him with a false and thus sinning identity).

D. *The death cannot be considered actual due to the fact that the time of the departure of the old man awaits either physical death or rapture.*

This view is pointedly expressed in the following quotations,

"Being an integral part of a human being, this evil nature cannot and will not be dismissed until the body itself in which it functions is redeemed, or until the separation between the body and the immaterial elements of soul and spirit is achieved by death."[50]

"Like physical death, the Adamic nature, which is the perpetuator of spiritual death, is not now dismissed, but, in the case of the redeemed, it is subject to gracious divine provisions whereby its injuries may be restrained. Salvation from the power of sin for the unsaved, depends upon two factors, namely, the divine provision and the human appropriation."[51]

"The state of sinless perfection can never be reached until the sin nature is cast out, and this is accomplished only through the death of the physical body or the transformation of the body without death at the rapture."[52]

It seems remarkable indeed with the total omission of any New Testament scriptural reference to such a departure of the old man (and the parallel terms used by the above writers) that theologians can feel free to be so dogmatic. Though it is true that our bodies will yet know a redemption (Romans 8:23), Paul completely avoids any connection between this fact and the deliverance from the old man. Such a view would seem to teach two deaths of the old man: a death in the sense of power being broken, or activity being controlled, and a death in the sense of total separation involving complete cessation of activity. Nowhere is this taught in the Bible.

The redemption of our bodies will be a marvelous moment for every believer for several reasons. *First*, we will be released from the heavy limitations of our bodies, to enjoy *"conformity with the body of His glory"* (Philippians 3:21, NASB). The result of this miracle will be that we will be able to *"see him as he is"* (1 John 3:2). In our present bodies we could not begin to endure the full frontal impact of the glory of God; our senses, our minds and emotions would indeed disintegrate before such inexpressible brilliance. But in that day *"we shall see him as he is!"* In that day *"I shall know fully, even as I am fully known"* (1 Corinthians 13:12).

Secondly, our bodies, "bodies in which sin tends to tyrannize still,"[53] (in this sense, "the body of sin") will be redeemed. This is well expressed by Lloyd-Jones in saying,

"The old man has gone. I am no longer that man; I am a new man in Christ Jesus. That is what is true about me. But though that is the truth about me, it is not yet the truth about my body, my mortal body. Sin is still in my mortal body, in my members, working as a 'law in my members,' having its effect upon my 'instruments,' 'my members,' the parts of my body."[54]

Enlarging upon this he adds,

"There is a day coming, says the Apostle, when even my body shall have been delivered from the final effects and influences of the reign and the rule of sin. Not yet! But it is coming. Even here and now, as I understand this, the evil effect of sin upon my body should be lessening, but finally I shall have a glorified body. I myself, in Christ, am already glorified—'Whom he hath called, them he hath also justified, and whom he hath justified, them he hath also glorified' (Romans 8:30). I am glorified, and a day is coming when my body shall be glorified."[55]

Summary

The "old self" (man) was who we *were*. "Flesh" was the stuff out of which life for us was made—fragile, mortal humanness severed from God's life and ultimate meaning. As such we *"were by nature children of wrath,"* living *"in the lusts of our flesh, indulging the desires of the flesh and of the mind* (literally 'thoughts')" (Ephesians 2:3, NASB).

We are *now* living spirits—living because Jesus' risen life is our life. Not only have each of us retained all of our unique humanness with its proneness for producing counterfeit life, but we actually value it as the means by which Christ may progressively be seen in this world "in the flesh." Happily some day we will exchange all that remains mortal about us for total immortality. In that day we will at last know fully "the glorious liberty of the sons of God."

Conclusion

By no means should this study be considered to be complete in the sense of considering every passage related to this issue. In view of the almost limitless potential of interpreting verses out of context or from a prior prejudice, I doubt if such a study could ever be considered as complete. My earnest desire is that you might praise God with me as we look together at the broad and bright picture of new covenant Christianity.

The fundamental question simply is: As you read the book of Acts and the epistles, what overall conclusion are you forced to draw as to the essential nature of one who has been born again?

Appendix B, Notes

1. John F. Walvoord, *Holy Spirit* (Wheaton: Van Kampen Press, 1954), p. 207.

2. Charles Hodge, *A Commentary on the Epistle to the Ephesians* (Grand Rapids: Eerdmans, n.d.), p. 259.

3. Tim La Haye, *Spirit Controlled Temperament* (Wheaton: Tyndale House Publishers, 1966), p. 5.

4. D. Martyn Lloyd-Jones, *Romans, The New Man, An Exposition of Chapter 6* (Grand Rapids: Zondervan, 1973), p. 62.

5. Ibid., p. 79.

6. John Murray, *Principles of Conduct* (Grand Rapids: Eerdmans, 1957), p. 218.

7. W. H. Griffith Thomas, *St. Paul's Epistle to the Romans* (Grand Rapids: Eerdmans, 1946), p. 167.

8. Lewis Sperry Chafer, *He That is Spiritual* (Wheaton: Van Kampen Press, 1918), p. 144.

9. Ibid., pp. 144-145.

10. Ruth Paxson, *Life on the Highest Plain* (Chicago: Moody Press, 1928), pp. 209-211.

11. Ibid., pp. 123-124.

12. Ibid., p. 227.

13. Ibid., p. 228.

14. Ibid., p. 218.

15. T.C. Hammon, *In Understanding Be Men* (Downers Grove, Ill.: InterVarsity Fellowship, 1963), p. 154.

16. J. Dwight Pentecost, *Pattern For Maturity* (Chicago: Moody Press, 1966), p. 100.

17. Francis Schaeffer, *True Spirituality* (Wheaton: Tyndale House, 1971), p. 40.

18. Ibid., p. 56.

19. Ranald Macaulay and Jerram Barrs, *Being Human: The Nature of Spiritual Experience* (Downers Grove, Ill.: InterVarsity Press, 1978), p. 82.

20. Murray, *Principles of Conduct,* p. 218.

21. Ibid., p. 208.

22. Ibid., pp. 211-212.

23. Ibid., pp. 212-213.

24. Ibid., p. 214.

25. John Murray, *The Epistle to the Romans* (Grand Rapids: Eerdmans, 1968), pp. 219-220.

26. Lloyd-Jones, *Romans, The New Man,* p. 68.

27. Norman Grubb, *Deep Things of God* (Ft. Washington, Pa.: Christian Literature Crusade, 1958), p. 31.

28. Thomas, *St. Paul's Epistle to the Romans,* p. 168.

29. Craig Massey, *Adjust or Self-Destruct, A Study of the Believer's Two Natures* (Chicago: Moody Press, 1977).

30. Pentecost, *Pattern for Maturity,* p. 99.

31. Lloyd-Jones, *Romans, The New Man*, pp. 68-70.

32. Ibid, p. 78.

33. Ibid., p. 72.

34. Ibid, p. 153. See also pp. 78, 83, 152, 222, 247.

35. Murray, *The Epistle to the Romans*, p. 220.

36. Ibid.

37. Ibid., p. 294.

38. Lloyd-Jones, *Romans, The New Man*, p. 83.

39. Murray, *The Epistle to the Romans*, p. 268.

40. Thomas, *St. Paul's Epistle to the Romans*, p. 168.

41. Lloyd-Jones, *Romans, The New Man,* pp. 165-166.

42. Ibid., p. 83.

43. Ibid., p. 74.

44. Pentecost, *Pattern for Maturity,* pp. 92-93.

45. Robert Law, *The Tests of Life, A Study in the First Epistle of St. John,* (Grand Rapids: Baker Book House, 1968), p. 130. Reference to this interpretation is also made in a footnote in *The Epistles of John, An Introduction and Commentary* by John Stott (Grand Rapids: Eerdmans, 1964), p. 77.

46. It might be suggested that the Christian's sin not only arises from his flesh, but also from his spirit because of Paul's statement in 2 Corinthians 7:1, "let us cleanse ourselves from all defilement of flesh and spirit, perfecting holiness in the fear of God." (Out of a desire to keep Paul from identifying the source of sin as being the spirit, Nestle suggested that the grammar would allow for the following translation, "from all defilement of the flesh; in spirit perfecting holiness in the fear of God." Augustine considered this to be a possibility although not acceptable to him. See Alfred Plummer, *Second Epistle of St. Paul to the Corinthians,* The International Critical Commentary, [Edinburgh: T & T Clark, 1956], p. 212. But since such a translation would be abnormal, we should look for an explanation of the passage elsewhere.) I believe the context provides an adequate explanation. Paul is in no way suggesting that the source of sin is one's spirit (or for that matter in this case, one's flesh). The entire issue has to do with the *defilement* that can take place because of the association of something holy with something that is unholy. To say that one's spirit could possibly be defiled is to say something very different from the thought that one's spirit is a source of sin. It is significant that L.S. Chafer believed that it was impossible for the new nature to be the source of sin. See L.S. Chafer, *He That Is Spiritual,* p. 148; see Paxson, *Life on the Highest Plain,* p. 293. Also Craig Massey, *Adjust or Self-Destruct, A Study of the Believer's Two Natures,* p. 91. Nor can 1 Thessalonians 5:23 demand the idea that one's spirit can be "with blame" when Christ returns. One final factor has to do with the fact that we cannot always be sure when Paul is using the term "spirit" in the

sense of deepest being and when he is using it simply to express the non-material aspect of humanness which would then make it parallel to similar usages of the word "soul."

47. See *The American Heritage Dictionary of the English Language* (Boston: Houghton Miflin Co., 1969).

48. This entire consideration of 1 John 1:6-10 is based upon the common view that these verses are describing those who are born again. Though I open myself to a variety of raised eyebrows, I believe that the non-traditional interpretation given to this passage by Peter Gillquist in *Love is Now*, (Grand Rapids: Zondervan, 1970), pp. 55-65, has never successfully been refuted, Zane C. Hodge's article, "Fellowship and Confession in 1 John 1:5-10," *Bibliotheca Sacra*, 129 (January-March 1972), pp. 48-60, notwithstanding.

49. Charles Ryrie, *Balancing the Christian Life* (Chicago: Moody Press, 1969), p. 54.

50. L.S. Chafer, *Systematic Theology*. 8 vols., vol 2: *Angelology, Anthropology, Hamartiology* (Dallas: Dallas Seminary Press, 1947-48), 2: 183.

51. Ibid., p. 349.

52. Walvoord, *Holy Spirit*, p. 136.

53. Lloyd-Jones, *Romans, The New Man*, p. 79.

54. Ibid., p. 73.

55. Ibid., p. 77.

Appendix C

The Term "Flesh" and Galatians 5:24

"Now those who belong to Christ have crucified the flesh with its passions and desires."
(Galatians 5:24, NASB)

According to the apostle, every person belonging to Christ has taken this decisive action of crucifying the flesh (as used in a negative ethical sense, "passions and desires"[1]). It is not something a believer is urged to do, nor certainly is it an option. It is an accomplished fact.

In view of the distinction already made between the terms "old self" (or "man"), and the "flesh," it is most important to appreciate the place of this truth within the overall subject of personal holiness. To do so, we must first remember the fundamental distinction Paul underlines in Romans 6-8, Colossians 2-3, 2 Corinthians 2-5 and most briefly in Ephesians 2:1-10 (especially verse 3). A Christian simply is not the same person he once was. Prior to regeneration he was an "in the flesh" person. That is, life, such as it was, had to be found in the sphere of his independent mortal humanness. And why? Simply because it wasn't to be found anywhere else. Such a person was the "old man." Upon regeneration, every believer becomes (in the sense of truest personhood) one who has died to sin and who is no longer "in the flesh," but rather "in the Spirit." It is within this perspective that Galatians must be understood. A Christian is one who because he "is Christ's" has of necessity declared death to "in the flesh" life in terms of its passions and desires. Since God has finished off the person I once was by the crucifixion of Christ, I as a new man have made my declaration concerning the finishing off of my flesh. Every Christian has done this whether in his mortal consciousness he is always aware of it or not. Awareness, though, is assumed as seen in Romans 7:21-22.

To put it another way, to be a Christian is not only to say "Yes!" to Jesus as Lord, but it also most emphatically is to say "No!" to everything contrary to His Lordship. "In the flesh" existence is precisely that. Romans 8:9 forbids any possibility that a person can both be "in the flesh" and "in the Spirit."[2] It is so crucial that we do not minimize the revolutionary miracle of regeneration.[3]

In contrast with the declaration ("I 'have crucified the flesh' "), Romans 6 states that the death of the old self and the resurrection of the new self is something God has done. God's declaration was fully actualized by His divine power in joining the person I once was (the old self) to Jesus in His death. Because of this I am "to reckon" it so *because it is so.* By contrast, the declaration that I 'have crucified the flesh' has with it no actualizing power in terms of experience even though it is an honest evaluation in harmony with the person I now most deeply am. Hence there is the necessity of the Spirit's power in "putting to death the deeds of the body" (Romans 8:13; cf. Colossians 3:5). Clearly this involves a continuing and progressive action in a believer's life.[4] This awareness of being a new person and the alertness as to the specific deeds of one's body which are not the expressions of resurrection life are brought about by Word of God and the Holy Spirit in the supportive fellowship of believers.

It should be noted, though it is quite obvious, that when Paul speaks of the crucifixion of the flesh, he is not speaking of pounds and ounces or of brain waves. He is thinking metaphorically of the productions of "the earthy part of man"[5] that are sinful because they are not the expressions of the life of Christ in me. In this sense flesh "represents human self-sufficiency."[6]

On one hand the new man rejects the idea that life is to be found in the "passions and lusts" of his flesh, but on the other hand he gladly appreciates the fact that his as yet unredeemed physical and aesthetic senses can be used to appreciate the many good things from God *"who richly provides us with everything for enjoyment"* (1 Timothy 6:17). It is in this sense that the contentment described in Philippians 4:11-12 can be fully appreciated—*"having plenty," "well fed,"* and *"living in plenty."* But since ultimate meaning is in receiving and displaying Jesus, the same believer may know full contentment *"in need," "hungry,"* and *"in want."* Authentic life can function just as well in either circumstance.

To see this more clearly, let's take a very graphic illustration. I have a nose that prefers good smells over bad ones. Now let's assume that God places me in some filthy aboriginal village where the stench is so intense I can scarcely breathe—even through my mouth. In this state I will find it most difficult to be content. And to be discontented with the will of God is sin.

Obviously the mechanics of my problem are quite simple even though the resulting sin is among the most pervasive of all sins. My nose simply sends a message to its control center in my brain. Because of its urgency, it interrupts all other communications with one loud "I can't take this any longer!! I deserve some fulfillment. I demand something pleasant to smell." Before long the console of the conscience department of my brain flashes in bright red "COVETING."

At this point, unless my true personhood comes across with overriding decisiveness, I will be in real trouble. Either I will struggle on, bombarded with guilt and repeated confessions, or I may simply pack up and leave. But wait a minute. Life for me is *not* what I smell. "Sorry nose, you simply are going to have to suffer. Life for me is in displaying Jesus and believe me, this place needs Him—'a fragrance of life unto life!'"

In dealing so harshly with the desires of the flesh, I am really only agreeing with the ground on which I stand. As a believer I have "crucified the flesh with its passions and desires." But from that point on "by the Spirit" I must "put to death the deeds of the body." Is that negative? Absolutely not! It liberates me in order to experience authentic life.

Certainly the overall tone of the Scriptures is that a believer should exercise the fullest potential of all that he is "in the flesh" (in the positive sense of Galatians 2:20) to the glory of God. But if he is not careful, he may so focus on his aptitudes, talents, health, etc. that he forgets that these are the channels through which ultimate meaning is expressed rather than being ends in themselves.[7]

Can you imagine standing before God's judgment seat some day and hearing Him say to you, "Well done, my child, you discovered a cure for cancer — you won an Olympic medal — you made it to the top of your chosen field — you fulfilled 'the American character.'" Or even "Well done, my child, you didn't let your birth defect, your blindness, your miserable childhood break you. No, instead you proved to the world that you could still earn that college degree, support your family. Congratulations!"

What will God say?

How does He measure the quality of the life lived?

Certainly He will evaluate our stewardship of every aspect of life. But the fundamental, overriding issue is Christ. The sphere of expression may be the Olympics or a medical lab — health or sickness, abundance or poverty. But the sphere will always be secondary to the essence — the Christ-displaying "prism" life. Apart from this even the most determined commitment to know one's fullest potential may in the end be nothing more than "the flesh with its passions and desires."

It is more than coincidence that Galatians 5:24 is preceeded by that classic description of the fruit of the Spirit!

Appendix C, Notes

1. "The two words are chiefly distinguished as presenting vice in its passive and its active side respectively." J.B. Lightfoot, *The Epistle of St. Paul to the Galatians* (Grand Rapids: Zondervan, 1905), p. 213.

2. When Paul says *"I am of the flesh, sold under sin"* in Romans 7:14, NASB, he is viewing himself from the perspective of one who on a flesh level is attempting to satisfy God's law, which of course a Christian is never supposed to do. This whole approach to the problem of sin (Romans 7:14-24) is soundly rejected by Paul as unworthy of the miracle of *"the Spirit of life in Christ Jesus"* (Romans 8:2, NASB). Paul then declares authentic Christian personhood as being that which is *"not in the flesh,"* a direct contradiction with his statement in 7:14.

3. Regeneration is basically, therefore, an act of God through the immediate agency of the Holy Spirit operative in man (Colossians 2:13), originating in him a new dimension of moral life; a resurrection to new life in Christ. This new life is not merely a neutral state arising out of forgiveness of sin, but a positive implantation of Christ's righteousness in man, by which he is quickened (John 5:21), begotten (1 John 5:1), made a new creation (2 Corinthians 5:17), and given a new life (Romans 6:4).

"Regeneration involves an illumination of the mind, a change in the will, and a renewed nature. It extends to the total nature of man, irrevocably altering his governing disposition, and restoring him to a true experiential knowledge in Christ. It is a partaking of the divine nature (2

Peter 1:4), a principle of spiritual life implanted in the heart"
(*Zondervan Pictorial Bible Dictionary,* 1963 ed., s.v. "Regeneration," by Clarence B. Bass).

"We must fully appreciate the strength of Paul's statement, 'we died to sin.' The simple and apodictic directness
must not be allowed to obscure the far-reaching implications.
Our understanding of the force of this description must be
derived from the obvious meaning of the phenomenal,
psychico-physical death with which we are so well ac-
quainted. When a person dies we know from bitter experience that the bond which united that person to life and
activity in this world has been severed. He is no longer active
in the sphere, realm, or relationship in reference to which he
has died; he is no longer *en rapport* with life here. The Scripture graphically portrays this obvious fact. *'But he passed
away, and lo, he was not; yea, I sought him but he could not
be found'* (Psalm 37:36). *'As for man, his days are as grass: as
a flower of the field, so he flourisheth. For the wind passeth
over it, and it is gone; and the place thereof shall know it no
more'* (Psalm 103:15, 16).

"It is this analogy that must be applied to death to sin.
The person who has died to sin no longer lives and acts in the
sphere or realm of sin. *In the moral and spiritual realm there
is a translation as real and decisive as in the realm of the
psychico-physical on the event of ordinary death.* Those who
still live in the realm of sin and whose life is constituted by sin
may say with reference to the person translated from it, 'he
passed away, and, lo, he was not: yea, I sought him, but he
could not be found.' The place that knew him knows him no
more.

"There is a kingdom of sin, of darkness, and of death.
The forces of iniquity rule there. It is the kingdom of this
world and it lies in the wicked one (cf. 2 Corinthians 4:3, 4;
Ephesians 2:1-3; 1 John 5:19). The person who has died to sin
no longer lives there; it is no more the world of his thought,
affection, will, life, and action. His well-springs are now in
the kingdom which is totally antithetical, the kingdom of

God and of his righteousness. It is of this translation that Paul speaks elsewhere when he gives thanks to the Father *'who hath delivered us from the power of darkness and hath translated us into the kingdom of the Son of his love'* and *'made us meet to be partakers of the inheritance of the saints in light'* (Colossians 1:12, 13; cf. Galatians 1:4). And Peter reflects on the consternation of those who are left behind in the world of iniquity: *'they think it strange that ye run not with them into the same excess of riot, speaking evil of you'* (1 Peter 4:4; cf. verses 1-3).

"*We are too ready to give heed to what we deem to be the hard, empirical facts of Christian profession, and we have erased the clear line of demarcation which Scripture defines.* As a result we have lost our vision of the high calling of God in Christ Jesus. Our ethic has lost its dynamic and we have become conformed to this world. We know not the power of death to sin in the death of Christ, and we are not able to bear the rigour of the liberty of redemptive emancipation. We died to sin: the glory of Christ's accomplishment and the guarantee of the Christian ethic are bound up with that doctrine. *If we live in sin we have not died to it, and if we have not died to it we are not Christ's.*"
(John Murray, *Principles of Conduct* [Grand Rapids: Eerdmans, 1957], pp. 204-205.)

4.   In view of the behavioral context of Colossians 3, Paul in the statement "you have laid aside the old self" (verse 9) seems to have had in mind the character of life which was typical of the old self, that is, living according to the flesh. Therefore the past tense laying aside or putting off action would be closely parallel with the thought of Galatians 5:24. See chapter 2, footnote 14, p. 67, concerning the parallel passage, Ephesians 4:22-24.

5.   *New Bible Dictionary*, 1962 ed., s.v. "Flesh," by L.L. Morris.

6.   J.A.T. Robinson, *The Body: A Study of Pauline Theology* (London: S.M.C., 1952), pp. 25-27. Also: It is with only minor reservations that I recommend the excellent analysis of the word "flesh" by A.C. Thiselton as corresponding very closely with the emphasis I wish to present. (Colin Brown, ed., *The New International Dictionary of New Testament Theology*, 3 vols. [Grand Rapids: Zondervan, 1975], 1:675-676.)

7.   "Human nature, being inferior to spiritual, is to be in subjection to it. If man refuses to be under his higher law, and as a free agent permits the lower nature to gain ascendancy over the spirit, the 'flesh' becomes a revolting force." *The International Standard Bible Encyclopedia*, 1949 ed., s.v. "Flesh," by H.L.E. Luering.

Appendix D

Spiritual Identity and Physical and Psychological Problems

The scriptural norm for a believer is that one's inner man would be so strengthened by the Spirit that his body would indeed be "a slave to righteousness," that his body would actually manifest by word, expression, and action, the attractiveness of Jesus Christ.

But the fact is that there may be times when the travailings of our bodies will be so intense, that this norm is virtually impossible. (See p. 90.)

The Bible also assumes that the reader is capable of logical thinking, adequate enough to handle, for example, the careful progression of the book of Romans. Yet there may be extended periods when, for example, a person is so plagued with migraine headaches that he despairs of such a prospect.

We must therefore conclude that God knows and delights in the *true nature* of every child of His, whether he is an aged saint with a stroke who pinches cute nurses and delights in children's cartoons or an emotionally distraught mother with an endocrine gland malfunction who through her tears cries out, "I don't know what's wrong with me. I don't want to be irritable, I don't want to be depressed. God knows I want to please Him!"

By all means the world desperately needs to see Jesus Christ in our flesh. But it would be a most serious error for us to conclude that one of God's children is of less worth when an affliction would limit or even appear to oppose that purpose as though that were the only reason for which God made him part of His family. Just try for a moment to visualize the thousands of horribly treated human beings (some of them Christians) who down through the centuries have been locked and chained and mocked and tortured and killed because they were spastic or epileptic or abnormally intelligent or stupid.

Awareness of spiritual identity is fundamental to any comprehensive appreciation of the value of persons. The new birth always, *always* produces God's workmanship. Whatever is born of God "is spirit." Every child of God is after God's own nature whether outwardly seen or not. How carefully we must guard ourselves from misjudging God's precious creations. Perhaps if we only knew the intensity of the pressures some have known, we would have to admit that we would have been crushed by them long ago. Could it be that unknown and unseen to us and to them, God is facetting their deep, inner selves with the most marvelous reflective surfaces which will shine throughout eternity with a brilliance beyond all others? Who knows, perhaps too, though their witness to men in the world may be tragically limited, their inner witness to principalities and powers in the spirit may be bringing glory to God in dimensions we cannot comprehend?

When some problem which is temporary in nature strikes someone, we rightly cover for him by saying, "He just is not himself today." The same is true for those whose lifelong circumstances produce behavior that is far removed from the fruit of the Spirit. The speechless spastic, the eccentric, even offensive person who unknown to everyone carries with him a slowly growing brain tumor; the once cheerful little lady now wasting away with Parkinson's disease who can only read Galatians 5 and weep. May God protect us from the horrid cruelty of judging men according to the flesh!

In our contemporary obsession with personality we must be careful to communicate that true personal worth is first of all in the spirit. God always produces masterpieces![1]

A somewhat different danger we Christians have is that of evaluating individuals on the basis of actions rather than motives. Romans 14:1-13 speaks volumes to this point. Certainly God is not honored by wrong actions, but we may be confident that in spite of the actions He *is* honored by the right motives behind the wrong actions. That is an overwhelmingly wonderful fact for all of us!

Appendix D, Notes

1. "That man is human spirit is a profound and difficult thought. It means that an imaginable gift has come to us, that we are in the same spiritual order as God. It means that we are not what we externally appear to be. It also means that man is quite as indefinable and as descriptively elusive as God Himself. The most the word *spirit* can do is tell us that we really cannot be seen." (Earl Jabay, *The God Players* [Grand Rapids: Zondervan, 1969], p. 14.)

Scripture Index

I Corinthians

Subject Index

Accountability, 228
Adam, 21, 22
  fall of, 38
  man child of, 26, 27, 30
  rejected life, 35
Aliens, 15
Ambassador, 113
Anointing, 50
Assurance:
  and security, 174
  definition of, 174
  of salvation, 173ff, 180
Authority:
  of Paul, 71
  of Scriptures, 208, 221
  submission to, 208

Babel, 26
Behavior, Christlike, 76
Being, spiritual, 75, 91, 95, 99
Believer, 123, 41
  scriptural norm, 273
Birth, see New Birth
Birthright, 68, 153, 156, 216
Body (Bodies), 85, 88
Body of Christ, 207
Body life:
  active participation in, 145
  rediscovery of, 208
  related to spiritual warfare,
    227
"Body-Spirit," 89
Born again, 48, 49, 53, 60, 61,
  103, 137, 174, 258

Capacity, 46, 80
  man's two natures, 76, 78, 80,
    138

Children:
  of God, 51
  of Light, 17, 47
Christian, 39, 42, 44, 51, 52, 170
  essential nature of, 114
  fundamental issue, 114
  God's new creation, 164
  his harmony with God, 138
  identity of, 47, 74-75
  knowledge of first generation,
    120
  two portraits of, 77-78
Christian life, 12, 13, 14, 47, 64,
  149-153
Christianity:
  definition of, 158
  illustration of, 149
  radical, 96
Citizenship in heaven, 52
Communicate, 26
Communication:
  of biblical truth, 11
Conflict:
  explained, 139
  defined, 138
  the real, 82
Convictions, 62
Corporeal, 36
Covenant, 63, 160
  general use, 18
  life under old and new,
    101-105
  new, 15, 102, 103, 104, 113,
    191
  old, 52, 116n, 190
Coveting, sin of, 55, 267
Creation:
  new, 58, 269n
  of man, 23, 66